Embedded Linux Projects Using Yocto Project Cookbook

Over 70 hands-on recipes for professional embedded
Linux developers to optimize and boost their
Yocto know-how

Alex González

[PACKT] open source *
PUBLISHING   community experience distilled

BIRMINGHAM - MUMBAI

Embedded Linux Projects Using Yocto Project Cookbook

First published: March 2015

Production reference: 1240315

Published by Packt Publishing Ltd.
Livery Place
35 Livery Street
Birmingham B3 2PB, UK.

ISBN 978-1-78439-518-6

www.packtpub.com

Cover image by Alex González (alex@lindusphoto.com)

Credits

Author
Alex González

Reviewers
Burt Janz

Dave (Jing) Tian

Javier Viguera

Commissioning Editor
Nadeem N. Bagban

Acquisition Editor
Owen Roberts

Content Development Editor
Natasha DSouza

Technical Editor
Prajakta Mhatre

Copy Editors
Puja Lalwani

Aditya Nair

Vikrant Phadke

Project Coordinator
Rashi Khivansara

Proofreaders
Simran Bhogal

Clyde Jenkins

Indexer
Tejal Soni

Production Coordinator
Alwin Roy

Cover Work
Alwin Roy

Foreword

If we look back at the last 15 years of the field of embedded systems, we will see that everything has changed radically. Embedded systems have become more and more powerful and have gained new functionalities. Today, you can find "embedded" quad-core systems with 1 GB of RAM and several GBs of storage, comparable to a few-years-old desktop computer. Nowadays, it is not unusual that the requirements of an embedded system are low consumption, graphic acceleration, multimedia capabilities, sufficient storage, and so on.

On the software side, if we look back again at those 15 years, we will notice that most of the Linux-running embedded systems at that time were in-house developments built from the ground up. Their main functionality was to boot the device and run the specific application (usually not graphical) the device was designed for. A typical system from those days contained a minimal Linux kernel, a small C library (uclibc), BusyBox as the base user space, and then the specific application or set of applications.

As the hardware became more powerful and gained more functionalities, the requirements of the software also increased. With embedded systems becoming powerful enough to run distributions that were considered mostly for desktops (such as Debian or Ubuntu), it's no longer as easy as building a minimal set of software packages (uclibc, BusyBox, and a command-line application) anymore. You now have to choose between different windowing systems (X11, Wayland, and so on) and different graphic libraries (Qt, GTK, and so on). Maybe your hardware has dedicated units for video processing (VPU) or graphics processing (GPU) and is running its own firmware, and so on.

All of this extra difficulty is what makes an embedded software engineer look for new tools that ease their work and speed up the development. This is the context where different Linux build systems began to appear.

The first build system to show up was Buildroot. It has its roots in the uClibc project. The initial goal of Buildroot was to build a root filesystem based on the uclibc library for testing purposes. Buildroot is based on a Makefile's structure, kconfig as the configuration tool, and patches that apply to the different software packages before being built. These days, Buildroot supports multiple architectures, and apart from root filesystem images, it also can build kernel and bootloader images.

A bit later, OpenEmbedded was born. Its goal is a bit different because it is defined as a Linux distribution builder. OpenEmbedded is based on recipes interpreted by the BitBake build engine. BitBake in turn is a tool derived from portage (Gentoo's distribution package manager). An interesting feature about OpenEmbedded is that the recipes can specify dependencies between packages, and later on, BitBake parses all the recipes and creates a queue of tasks in the correct order to fulfill the dependencies. Two examples of distributions created with OpenEmbedded are Angstrom and OpenMoko.

Another OpenEmbedded-based distribution was Poky Linux. This has special importance because it's the way that leads to Yocto. The Yocto Project is an open source project whose goal is to provide the tools that help build Linux-based embedded systems. Under the umbrella of the Yocto Project, there are multiple software projects, such as Poky, the BitBake build engine, and even OpenEmbedded-Core. These are probably the main projects, but by no means, the only projects. In this new phase, Poky (the former Linux distribution) became the reference system of the Yocto Project, being the build system of the Yocto Project these days and using the BitBake build engine and OpenEmbedded-Core metadata (recipes, classes, and configuration files) underneath. This is the reason people tend to confuse the Yocto Project with the Poky build system.

Poky is a nearly complete solution for embedded software engineering teams. It allows you to create a distribution for your hardware. It also allows you to create a software development kit (SDK) tailored for your distribution. This SDK may be used by other engineers in a team to compile the user-space applications that will later run on your Linux system. The price to pay for the functionality Poky provides is a steep learning curve compared to other build systems.

Alex González's contribution with *Embedded Linux Projects Using Yocto Project Cookbook* is of great help to overcome that steep learning curve. The practical focus of this book and its structure in the form of short recipes help you resolve specific problems that you may find along the way when building an embedded product.

So please enjoy and learn from this book. In return for the invested time, you will get deeper knowledge of embedded system development with the help of the Yocto Project.

Javier Viguera
Embedded Software Engineer at Digi International

About the Author

Alex González is software engineering supervisor at Digi International and one of the maintainers of the Digi Embedded Yocto distribution.

He started working professionally with embedded systems in 1999 and the Linux kernel in 2004, designing products for voice and video over IP networks, and followed his interests into machine-to-machine (M2M) technologies and the Internet of Things.

Born and raised in Bilbao, Spain, Alex has his second home in the UK, where he lived for over 10 years and received his MSc in communication systems from the University of Portsmouth. He currently lives in La Rioja, where he enjoys photography and a good Riojan wine.

I would like to thank the Yocto and OpenEmbedded communities, whose dedication keeps the Yocto project running, and the people involved with the Freescale BSP community layer, whose work is the basis for this book.

I would also like to thank my family, for the time, space, and support that made this possible, and especially my mum for showing me how to be brave—gracias Ama por enseñarme a ser valiente.

About the Reviewers

Burt Janz has been involved with computing systems since he assembled his first microcomputer in the US Navy in 1975. Starting with the development of device drivers and low-level interfaces on *NIX systems in the early 1980s, he has been creating complex software products for over 30 years. His expertise includes the design and implementation of low-level operating system internals and device drivers, complex applications for embedded and handheld devices, and government- and enterprise-level systems.

A graduate of Franklin Pierce College in 1988 (BSCS with high honors), Burt was an adjunct professor at Daniel Webster College for 11 years in their evening-based continuing education program, while developing embedded and enterprise-level software during the day. His curricula of instruction included courses ranging from a basic introduction to computers and programming languages (C, C++, and Java), networking theory and network programming, database theory, and schema design to artificial intelligence systems. Along the way, Burt has written magazine articles and other technical commentaries. He was also involved in one of the first over-the-counter Linux distributions, Yggdrasil, in 1994.

Burt has designed complete embedded and enterprise-level software systems as a lead architect and has led teams from the requirements and design phases of new products to the phases of completion and delivery to customers. He has experience with x86, 68xxx, PPC, ARM, and SPARC processors. He continues to write kernel threads and kmods, open firmware device trees, drivers for new and proprietary hardware, FPGA I/P core interfaces, applications, libraries, and boot manager code.

He can be contacted directly by e-mail at `bhjanz@ccsneinc.com` or `burt.janz@gmail.com` or via LinkedIn.

Dave (Jing) Tian is a graduate research fellow and PhD student in the Computer and Information Science and Engineering (CISE) Department at the University of Florida. He is a founding member of the SENSEI center. His research direction involves system security, embedded system security, trusted computing, and static code analysis for security and virtualization. He is interested in Linux kernel hacking and compiler hacking. He also spent a year on AI and machine learning and taught Python and operating systems in the University of Oregon. Before that, he worked as a software developer in the LCP (Linux Control Platform) group in Alcatel-Lucent (formerly, Lucent Technologies) for approximately 4 years. This role was associated with research and development. He holds BS and ME degrees in electronics engineering from China.

He can be contacted directly by e-mail at root@davejingtian.org or you can visit his website at http://davejingtian.org.

> Thanks to the author of this book, who has done a good job for embedded Linux and Yocto, and thanks to the editors of the book, who made it perfect and offered the opportunity to review such a nice book.

Javier Viguera has been a Linux fan since the mid-1990s, when he managed to install a Slackware distribution in his home computer from a set of floppy disks. This was a milestone because it allowed him to manage his programming practice comfortably at home instead of fighting for a 2-hour slot in the university's computer lab.

With a master's degree in telecommunications engineering and a bachelor's degree in computer science, he is currently working at Digi International as an embedded software engineer. He is one of the maintainers of the former Digi Embedded Linux, now Digi Embedded Yocto, distributions.

Javier lives in La Rioja, Spain. In his spare time, he likes to see good, classic movies, but you can also find him looking at the sky, as he is a fan of planes and aviation. He still dreams of getting a private pilot license.

www.PacktPub.com

Support files, eBooks, discount offers, and more

For support files and downloads related to your book, please visit www.PacktPub.com.

Did you know that Packt offers eBook versions of every book published, with PDF and ePub files available? You can upgrade to the eBook version at www.PacktPub.com and as a print book customer, you are entitled to a discount on the eBook copy. Get in touch with us at service@packtpub.com for more details.

At www.PacktPub.com, you can also read a collection of free technical articles, sign up for a range of free newsletters and receive exclusive discounts and offers on Packt books and eBooks.

https://www2.packtpub.com/books/subscription/packtlib

Do you need instant solutions to your IT questions? PacktLib is Packt's online digital book library. Here, you can search, access, and read Packt's entire library of books.

Why Subscribe?

- Fully searchable across every book published by Packt
- Copy and paste, print, and bookmark content
- On demand and accessible via a web browser

Free Access for Packt account holders

If you have an account with Packt at www.PacktPub.com, you can use this to access PacktLib today and view 9 entirely free books. Simply use your login credentials for immediate access.

Table of Contents

Preface

The Linux kernel is at the heart of a large number of embedded products being designed today. Over the last 10 years, this operating system has developed from dominating the server market to being the most used operating system in embedded systems, even those with real-time requirements. On the way, Linux has evolved, and the embedded industry has realized it has some key and unique characteristics:

- Linux is quick to adapt to new technologies and it's the place where innovation happens first
- It is robust, and the development community is quick to react to problems
- It is secure, and vulnerabilities are discovered and dealt with in a much quicker way than in competing proprietary products
- It is open, which means your company is able to own, modify, and understand the technology
- Finally, Linux is free

All of these make it a very compelling choice for embedded development.

But at the same time, an embedded Linux product is not only the Linux kernel. Companies need to build an embedded system over the operating system, and that's where embedded Linux was finding it difficult to make its place—until Yocto arrived.

The Yocto Project brings all the benefits of Linux into the development of embedded systems. It provides a standard build system that allows you to develop embedded products in a quick, reliable, and controlled way. Just as Linux has its strong points for embedded development, Yocto has its own too:

- Yocto is secure, as it uses recent sources and provides the means to quickly apply security vulnerabilities to your products
- It is robust, as it is used by a large community, which is quick to react to problems

> ▶ It is open, so your company can own the technology, understand it, and make it fit for specific needs

> ▶ It is free

With the Yocto Project's 6-month stable release process, package management updates, and flexibility, you will be able to focus on your embedded application, knowing that you are building it on top of a trusted system. You will speed up your development cycles and produce outstanding products.

But Yocto is a new technology, and developers need to adapt to it. This books aims to provide a practical guide for readers with basic knowledge of Linux and Yocto to develop a production-ready industrial system based on the ARM architecture.

What this book covers

Chapter 1, The Build System, describes the use of the Poky build system and extends it with the Freescale BSP community layer. It also describes common build system configurations and features used to optimize the building of target images.

Chapter 2, The BSP Layer, guides you through the customization of the BSP for your own product. It then explains how to configure, modify, build, and debug the U-Boot bootloader, the Linux kernel, and its device tree.

Chapter 3, The Software Layer, describes the process of creating a new software layer to hold new applications, services, or modifications to existing packages, as well as discussing a release process for license compliance.

Chapter 4, Application Development, starts with toolchains and the Application Development Toolkit (ADT), and deals with application development in detail, including development environments such as Eclipse and Qt creator.

Chapter 5, Debugging, Tracing, and Profiling, discusses debugging tools and techniques, and explores the tracing functionalities offered by the Linux kernel, along with some of the user-space-tracing and profiling tools that make use of them.

What you need for this book

This book assumes some basic working knowledge with GNU/Linux systems; applications such as the bash shell and derivatives; as well as standard tools such as grep, patch, diff, and so on. The examples have been tested with an Ubuntu 14.04 LTS system, but any Linux distribution supported by the Yocto Project can be used.

This is not meant to be an introductory book to the Yocto project, and reading an introductory book, such as *Embedded Linux Development with Yocto Project* by Otavio Salvador and Daiane Angolini, also from Packt Publishing, is recommended.

This book is structured to follow the usual development workflow of an embedded Linux product, but chapters or even single recipes can be read independently.

The recipes take a practical hands-on approach using a Freescale i.MX6-based system, the wandboard-quad, as base hardware. However, any other piece of i.MX-based hardware can be used to follow the examples.

Who this book is for

This book is the ideal way for embedded developers learning about embedded Linux and the Yocto Project to become proficient and broaden their knowledge with examples that are immediately applicable to embedded developments.

Experienced embedded Yocto developers will find new insights into working methodologies and ARM-specific development competence.

Sections

In this book, you will find several headings that appear frequently (Getting ready, How to do it, How it works, There's more, and See also).

To give clear instructions on how to complete a recipe, we use these sections:

Getting ready

This section tells you what to expect in the recipe, and describes how to set up any software or any preliminary settings required for the recipe.

How to do it...

This section contains the steps required to follow the recipe.

How it works...

This section usually consists of a detailed explanation of what happened in the previous section.

There's more...

This section consists of additional information about the recipe in order to make you more knowledgeable about the recipe.

See also

This section provides helpful links to other useful information for the recipe

Conventions

In this book, you will find a number of text styles that distinguish between different kinds of information. Here are some examples of these styles and an explanation of their meaning.

Code words in text, database table names, folder names, filenames, file extensions, pathnames, dummy URLs, user input, and Twitter handles are shown as follows: "You can add a list of packages to exclude from cleaning by adding them to the RM_WORK_EXCLUDE variable."

A block of code is set as follows:

```
SRC_URI = "file://helloworld.c"

S = "${WORKDIR}"
```

When we wish to draw your attention to a particular part of a code block, the relevant lines or items are set in bold:

```
SRC_URI = "file://helloworld.c"
DEPENDS = "lttng-ust"

S = "${WORKDIR}"
```

Any command-line input or output is written as follows:

```
$ ls sources/meta-fsl*/conf/machine/*.conf
```

New terms and **important words** are shown in bold. Words that you see on the screen, for example, in menus or dialog boxes, appear in the text like this: "Build the project by navigating to **Project | Build Project**."

> Warnings or important notes appear in a box like this.

> Tips and tricks appear like this.

Reader feedback

Feedback from our readers is always welcome. Let us know what you think about this book—what you liked or disliked. Reader feedback is important for us as it helps us develop titles that you will really get the most out of.

To send us general feedback, simply e-mail feedback@packtpub.com, and mention the book's title in the subject of your message.

If there is a topic that you have expertise in and you are interested in either writing or contributing to a book, see our author guide at www.packtpub.com/authors.

Customer support

Now that you are the proud owner of a Packt book, we have a number of things to help you to get the most from your purchase.

Downloading the example code

You can download the example code files from your account at http://www.packtpub.com for all the Packt Publishing books you have purchased. If you purchased this book elsewhere, you can visit http://www.packtpub.com/support and register to have the files e-mailed directly to you.

The example code in the book can be accessed through several GitHub repositories at https://github.com/yoctocookbook. Follow the instructions on GitHub to obtain a copy of the source in your computer.

Errata

Although we have taken every care to ensure the accuracy of our content, mistakes do happen. If you find a mistake in one of our books—maybe a mistake in the text or the code—we would be grateful if you could report this to us. By doing so, you can save other readers from frustration and help us improve subsequent versions of this book. If you find any errata, please report them by visiting `http://www.packtpub.com/submit-errata`, selecting your book, clicking on the **Errata Submission Form** link, and entering the details of your errata. Once your errata are verified, your submission will be accepted and the errata will be uploaded to our website or added to any list of existing errata under the Errata section of that title.

To view the previously submitted errata, go to `https://www.packtpub.com/books/content/support` and enter the name of the book in the search field. The required information will appear under the **Errata** section.

Piracy

Piracy of copyrighted material on the Internet is an ongoing problem across all media. At Packt, we take the protection of our copyright and licenses very seriously. If you come across any illegal copies of our works in any form on the Internet, please provide us with the location address or website name immediately so that we can pursue a remedy.

Please contact us at `copyright@packtpub.com` with a link to the suspected pirated material.

We appreciate your help in protecting our authors and our ability to bring you valuable content.

Questions

If you have a problem with any aspect of this book, you can contact us at `questions@packtpub.com`, and we will do our best to address the problem.

1
The Build System

In this chapter, we will cover the following recipes:

- ▸ Setting up the host system
- ▸ Installing Poky
- ▸ Creating a build directory
- ▸ Building your first image
- ▸ Explaining the Freescale Yocto ecosystem
- ▸ Installing support for Freescale hardware
- ▸ Building Wandboard images
- ▸ Troubleshooting your Wandboard's first boot
- ▸ Configuring network booting for a development setup
- ▸ Sharing downloads
- ▸ Sharing the shared state cache
- ▸ Setting up a package feed
- ▸ Using build history
- ▸ Working with build statistics
- ▸ Debugging the build system

Introduction

The Yocto project (`http://www.yoctoproject.org/`) is an embedded Linux distribution builder that makes use of several other open source projects.

The Yocto project provides a reference build system for embedded Linux, called **Poky**, which has the **BitBake** and **OpenEmbedded-Core** (**OE-Core**) projects at its base. The purpose of Poky is to build the components needed for an embedded Linux product, namely:

- ▸ A bootloader image
- ▸ A Linux kernel image
- ▸ A root filesystem image
- ▸ Toolchains and **software development kits** (**SDKs**) for application development

With these, the Yocto project covers the needs of both system and application developers. When the Yocto project is used as an integration environment for bootloaders, the Linux kernel, and user space applications, we refer to it as system development.

For application development, the Yocto project builds SDKs that enable the development of applications independently of the Yocto build system.

The Yocto project makes a new release every six months. The latest release at the time of this writing is Yocto 1.7.1 Dizzy, and all the examples in this book refer to the 1.7.1 release.

A Yocto release comprises the following components:

- ▸ Poky, the reference build system
- ▸ A build appliance; that is, a VMware image of a host system ready to use Yocto
- ▸ An **Application Development Toolkit** (**ADT**) installer for your host system
- ▸ And for the different supported platforms:
    - ❑ Prebuilt toolchains
    - ❑ Prebuilt packaged binaries
    - ❑ Prebuilt images

The Yocto 1.7.1 release is available to download from `http://downloads.yoctoproject.org/releases/yocto/yocto-1.7.1/`.

Setting up the host system

This recipe will explain how to set up a host Linux system to use the Yocto project.

Getting ready

The recommended way to develop an embedded Linux system is using a native Linux workstation. Development work using virtual machines is discouraged, although they may be used for demo and test purposes.

Yocto builds all the components mentioned before from scratch, including the cross-compilation toolchain and the native tools it needs, so the Yocto build process is demanding in terms of processing power and both hard drive space and I/O.

Although Yocto will work fine on machines with lower specifications, for professional developer's workstations, it is recommended to use **symmetric multiprocessing** (**SMP**) systems with 8 GB or more system memory and a high capacity, fast hard drive. Build servers can employ distributed compilation, but this is out of the scope of this book. Due to different bottlenecks in the build process, there does not seem to be much improvement above 8 CPUs or around 16 GB RAM.

The first build will also download all the sources from the Internet, so a fast Internet connection is also recommended.

How to do it...

Yocto supports several distributions, and each Yocto release will document a list of the supported ones. Although the use of a supported Linux distribution is strongly advised, Yocto is able to run on any Linux system if it has the following dependencies:

- ▶ Git 1.7.8 or greater
- ▶ Tar 1.24 or greater
- ▶ Python 2.7.3 or greater (but not Python 3)

Yocto also provides a way to install the correct version of these tools by either downloading a *buildtools-tarball* or building one on a supported machine. This allows virtually any Linux distribution to be able to run Yocto, and also makes sure that it will be possible to replicate your Yocto build system in the future. This is important for embedded products with long-term availability requirements.

This book will use the Ubuntu 14.04 **Long-Term Stable** (**LTS**) Linux distribution for all examples. Instructions to install on other Linux distributions can be found on the *Supported Linux Distributions* section of the *Yocto Project Development Manual*, but the examples will only be tested with Ubuntu 14.04 LTS.

To make sure you have the required package dependencies installed for Yocto and to follow the examples in the book, run the following command from your shell:

```
$ sudo apt-get install gawk wget git-core diffstat unzip texinfo gcc-
   multilib build-essential chrpath socat libsdl1.2-dev xterm make
   xsltproc docbook-utils fop dblatex xmlto autoconf automake libtool
   libglib2.0-dev python-gtk2 bsdmainutils screen
```

How it works...

The preceding command will use `apt-get`, the **Advanced Packaging Tool** (**APT**), command-line tool. It is a frontend of the **dpkg** package manager that is included in the Ubuntu distribution. It will install all the required packages and their dependencies to support all the features of the Yocto project.

There's more...

If build times are an important factor for you, there are certain steps you can take when preparing your disks to optimize them even further:

▶ Place the `build` directories on their own disk partition or a fast external drive.

▶ Use the ext4 filesystem but configure it not to use journalism on your Yocto-dedicated partitions. Be aware that power losses may corrupt your build data.

▶ Mount the filesystem in such a way that read times are not written/recorded on file reads, disable write barriers, and delay committing filesystem changes with the following mount options:

`noatime,barrier=0,commit=6000.`

▶ Do not build on network-mounted drives.

These changes reduce the data integrity safeguards, but with the separation of the `build` directories to their own disk, failures would only affect temporary build data, which can be erased and regenerated.

See also

▸ The complete Yocto project installation instructions for Ubuntu and other supported distributions can be found on the *Yocto Project Reference Manual* at `http://www.yoctoproject.org/docs/1.7.1/ref-manual/ref-manual.html`

Installing Poky

This recipe will explain how to set up your host Linux system with Poky, the Yocto project reference system.

Getting ready

Poky uses the OpenEmbedded build system, and as such, uses the BitBake tool, a task scheduler written in Python which forked from Gentoo's Portage tool. You can think of BitBake as the make utility in Yocto. It will parse the configuration and recipe metadata, schedule a task list, and run through it.

BitBake is also the command-line interface to Yocto.

Poky and BitBake are two of the open source projects used by Yocto. The Poky project is maintained by the Yocto community. You can download Poky from its Git repository at `http://git.yoctoproject.org/cgit/cgit.cgi/poky/`.

Development discussions can be followed and contributed to by visiting the development mailing list at `https://lists.yoctoproject.org/listinfo/poky`.

BitBake, on the other hand, is maintained by both the Yocto and OpenEmbedded communities, as the tool is used by both. BitBake can be downloaded from its Git repository at `http://git.openembedded.org/bitbake/`.

Development discussions can be followed and contributed to by visiting the development mailing list at `http://lists.openembedded.org/mailman/listinfo/bitbake-devel`.

The Poky build system only supports virtualized QEMU machines for the following architectures:

▸ ARM (qemuarm)

▸ x86 (qemux86)

▸ x86-64 (qemux86-64)

▸ PowerPC (qemuppc)

▸ MIPS (qemumips, qemumips64)

Apart from these, it also supports some reference hardware **Board Support Packages** (**BSPs**), representative of the architectures just listed. These are those BSPs:

- ▶ Texas Instruments Beaglebone (beaglebone)
- ▶ Freescale MPC8315E-RDB (mpc8315e-rdb)
- ▶ Intel x86 based PCs and devices (genericx86 and genericx86-64)
- ▶ Ubiquiti Networks EdgeRouter Lite (edgerouter)

To develop on different hardware, you will need to complement Poky with hardware-specific Yocto layers. This will be covered later on.

How to do it...

The Poky project incorporates a stable BitBake release, so to get started with Yocto, we only need to install Poky in our Linux host system.

> Note that you can also install BitBake independently through your distribution's package management system. This is not recommended and can be a source of problems, as BitBake needs to be compatible with the metadata used in Yocto. If you have installed BitBake from your distribution, please remove it.

The current Yocto release is 1.7.1, or Dizzy, so we will install that into our host system. We will use the /opt/yocto folder as the installation path:

```
$ sudo install -o $(id -u) -g $(id -g) -d /opt/yocto
$ cd /opt/yocto
$ git clone --branch dizzy git://git.yoctoproject.org/poky
```

How it works...

The previous instructions will use Git (the source code management system command-line tool) to clone the Poky repository, which includes BitBake, into a new poky directory on our current path, and point it to the Dizzy stable branch.

There's more...

Poky contains three metadata directories, `meta`, `meta-yocto`, and `meta-yocto-bsp`, as well as a template metadata layer, `meta-skeleton`, that can be used as a base for new layers. Poky's three metadata directories are explained here:

- ▸ `meta`: This directory contains the OpenEmbedded-Core metadata, which supports the ARM, x86, x86-64, PowerPC, MIPS, and MIPS64 architectures and the QEMU emulated hardware. You can download it from its Git repository at `http://git.openembedded.org/openembedded-core/`.

  Development discussions can be followed and contributed to by visiting the development mailing list at `http://lists.openembedded.org/mailman/listinfo/openembedded-core`.

- ▸ `meta-yocto`: This contains Poky's distribution-specific metadata.

- ▸ `meta-yocto-bsp`: This contains metadata for the reference hardware boards.

See also

- ▸ There is documentation about Git, the distributed version control system, at `http://git-scm.com/doc`

Creating a build directory

Before building your first Yocto image, we need to create a `build` directory for it.

The build process, on a host system as outlined before, can take up to one hour and need around 20 GB of hard drive space for a console-only image. A graphical image, like `core-image-sato`, can take up to 4 hours for the build process and occupy around 50 GB of space.

How to do it...

The first thing we need to do is create a `build` directory for our project, where the build output will be generated. Sometimes, the `build` directory may be referred to as the project directory, but `build` directory is the appropriate Yocto term.

There is no right way to structure the `build` directories when you have multiple projects, but a good practice is to have one `build` directory per architecture or machine type. They can all share a common `downloads` folders, and even a shared state cache (this will be covered later on), so keeping them separate won't affect the build performance, but it will allow you to develop on multiple projects simultaneously.

To create a `build` directory, we use the `oe-init-build-env` script provided by Poky. The script needs to be sourced into your current shell, and it will set up your environment to use the OpenEmbedded/Yocto build system, including adding the BitBake utility to your path. You can specify a `build` directory to use or it will use `build` by default. We will use `qemuarm` for this example.

```
$ cd /opt/yocto/poky
$ source oe-init-build-env qemuarm
```

The script will change to the specified directory.

> As `oe-init-build-env` only configures the current shell, you will need to source it on every new shell. But, if you point the script to an existing `build` directory, it will set up your environment but won't change any of your existing configurations.

> BitBake is designed with a client/server abstraction, so we can also start a memory resident server and connect a client to it. With this setup, loading cache and configuration information each time is avoided, which saves some overhead. To run a memory resident BitBake that will always be available, you can use the `oe-init-build-env-memres` script as follows:
>
> ```
> $ source oe-init-build-env-memres 12345 qemuarm
> ```
>
> Here `12345` is the local port to be used.
>
> Do not use both BitBake flavors simultaneously, as this can be a source of problems.
>
> You can then kill the memory resident BitBake by executing the following command:
>
> ```
> $ bitbake -m
> ```

How it works...

Both scripts call the `scripts/oe-setup-builddir` script inside the `poky` directory to create the `build` directory.

On creation, the `build` directory contains a `conf` directory with the following three files:

- ▶ `bblayers.conf`: This file lists the metadata layers to be considered for this project.
- ▶ `local.conf`: This file contains the project-specific configuration variables. You can set common configuration variables to different projects with a `site.conf` file, but this is not created by default.

▶ `templateconf.cfg`: This file contains the directory that includes the template configuration files used to create the project. By default it uses the one pointed to by the `templateconf` file in your Poky installation directory, which is `meta-yocto/conf` by default.

> To start a build from scratch, that's all the `build` directory needs. Erasing everything apart from these files will recreate your build from scratch.
>
> ```
> $ cd /opt/yocto/poky/qemuarm
> $ rm -Rf tmp sstate-cache
> ```

There's more...

You can specify a different template configuration file to use when you create your `build` directory using the `TEMPLATECONF` variable; for example:

```
$ TEMPLATECONF=meta-custom/config source oe-init-build-env <build-dir>
```

The `TEMPLATECONF` variable needs to refer to a directory containing templates for both `local.conf` and `bblayer.conf`, but named `local.conf.sample` and `bblayers.conf.sample`.

For our purposes, we can use the unmodified default project configuration files.

Building your first image

Before building our first image, we need to decide what type of image we want to build. This recipe will introduce some of the available Yocto images and provide instructions to build a simple image.

Getting ready

Poky contains a set of default target images. You can list them by executing the following commands:

```
$ cd /opt/yocto/poky
$ ls meta*/recipes*/images/*.bb
```

A full description of the different images can be found on the *Yocto Project Reference Manual*. Typically, these default images are used as a base and customized for your own project needs. The most frequently used base default images are:

- ▶ `core-image-minimal`: This is the smallest BusyBox-, sysvinit-, and udev-based console-only image

- ▶ `core-image-full-cmdline`: This is the BusyBox-based console-only image with full hardware support and a more complete Linux system, including bash

- ▶ `core-image-lsb`: This is a console-only image that is based on Linux Standard Base compliance

- ▶ `core-image-x11`: This is the basic X11 Windows-system-based image with a graphical terminal

- ▶ `core-image-sato`: This is the X11 Window-system-based image with a SATO theme and a GNOME Mobile desktop environment

- ▶ `core-image-weston`: This is a Wayland protocol and Weston reference compositor-based image

You will also find images with the following suffixes:

- ▶ `dev`: These images are suitable for development work, as they contain headers and libraries.

- ▶ `sdk`: These images include a complete SDK that can be used for development on the target.

- ▶ `initramfs`: This is an image that can be used for a RAM-based root filesystem, which can optionally be embedded with the Linux kernel.

How to do it...

To build an image, we need to configure the MACHINE we are building it for and pass its name to BitBake. For example, for the `qemuarm` machine, we would run the following:

```
$ cd /opt/yocto/poky/qemuarm
$ MACHINE=qemuarm bitbake core-image-minimal
```

Or we could export the MACHINE variable to the current shell environment with the following:

```
$ export MACHINE=qemuarm
```

But the preferred and persistent way to do it is to edit the `conf/local.conf` configuration file to change the default machine to `qemuarm`:

```
- #MACHINE ?= "qemuarm"
+ MACHINE ?= "qemuarm"
```

Then you can just execute the following:

```
$ bitbake core-image-minimal
```

How it works...

When you pass a target recipe to BitBake, it first parses the following configuration files:

- ▶ `conf/bblayers.conf`: This file is used to find all the configured layers
- ▶ `conf/layer.conf`: This file is used on each configured layer
- ▶ `meta/conf/bitbake.conf`: This file is used for its own configuration
- ▶ `conf/local.conf`: This file is used for any other configuration the user may have for the current build
- ▶ `conf/machine/<machine>.conf`: This file is the machine configuration; in our case, this is `qemuarm.conf`
- ▶ `conf/distro/<distro>.conf`: This file is the distribution policy; by default, this is the `poky.conf` file

And then BitBake parses the target recipe that has been provided and its dependencies. The outcome is a set of interdependent tasks that BitBake will then execute in order.

There's more...

Most developers won't be interested in keeping the whole build output for every package, so it is recommended to configure your project to remove it with the following configuration in your `conf/local.conf` file:

```
INHERIT += "rm_work"
```

But at the same time, configuring it for all packages means that you won't be able to develop or debug them.

You can add a list of packages to exclude from cleaning by adding them to the `RM_WORK_EXCLUDE` variable. For example, if you are going to do BSP work, a good setting might be:

```
RM_WORK_EXCLUDE += "linux-yocto u-boot"
```

Remember that you can use a custom template `local.conf.sample` configuration file in your own layer to keep these configurations and apply them for all projects so that they can be shared across all developers.

Once the build finishes, you can find the output images on the `tmp/deploy/images/qemuarm` directory inside your `build` directory.

By default, images are not erased from the `deploy` directory, but you can configure your project to remove the previously built version of the same image by adding the following to your `conf/local.conf` file:

```
RM_OLD_IMAGE = "1"
```

You can test run your images on the QEMU emulator by executing this:

```
$ runqemu qemuarm core-image-minimal
```

The `runqemu` script included in Poky's `scripts` directory is a launch wrapper around the QEMU machine emulator to simplify its usage.

Explaining the Freescale Yocto ecosystem

As we saw, Poky metadata starts with the `meta`, `meta-yocto`, and `meta-yocto-bsp` layers, and it can be expanded by using more layers.

An index of the available OpenEmbedded layers that are compatible with the Yocto project is maintained at `http://layers.openembedded.org/`.

An embedded product's development usually starts with hardware evaluation using a manufacturer's reference board design. Unless you are working with one of the reference boards already supported by Poky, you will need to extend Poky to support your hardware.

Getting ready

The first thing to do is to select which base hardware your design is going to be based on. We will use a board that is based on a Freescale i.MX6 **System on Chip** (**SoC**) as a starting point for our embedded product design.

This recipe gives an overview of the support for Freescale hardware in the Yocto project.

How to do it...

The SoC manufacturer (in this case, Freescale) has a range of reference design boards for purchase, as well as official Yocto-based software releases. Similarly, other manufacturers that use Freescale's SoCs offer reference design boards and their own Yocto-based software releases.

Selecting the appropriate hardware to base your design on is one of the most important design decisions for an embedded product. Depending on your product needs, you will decide to either:

- ▶ Use a production-ready board, like a **single-board computer** (**SBC**)
- ▶ Use a module and build your custom carrier board around it
- ▶ Use Freescale's SoC directly and design your own board

Most of the times, a production-ready board will not match the specific requirements of an professional embedded system, and the process of designing a complete carrier board using Freescale's SoC would be too time consuming. So, using an appropriate module that already solves the most technically challenging design aspects is a common choice.

Some of the characteristics that are important to consider are:

- Industrial temperature ranges
- Power management
- Long-term availability
- Precertified wireless and Bluetooth (if applicable)

The Yocto community layers that support Freescale-based boards are called `meta-fsl-arm` and `meta-fsl-arm-extras`. The selection of boards that are supported on `meta-fsl-arm` is limited to Freescale reference designs, which would be the starting point if you are considering designing your own carrier board around Freescale's SoC. Boards from other vendors are maintained on the `meta-fsl-arm-extras` layer.

There are other embedded manufacturers that use `meta-fsl-arm`, but they have not integrated their boards in the `meta-fsl-arm-extras` community layer. These manufacturers will keep their own BSP layers, which depend on `meta-fsl-arm`, with specific support for their hardware. An example of this is Digi International and its ConnectCore 6 module, which is based on the i.MX6 SoC.

How it works...

To understand Freescale Yocto ecosystem, we need to start with the Freescale community BSP, comprising the `meta-fsl-arm` layer with support for Freescale reference boards, and its companion, `meta-fsl-arm-extra`, with support for boards from other vendors, and its differences with the official Freescale Yocto releases that Freescale offers for their reference designs.

There are some key differences between the community and Freescale Yocto releases:

- Freescale releases are developed internally by Freescale without community involvement and are used for BSP validation on Freescale reference boards.
- Freescale releases go through an internal QA and validation test process, and they are maintained by Freescale support.
- Freescale releases for a specific platform reach a maturity point, after which they are no longer worked on. At this point, all the development work has been integrated into the community layer and the platforms are further maintained by the Freescale BSP community.
- Freescale Yocto releases are not Yocto compatible, while the community release is.

Freescale's engineering works very closely with the Freescale BSP community to make sure that all development in their official releases is integrated in the community layer in a reliable and quick manner.

Usually, the best option is to use the Freescale BSP community release but stay with the U-Boot and Linux kernel versions that were released as part of the manufacturer's stable BSP release.

This effectively means that you get the latest updates to the Linux kernel and U-Boot from the manufacturer while simultaneously getting the latest updates to the root filesystem from the community, extending the lifetime of your product, and making sure you are up to date with applications, bug fixes, and security updates.

This takes advantage of the manufacturer's QA process for the system components that are closer to the hardware, and makes it possible to use the manufacturer's support while simultaneously getting user space updates from the community. The Freescale BSP community is also very responsive and active, so problems can usually be worked on with them to benefit all parts.

There's more...

The Freescale BSP community extends Poky with the following layers:

> ▶ `meta-fsl-arm`: This is the community layer that supports Freescale reference designs. It has a dependency on OpenEmbedded-Core. Machines in this layer will be maintained even after Freescale stops active development on them. You can download `meta-fsl-arm` from its Git repository at `http://git.yoctoproject.org/cgit/cgit.cgi/meta-fsl-arm/`.
>
> Development discussions can be followed and contributed to by visiting the development mailing list at `https://lists.yoctoproject.org/listinfo/meta-freescale`.
>
> The `meta-fsl-arm` layer pulls both the Linux kernel and the U-Boot source from Freescale's repositories using the following links:
>
> > ❑ **Freescale Linux kernel Git repository**: `http://git.freescale.com/git/cgit.cgi/imx/linux-2.6-imx.git/`
> >
> > ❑ **Freescale U-Boot Git repository**: `http://git.freescale.com/git/cgit.cgi/imx/uboot-imx.git/`
>
> Other Linux kernel and U-Boot versions are available, but keeping the manufacturer's supported version is recommended.

The `meta-fsl-arm` layer includes Freescale's proprietary binaries to enable some hardware features – most notably its hardware graphics, multimedia, and encryption capabilities. To make use of these capabilities, the end user needs to accept Freescale's **End-User License Agreement** (**EULA**), which is included in the `meta-fsl-arm` layer. To accept the license, the following line needs to be added to the project's `conf/local.conf` configuration file:

```
ACCEPT_FSL_EULA = "1"
```

▶ `meta-fsl-arm-extra`: This layer adds support for other community-maintained boards; for example, the Wandboard. To download the layer's content, you may visit `https://github.com/Freescale/meta-fsl-arm-extra/`.

▶ `meta-fsl-demos`: This layer adds a metadata layer for demonstration target images. To download the layer's content, you may visit `https://github.com/Freescale/meta-fsl-demos`.

Freescale uses another layer on top of the layers above for their official software releases: `meta-fsl-bsp-release`.

▶ `meta-fsl-bsp-release`: This is a Freescale-maintained layer that is used in the official Freescale software releases. It contains modifications to both `meta-fsl-arm` and `meta-fsl-demos`. It is not part of the community release.

See also

▶ For more information, refer to the FSL community BSP release notes available at `http://freescale.github.io/doc/release-notes/1.7/`

Installing support for Freescale hardware

In this recipe, we will install the community Freescale BSP Yocto release that adds support for Freescale hardware to our Yocto installation.

Getting ready

With so many layers, manually cloning each of them and adding them to your project's `conf/bblayers.conf` file is cumbersome. The community is using the `repo` tool developed by Google for their community Android to ease the installation of Yocto.

To install `repo` in your host system, type in the following commands:

```
$ sudo curl http://commondatastorage.googleapis.com/git-repo-
  downloads/repo > /usr/local/sbin/repo
$ sudo chmod a+x /usr/local/sbin/repo
```

The `repo` tool is a Python utility that parses an XML file, called `manifest`, with a list of Git repositories. The `repo` tool is then used to manage those repositories as a whole.

How to do it...

For example, we will use `repo` to download all the repositories listed in the previous recipe to our host system. For that, we will point it to the Freescale community BSP `manifest` for the Dizzy release:

```xml
<?xml version="1.0" encoding="UTF-8"?>
<manifest>
  <default sync-j="4" revision="master"/>
  <remote fetch="git://git.yoctoproject.org" name="yocto"/>
  <remote fetch="git://github.com/Freescale" name="freescale"/>
  <remote fetch="git://git.openembedded.org" name="oe"/>
  <project remote="yocto" revision="dizzy" name="poky"
  path="sources/poky"/>
  <project remote="yocto" revision="dizzy" name="meta-fsl-arm"
  path="sources/meta-fsl-arm"/>
  <project remote="oe" revision="dizzy" name="meta-openembedded"
  path="sources/meta-openembedded"/>
  <project remote="freescale" revision="dizzy" name="fsl-
  community-bsp-base" path="sources/base">
        <copyfile dest="README" src="README"/>
        <copyfile dest="setup-environment" src="setup-
  environment"/>
  </project>
  <project remote="freescale" revision="dizzy" name="meta-fsl-arm-
  extra" path="sources/meta-fsl-arm-extra"/>
  <project remote="freescale" revision="dizzy" name="meta-fsl-
  demos" path="sources/meta-fsl-demos"/>
  <project remote="freescale" revision="dizzy"
  name="Documentation" path="sources/Documentation"/>
</manifest>>
```

The `manifest` file shows all the installation paths and repository sources for the different components that are going to be installed.

How it works...

The `manifest` file is a list of the different layers that are needed for the Freescale community BSP release. We can now use `repo` to install it. Run the following:

```
$ mkdir /opt/yocto/fsl-community-bsp
```

```
$ cd /opt/yocto/fsl-community-bsp
```

```
$ repo init -u https://github.com/Freescale/fsl-community-bsp-
  platform -b dizzy
```

```
$ repo sync
```

You can optionally pass a `-jN` argument to sync if you have a multicore machine for multithreaded operations; for example, you could pass `repo sync -j8` in an 8-core host system.

There's more...

To list the hardware boards supported by the different layers, we may run:

```
$ ls sources/meta-fsl*/conf/machine/*.conf
```

And to list the newly introduced target images, use the following:

```
$ ls sources/meta-fsl*/recipes*/images/*.bb
```

The community Freescale BSP release introduces the following new target images:

- ▸ `fsl-image-mfgtool-initramfs`: This is a small, RAM-based `initramfs` image used with the Freescale manufacturing tool
- ▸ `fsl-image-multimedia`: This is a console-only image that includes the `gstreamer` multimedia framework over the framebuffer, if applicable
- ▸ `fsl-image-multimedia-full`: This is an extension of `fsl-image-multimedia`, but extends the `gstreamer` multimedia framework to include all available plugins
- ▸ `fsl-image-machine-test`: This is an extension on `fsl-image-multimedia-full` for testing and benchmarking
- ▸ `qte-in-use-image`: This is a graphical image that includes support for Qt4 over the framebuffer
- ▸ `qt-in-use-image`: This is a graphical image that includes support for Qt4 over the X11 Windows system

See also

- ▸ Instructions to use the `repo` tool, including using `repo` with proxy servers, can be found in the Android documentation at `https://source.android.com/source/downloading.html`

Building Wandboard images

Building images for one of the supported boards (for example, `Wandboard Quad`) follows the same process we described earlier for the QEMU machines, with the exception of using the `setup-environment` script, which is a wrapper around `oe-init-build-env`.

How to do it...

To build an image for the `wandboard-quad` machine, use the following commands:

```
$ cd /opt/yocto/fsl-community-bsp
$ mkdir -p wandboard-quad
$ MACHINE=wandboard-quad source setup-environment wandboard-quad
$ bitbake core-image-minimal
```

> The current version of the `setup-environment` script only works if the `build` directory is under the installation folder; in our case, `/opt/yocto/fsl-community-bsp`.

How it works...

The `setup-environment` script will create a `build` directory, set up the `MACHINE` variable, and prompt you to accept the Freescale EULA as described earlier. Your `conf/local.conf` configuration file will be updated both with the specified machine and the EULA acceptance variable.

> Remember that if you close your terminal session, you will need to set up the environment again before being able to use BitBake. You can safely rerun the `setup-environment` script as seen previously, as it will not touch an existing `conf/local.conf` file. Run the following:
> ```
> $ cd /opt/yocto/fsl-community-bsp/
> $ source setup-environment wandboard-quad
> ```

The resulting image, `core-image-minimal.sdcard`, which is created inside the `build` directory, can be programmed into a microSD card, inserted into the primary slot in the Wandboard CPU board, and booted using the following commands:

```
$ cd /opt/yocto/fsl-community-bsp/wandboard-
  quad/tmp/deploy/images/wandboard-quad/
$ sudo dd if=core-image-minimal.sdcard of=/dev/sdN bs=1M && sync
```

Here, `/dev/sdN` corresponds to the device node assigned to the microSD card in your host system.

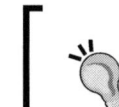

> Be careful when running the `dd` command, as it could harm your machine. You need to be absolutely sure that the *sdN* device corresponds to your microSD card and not a drive on your development machine.

See also

▶ You can find more information regarding the `repo` tool on Android's documentation at `https://source.android.com/source/using-repo.html`

Troubleshooting your Wandboard's first boot

If you have problems booting your image, follow this recipe to troubleshoot.

Getting ready

1. Without the microSD card inserted, plug in a microUSB-to-USB cable to the USB OTG interface of your Wandboard. Check the `lsusb` utility on your Linux host to see whether the Wandboard appears as follows:

   ```
   Bus 002 Device 006: ID 15a2:0054 Freescale Semiconductor, Inc.
     i.MX6Q SystemOnChip in RecoveryMode
   ```

   If you don't see this, try a different power supply. It should be 5V, 10W.

2. Make sure you connect a NULL modem serial cable between the RS232 connector in your Wandboard target and a serial port on your Linux host. Then open a terminal program like minicom with the following:

   ```
   $ minicom -D /dev/ttyS0 -b 115200
   ```

   > You will need to add your user to the dialout group, or try to run the command as sudo. This should open a 115200 8N1 serial connection. The serial device may vary in your Linux host. For example, a USB-to-serial adapter may be detected as `/dev/ttyUSB0`. Also, make sure both hardware and software flow control are disabled.

How to do it...

1. Insert the microSD card image to the module slot, not the base board, as the latter is only used for storage and not for booting, and power it. You should see the U-Boot banner in the minicom session output.

2. If not, you may have a problem with the serial communication. By default, the Ethernet interface in the FSL community BSP image is configured to request an address by DHCP, so you can use that to connect to the target.

   Make sure you have a DHCP server running on the test network where the target is.

You can use a packet sniffer like **Wireshark** to capture a network trace on your Linux host and filter packages like the `bootp` protocol. At the least, you should see some broadcasts from your target, and if you use an Ethernet hub, you should also see the DHCP replies.

Optionally, you can log in to your DHCP server and check the logs to see if a new IP address has been assigned. If you see an IP address being assigned, you might want to consider adding an SSH server, like **Dropbear**, to your core-image-minimal image so that you can establish a network connection with the target. You can do this by adding the following line to the `conf/local.conf` configuration file:

```
IMAGE_INSTALL_append = " dropbear"
```

Note the space after the initial quote.

After building and reprogramming, you can then start an SSH session to the Wandboard from your Linux host with:

```
$ ssh root@<ip_address>
```

The connection should automatically log in without a password prompt.

3. Try to program the default microSD card images from `http://www.wandboard.org/index.php/downloads` to make sure the hardware and your setup is valid.

4. Try to reprogram your microSD card. Make sure you are using the correct images for your board (for example, do not mix dual and quad images). Also, try different cards and card readers.

These steps will have your Wandboard start booting, and you should have some output in your serial connection.

There's more...

If everything else fails, you can verify the position of the bootloader on your microSD card. You can dump the contents of the first blocks of your microSD card with:

```
$ sudo dd if=/dev/sdN of=/tmp/sdcard.img count=10
```

You should see a U-Boot header at offset 0x400. That's the offset where the i.MX6 boot ROM will be looking for the bootloader when bootstrapped to boot from the microSD interface. Use the following commands:

```
$ head /tmp/sdcard.img | hexdump
0000400 00d1 4020 0000 1780 0000 0000 f42c 177f
```

You can recognize the U-Boot header by dumping the U-Boot image from your build. Run the following commands:

```
$ head u-boot-wandboard-quad.imx | hexdump
0000000 00d1 4020 0000 1780 0000 0000 f42c 177f
```

Configuring network booting for a development setup

Most professional i.MX6 boards will have an internal **embedded MMC** (**eMMC**) flash memory, and that would be the recommended way to boot firmware. The Wandboard is not really a product meant for professional use, so it does not have one. But neither the eMMC nor the microSD card are ideal for development work, as any system change would involve a reprogramming of the firmware image.

Getting ready

The ideal setup for development work is to use both TFTP and NFS servers in your host system and to only store the U-Boot bootloader in either the eMMC or a microSD card. With this setup, the bootloader will fetch the Linux kernel from the TFTP server and the kernel will mount the root filesystem from the NFS server. Changes to either the kernel or the root filesystem are available without the need to reprogram. Only bootloader development work would need you to reprogram the physical media.

Installing a TFTP server

If you are not already running a TFTP server, follow the next steps to install and configure a TFTP server on your Ubuntu 14.04 host:

```
$ sudo apt-get install tftpd-hpa
```

The `tftpd-hpa` configuration file is installed in `/etc/default/tftpd-hpa`. By default, it uses `/var/lib/tftpboot` as the root `TFTP` folder. Change the folder permissions to make it accessible to all users using the following command:

```
$ sudo chmod 1777 /var/lib/tftpboot
```

Now copy the Linux kernel and device tree from your `build` directory as follows:

```
$ cd /opt/yocto/fsl-community-bsp/wandboard-
  quad/tmp/deploy/images/wandboard-quad/
$ cp zImage-wandboard-quad.bin zImage-imx6q-wandboard.dtb
  /var/lib/tftpboot
```

Installing an NFS server

If you are not already running an NFS server, follow the next steps to install and configure one on your Ubuntu 14.04 host:

```
$ sudo apt-get install nfs-kernel-server
```

We will use the /nfsroot directory as the root for the NFS server, so we will "untar" the target's root filesystem from our Yocto build directory in there:

```
$ sudo mkdir /nfsroot
$ cd /nfsroot
$ sudo tar xvf /opt/yocto/fsl-community-bsp/wandboard-
  quad/tmp/deploy/images/wandboard-quad/core-image-minimal-wandboard-
  quad.tar.bz2
```

Next, we will configure the NFS server to export the /nfsroot folder:

```
/etc/exports:
/nfsroot/ *(rw,no_root_squash,async,no_subtree_check)
```

We will then restart the NFS server for the configuration changes to take effect:

```
$ sudo service nfs-kernel-server restart
```

How to do it...

Boot the Wandboard and stop at the U-Boot prompt by pressing any key on the serial console. Then run through the following steps:

1. Get an IP address by DHCP:

   ```
   > dhcp
   ```

   Alternatively, you can configure a static IP address with:

   ```
   > setenv ipaddr <static_ip>
   ```

2. Configure the IP address of your host system, where the TFTP and NFS servers have been set up:

   ```
   > setenv serverip <host_ip>
   ```

3. Configure the root filesystem mount:

   ```
   > setenv nfsroot /nfsroot
   ```

4. Configure the Linux kernel and device tree filenames:

   ```
   > setenv image zImage-wandboard-quad.bin
   > setenv fdt_file zImage-imx6q-wandboard.dtb
   ```

5. If you have configured a static IP address, you need to disable DHCP on boot by running:

   ```
   > setenv ip_dyn no
   ```

6. Save the U-Boot environment to the microSD card:

   ```
   > saveenv
   ```

7. Perform a network boot:

   ```
   > run netboot
   ```

The Linux kernel and device tree will be fetched from the TFTP server, and the root filesystem will be mounted by the kernel from the NFS share after getting a DHCP address from your network (unless using static IP addresses).

You should be able to log in with the root user without a password prompt.

Sharing downloads

You will usually work on several projects simultaneously, probably for different hardware platforms or different target images. In such cases, it is important to optimize the build times by sharing `downloads`.

Getting ready

The build system runs a search for downloaded sources in a number of places:

- It tries the local `downloads` folder.
- It looks into the configured premirrors, which are usually local to your organization.
- It then tries to fetch from the upstream source as configured in the package recipe.
- Finally, it checks the configured mirrors. Mirrors are public alternate locations for the source.

If a package source is not found in any of the these four, the package build will fail with an error. Build warnings are also issued when upstream fetching fails and mirrors are tried, so that the upstream problem can be looked at.

The Yocto project maintains a set of mirrors to isolate the build system from problems with the upstream servers. However, when adding external layers, you could be adding support for packages that are not in the Yocto project's mirror servers, or other configured mirrors, so it is recommended that you keep a local premirror to avoid problems with source availability.

The default Poky setting for a new project is to store the downloaded package sources on the current `build` directory. This is the first place the build system will run a search for source `downloads`. This setting can be configured in your project's `conf/local.conf` file with the `DL_DIR` configuration variable.

How to do it...

To optimize the build time, it is recommended to keep a shared `downloads` directory between all your projects. The `setup-environment` script of the `meta-fsl-arm` layer changes the default `DL_DIR` to the `fsl-community-bsp` directory created by the `repo` tool. With this setup, the `downloads` folder will already be shared between all the projects in your host system. It is configured as:

```
DL_DIR ?= "${BSPDIR}/downloads/"
```

A more scalable setup (for instance, for teams that are remotely distributed) is to configure a premirror. For example, adding the following to your `conf/local.conf` file:

```
INHERIT += "own-mirrors"
SOURCE_MIRROR_URL = "http://example.com/my-source-mirror"
```

A usual setup is to have a build server serve its `downloads` directory. The build server can be configured to prepare tarballs of the Git directories to avoid having to perform Git operations from upstream servers. This setting in your `conf/local.conf` file will affect the build performance, but this is usually acceptable in a build server. Add the following:

```
BB_GENERATE_MIRROR_TARBALLS = "1"
```

An advantage of this setup is that the build server's `downloads` folder can also be backed up to guarantee source availability for your products in the future. This is especially important in embedded products with long-term availability requirements.

In order to test this setup, you may check to see whether a build is possible just by using the premirrors with the following:

```
BB_FETCH_PREMIRRORONLY = "1"
```

This setting in your `conf/local.conf` file can also be distributed across the team with the `TEMPLATECONF` variable during the project's creation.

Sharing the shared state cache

The Yocto project builds everything from source. When you create a new project, only the configuration files are created. The build process then compiles everything from scratch, including the cross-compilation toolchain and some native tools important for the build.

This process can take a long time, and the Yocto project implements a shared state cache mechanism that is used for incremental builds with the aim to build only the strictly necessary components for a given change.

For this to work, the build system calculates a checksum of the given input data to a task. If the input data changes, the task needs to be rebuilt. In simplistic terms, the build process generates a run script for each task that can be checksummed and compared. It also keeps track of a task's output, so that it can be reused.

A package recipe can modify the shared state caching to a task; for example, to always force a rebuild by marking it as `nostamp`. A more in-depth explanation of the shared state cache mechanism can be found in the *Yocto Project Reference Manual* at `http://www. yoctoproject.org/docs/1.7.1/ref-manual/ref-manual.html`.

How to do it...

By default, the build system will use a shared state cache directory called `sstate-cache` on your `build` directory to store the cached data. This can be changed with the `SSTATE_DIR` configuration variable in your `conf/local.conf` file. The cached data is stored in directories named with the first two characters of the hash. Inside, the filenames contain the whole task checksum, so the cache validity can be ascertained just by looking at the filename. The build process set scene tasks will evaluate the cached data and use it to accelerate the build if valid.

When you want to start a build from a clean state, you need to remove both the `sstate-cache` directory and the `tmp` directory.

You can also instruct BitBake to ignore the shared state cache by using the `--no-setscene` argument when running it.

It's a good practice to keep backups of clean shared state caches (for example, from a build server), which can be used in case of shared state cache corruption.

There's more...

Sharing a shared state cache is possible; however, it needs to be approached with care. Not all changes are detected by the shared state cache implementation, and when this happens, some or all of the cache needs to be invalidated. This can cause problems when the state cache is being shared.

The recommendation in this case depends on the use case. Developers working on Yocto metadata should keep the shared state cache as default, separated per project.

However, validation and testing engineers, kernel and bootloader developers, and application developers would probably benefit from a well-maintained shared state cache.

To configure an NFS share drive to be shared among the development team to speed up the builds, you can add the following to your `conf/local.conf` configuration file:

```
SSTATE_MIRRORS ?= "\
    file://.* file:///nfs/local/mount/sstate/PATH"
```

The expression PATH in this example will get substituted by the build system with a directory named with the hash's first two characters.

Setting up a package feed

An embedded system project seldom has the need to introduce changes to the Yocto build system. Most of the time and effort is spent in application development, followed by a lesser amount in maybe kernel and bootloader development.

As such, a whole system rebuild is probably done very few times. A new project is usually built from a prebuilt shared state cache, and application development work only needs to be done to perform full or incremental builds of a handful of packages.

Once the packages are built, they need to be installed on the target system for testing. Emulated machines are fine for application development, but most hardware-related work needs to be done on embedded hardware.

Getting ready

An option is to manually copy the build binaries to the target's root filesystem, either copying it to the NFS share on the host system the target is mounting its root filesystem from (as explained in the *Configuring network booting for a development setup* recipe earlier) or using any other method like SCP, FTP, or even a microSD card.

This method is also used by IDEs like Eclipse when debugging an application you are working on. However, this method does not scale well when you need to install several packages and dependencies.

The next option would be to copy the packaged binaries (that is, the RPM, deb, or ipk packages) to the target's filesystem and then use the target's package management system to install them. For this to work, your target's filesystem needs to be built with package management tools. Doing this is as easy as adding the package-management feature to your root filesystem; for example, you may add the following line to your project's conf/local.conf file:

```
EXTRA_IMAGE_FEATURES += "package-management"
```

So for an RPM package, you will copy it to the target and use the **rpm** or **smart** utilities to install it. The smart package management tool is GPL licensed and can work with a variety of package formats.

However, the most optimized way to do this is to convert your host system package's output directory into a package feed. For example, if you are using the default RPM package format, you may convert `tmp/deploy/rpm` in your `build` directory into a package feed that your target can use to update.

For this to work, you need to configure an HTTP server on your computer that serves the packages.

Versioning packages

You also need to make sure that the generated packages are correctly versioned, and that means updating the recipe revision, **PR**, with every change. It is possible to do this manually, but the recommended—and compulsory way if you want to use package feeds—is to use a PR server.

However, the PR server is not enabled by default. The packages generated without a PR server are consistent with each other but offer no update guarantees for a system that is already running.

The simplest PR server configuration is to run it locally on your host system. To do this, you add the following to your `conf/local.conf` file:

```
PRSERV_HOST = "localhost:0"
```

With this setup, update coherency is guaranteed for your feed.

If you want to share your feed with other developers, or you are configuring a build server or package server, you would run a single instance of the PR server by running the following command:

```
$ bitbake-prserv --host <server_ip> --port <port> --start
```

And you will update the project's build configuration to use the centralized PR server, editing `conf/local.conf` as follows:

```
PRSERV_HOST = "<server_ip>:<port>"
```

Also, if you are using a shared state cache as described before, all of the contributors to the shared state cache need to use the same PR server.

Once the feed's integrity is guaranteed, we need to configure an HTTP server to serve the feed.

How to do it...

We will use `lighttpd` for this example, as it is lightweight and easy to configure. Follow these steps:

1. Install the web server:

   ```
   $ sudo apt-get install lighttpd
   ```

2. By default, the document root specified in the `/etc/lighttpd/lighttpd.conf` configuration file is `/var/www/`, so we only need a symlink to our package feed:

```
$ sudo mkdir /var/www/wandboard-quad
```

```
$ sudo ln -s /opt/yocto/fsl-community-bsp/wandboard-
  quad/tmp/deploy/rpm /var/www/wandboard-quad/rpm
```

Next, reload the configuration as follows:

```
$ sudo service lighttpd reload
```

3. Refresh the package index. This needs to be done manually to update the package feed after every build:

```
$ bitbake package-index
```

4. Then we need to configure our target filesystem with the new package feeds:

```
# smart channel --add all type=rpm-md \
  baseurl=http://<server_ip>/wandboard-quad/rpm/all
```

```
# smart channel --add wandboard_quad type=rpm-md \
  baseurl=http://<server_ip>/wandboard-quad/rpm/wandboard_quad
```

```
# smart channel --add cortexa9hf_vfp_neon type=rpm-md \
  baseurl=http://<server_ip>/wandboard-
  quad/rpm/cortexa9hf_vfp_neon
```

5. Once the setup is ready, we will be able to query and update packages from the target's root filesystem with the following:

```
# smart update
```

```
# smart query <package_name>
```

```
# smart install <package_name>
```

To make this change persistent in the target's root filesystem, we can configure the package feeds at compilation time by using the `PACKAGE_FEED_URIS` variable in `conf/local.conf` as follows:

```
PACKAGE_FEED_URIS = "http://<server_ip>/wandboard-quad"
```

See also

▸ More information and a user manual for the smart utility can be found at `https://labix.org/smart/`

Using build history

When maintaining software for an embedded product, you need a way to know what has changed and how it is going to affect your product.

On a Yocto system, you may need to update a package revision (for instance, to fix a security vulnerability), and you need to make sure what the implications of this change are; for example, in terms of package dependencies and changes to the root filesystem.

Build history enables you to do just that, and we will explore it in this recipe.

How to do it...

To enable build history, add the following to your `conf/local.conf` file:

```
INHERIT += "buildhistory"
```

The following enables information gathering, including dependency graphs:

```
BUILDHISTORY_COMMIT = "1"
```

The preceding line of code enables the storage of build history in a local Git repository.

The Git repository location can be set by the BUILDHISTORY_DIR variable, which by default is set to a `buildhistory` directory on your `build` directory.

By default, `buildhistory` tracks changes to packages, images, and SDKs. This is configurable using the BUILDHISTORY_FEATURES variable. For example, to track only image changes, add the following to your `conf/local.conf`:

```
BUILDHISTORY_FEATURES = "image"
```

It can also track specific files and copy them to the `buildhistory` directory. By default, this includes only `/etc/passwd` and `/etc/groups`, but it can be used to track any important files like security certificates. The files need to be added with the BUILDHISTORY_IMAGE_FILES variable in your `conf/local.conf` file as follows:

```
BUILDHISTORY_IMAGE_FILES += "/path/to/file"
```

Build history will slow down the build, increase the build size, and may also grow the Git directory to an unmanageable size. The recommendation is to enable it on a build server for software releases, or in specific cases, such as when updating production software.

How it works...

When enabled, it will keep a record of the changes to each package and image in the form of a Git repository in a way that can be explored and analyzed.

For a package, it records the following information:

▶ Package and recipe revision

▶ Dependencies

▶ Package size

▶ Files

For an image, it records the following information:

▶ Build configuration

▶ Dependency graphs

▶ A list of files that includes ownership and permissions

▶ List of installed packages

And for an SDK, it records the following information:

▶ SDK configuration

▶ List of both host and target files, including ownership and permissions

▶ Dependency graphs

▶ A list of installed packages

Looking at the build history

Inspecting the Git directory with the build history can be done in several ways:

▶ Using Git tools like gitk or git log.

▶ Using the **buildhistory-diff** command-line tool, which displays the differences in a human-readable format.

▶ Using a Django-1.4-based web interface. You will need to import the build history data to the application's database after every build. The details are available at `http://git.yoctoproject.org/cgit/cgit.cgi/buildhistory-web/tree/README`.

There's more...

To maintain the build history, it's important to optimize it and avoid it from growing over time. Periodic backups of the build history and clean-ups of older data are important to keep the build history repository at a manageable size.

Once the `buildhistory` directory has been backed up, the following process will trim it and keep only the most recent history:

1. Copy your repository to a temporary RAM filesystem (`tmpfs`) to speed things up. Check the output of the `df -h` command to see which directories are `tmpfs` filesystems and how much space they have available, and use one. For example, in Ubuntu, the `/run/shm` directory is available.

2. Add a graft point for a commit one month ago with no parents:

    ```
    $ git rev-parse "HEAD@{1 month ago}" > .git/info/grafts
    ```

3. Make the graft point permanent:

    ```
    $ git filter-branch
    ```

4. Clone a new repository to clean up the remaining Git objects:

    ```
    $ git clone file://${tmpfs}/buildhistory buildhistory.new
    ```

5. Replace the old `buildhistory` directory with the new cleaned one:

    ```
    $ rm -rf buildhistory
    $ mv buildhistory.new buildhistory
    ```

Working with build statistics

The build system can collect build information per task and image. The data may be used to identify areas of optimization of build times and bottlenecks, especially when new recipes are added to the system. This recipe will explain how the build statistics work.

How to do it...

To enable the collection of statistics, your project needs to inherit the `buildstats` class by adding it to `USER_CLASSES` in your `conf/local.conf` file. By default, the `fsl-community-bsp` build project is configured to enable them.

```
USER_CLASSES ?= "buildstats"
```

You can configure the location of these statistics with the `BUILDSTATS_BASE` variable, and by default it is set to the `buildstats` folder in the `tmp` directory under the `build` directory (tmp/buildstats).

The `buildstats` folder contains a folder per image with the build stats under a `timestamp` folder. Under it will be a subdirectory per package in your built image, and a `build_stats` file that contains:

- ▸ Host system information
- ▸ Root filesystem location and size
- ▸ Build time
- ▸ Average CPU usage
- ▸ Disk statistics

How it works...

The accuracy of the data depends on the download directory, `DL_DIR`, and the shared state cache directory, `SSTATE_DIR`, existing on the same partition or volume, so you may need to configure them accordingly if you are planning to use the build data.

An example `build-stats` file looks like the following:

```
Host Info: Linux agonzal 3.13.0-35-generic #62-Ubuntu SMP Fri Aug
   15 01:58:42 UTC 2014 x86_64 x86_64
Build Started: 1411486841.52
Uncompressed Rootfs size: 6.2M  /opt/yocto/fsl-community-
   bsp/wandboard-quad/tmp/work/wandboard_quad-poky-linux-
   gnueabi/core-image-minimal/1.0-r0/rootfs
Elapsed time: 2878.26 seconds
CPU usage: 51.5%
EndIOinProgress: 0
EndReadsComp: 0
EndReadsMerged: 55289561
EndSectRead: 65147300
EndSectWrite: 250044353
EndTimeIO: 14415452
EndTimeReads: 10338443
EndTimeWrite: 750935284
EndWTimeIO: 816314180
EndWritesComp: 0
StartIOinProgress: 0
StartReadsComp: 0
StartReadsMerged: 52319544
StartSectRead: 59228240
StartSectWrite: 207536552
StartTimeIO: 13116200
StartTimeReads: 8831854
StartTimeWrite: 3861639688
StartWTimeIO: 3921064032
StartWritesComp: 0
```

These disk statistics come from the Linux kernel disk I/O stats (`https://www.kernel.org/doc/Documentation/iostats.txt`). The different elements are explained here:

- `ReadsComp`: This is the total number of reads completed
- `ReadsMerged`: This is the total number of adjacent reads merged
- `SectRead`: This is the total number of sectors read
- `TimeReads`: This is the total number of milliseconds spent reading
- `WritesComp`: This is the total number of writes completed
- `SectWrite`: This is the total number of sectors written
- `TimeWrite`: This is the total number of milliseconds spent writing

`IOinProgress`: This is the total number of I/Os in progress when reading `/proc/diskstats`

- `TimeIO`: This is the total number of milliseconds spent performing I/O
- `WTimeIO`: This is the total number of weighted time while performing I/O

And inside each package, we have a list of tasks; for example, for `ncurses-5.9-r15.1`, we have the following tasks:

- `do_compile`
- `do_fetch`
- `do_package`
- `do_package_write_rpm`
- `do_populate_lic`
- `do_rm_work`
- `do_configure`
- `do_install`
- `do_packagedata`
- `do_patch`
- `do_populate_sysroot`
- `do_unpack`

Each one of them contain, in the same format as earlier, the following:

- Build time
- CPU usage
- Disk stats

You can also obtain a graphical representation of the data using the `pybootchartgui.py` tool included in the Poky source. From your project's `build` folder, you can execute the following command to obtain a `bootchart.png` graphic in `/tmp`:

```
$ ../sources/poky/scripts/pybootchartgui/pybootchartgui.py
  tmp/buildstats/core-image-minimal-wandboard-quad/ -o /tmp
```

Debugging the build system

In the last recipe of this chapter, we will explore the different methods available to debug problems with the build system and its metadata.

Getting ready

Let's first introduce some of the usual use cases on a debugging session.

Finding recipes

A good way to check whether a specific package is supported in your current layers is to search for it as follows:

```
$ find -name "*busybox*"
```

This will recursively search all layers for the BusyBox pattern. You can limit the search to recipes and append files by executing:

```
$ find -name "*busybox*.bb*"
```

Dumping BitBake's environment

When developing or debugging package or image recipes, it is very common to ask BitBake to list its environment both globally and for a specific target, be it a package or image.

To dump the global environment and `grep` for a variable of interest (for example, `DISTRO_FEATURES`), use the following command:

```
$ bitbake -e | grep -w DISTRO_FEATURES
```

Optionally, to locate the source directory for a specific package recipe like BusyBox, use the following command:

```
$ bitbake -e busybox | grep ^S=
```

You could also execute the following command to locate the working directory for a package or image recipe:

```
$ bitbake -e <target> | grep ^WORKDIR=
```

Using the development shell

BitBake offers the `devshell` task to help developers. It is executed with the following command:

```
$ bitbake -c devshell <target>
```

It will unpack and patch the source, and open a new terminal (it will autodetect your terminal type or it can be set with `OE_TERMINAL`) in the target source directory, which has the environment correctly setup.

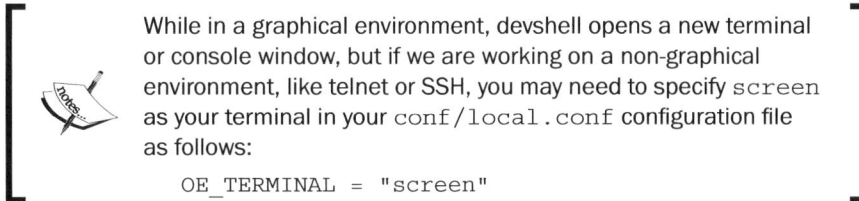

> While in a graphical environment, devshell opens a new terminal or console window, but if we are working on a non-graphical environment, like telnet or SSH, you may need to specify `screen` as your terminal in your `conf/local.conf` configuration file as follows:
>
> ```
> OE_TERMINAL = "screen"
> ```

Inside the devshell, you can run development commands like `configure` and `make` or invoke the cross-compiler directly (use the `$CC` environment variable, which has been set up already).

How to do it...

The starting point for debugging a package build error is the BitBake error message printed on the build process. This will usually point us to the task that failed to build.

To list all the tasks available for a given recipe, with descriptions, we execute the following:

```
$ bitbake -c listtasks <target>
```

If you need to recreate the error, you can force a build with the following:

```
$ bitbake -f <target>
```

Or you can ask BitBake to force-run only a specific task using the following command:

```
$ bitbake -c compile -f <target>
```

Task log and run files

To debug the build errors, BitBake creates two types of useful files per shell task and stores them in a `temp` folder in the working directory. Taking BusyBox as an example, we would look into:

```
/opt/yocto/fsl-community-bsp/wandboard-quad/tmp/work/cortexa9hf-
   vfp-neon-poky-linux-gnueabi/busybox/1.22.1-r32/temp
```

And find a list of log and run files. The filename format is

```
log.do_<task>.<pid>
```

and `run.do_<task>.<pid>`.

But luckily, we also have symbolic links, without the `pid` part, that link to the latest version.

The log files will contain the output of the task, and that is usually the only information we need to debug the problem. The run file contains the actual code executed by BitBake to generate the log mentioned before. This is only needed when debugging complex build issues.

Python tasks, on the other hand, do not currently write files as described previously, although it is planned to do so in the future. Python tasks execute internally and log information to the terminal.

Adding logging to recipes

BitBake recipes accept either bash or Python code. Python logging is done through the `bb` class and uses the standard logging Python library module. It has the following components:

- ▸ `bb.plain`: This uses `logger.plain`. It can be used for debugging, but should not be committed to the source.
- ▸ `bb.note`: This uses `logger.info`.
- ▸ `bb.warn`: This uses `logger.warn`.
- ▸ `bb.error`: This uses `logger.error`.
- ▸ `bb.fatal`: This uses `logger.critical` and exits BitBake.
- ▸ `bb.debug`: This should be passed log level as the first argument and uses `logger.debug`.

To print debug output from bash in our recipes, we need to use the `logging` class by executing:

```
inherit logging
```

The `logging` class is inherited by default by all recipes containing `base.bbclass`, so we don't usually have to inherit it explicitly. We will then have access to the following bash functions, which will output to the log files (not to the console) in the `temp` directory inside the working directory as described previously:

- ▸ `bbplain`: This function outputs literally what's passed in. It can be used in debugging but should not be committed to a recipe source.
- ▸ `bbnote`: This function prints with the NOTE prefix.
- ▸ `bbwarn`: This prints a non-fatal warning with the WARNING prefix.
- ▸ `bberror`: This prints a non-fatal error with the ERROR prefix.

- ► `bbfatal`: This function halts the build and prints an error message as with `bberror`.
- ► `bbdebug`: This function prints debug messages with log level passed as the first argument. It is used with the following format:

```
bbdebug [123] "message"
```

> The bash functions mentioned here do not log to the console but only to the log files.

Looking at dependencies

You can ask BitBake to print the current and provided versions of packages with the following command:

```
$ bitbake --show-versions
```

Another common debugging task is the removal of unwanted dependencies.

To see an overview of pulled-in dependencies, you can use BitBake's verbose output by running this:

```
$ bitbake -v <target>
```

To analyze what dependencies are pulled in by a package, we can ask BitBake to create DOT files that describe these dependencies by running the following:

```
$ bitbake -g <target>
```

The DOT format is a text description language for graphics that is understood by the **GraphViz** open source package and all the utilities that use it. DOT files can be visualized or further processed.

You can omit dependencies from the graph to produce more readable output. For example, to omit dependencies from `glibc`, you would run the following command:

```
$ bitbake -g <target> -I glibc
```

Once the preceding commands have been run, we get three files in the current directory:

- ► `package-depends.dot`: This file shows the dependencies between runtime targets
- ► `pn-depends.dot`: This file shows the dependencies between recipes
- ► `task-depends.dot`: This file shows the dependencies between tasks

There is also a `pn-buildlist` file with a list of packages that would be built by the given target.

To convert the `.dot` files to postscript files (`.ps`), you may execute:

```
$ dot -Tps filename.dot -o outfile.ps
```

However, the most useful way to display dependency data is to ask BitBake to display it graphically with the dependency explorer, as follows:

```
$ bitbake -g -u depexp <target>
```

The result may be seen in the following screenshot:

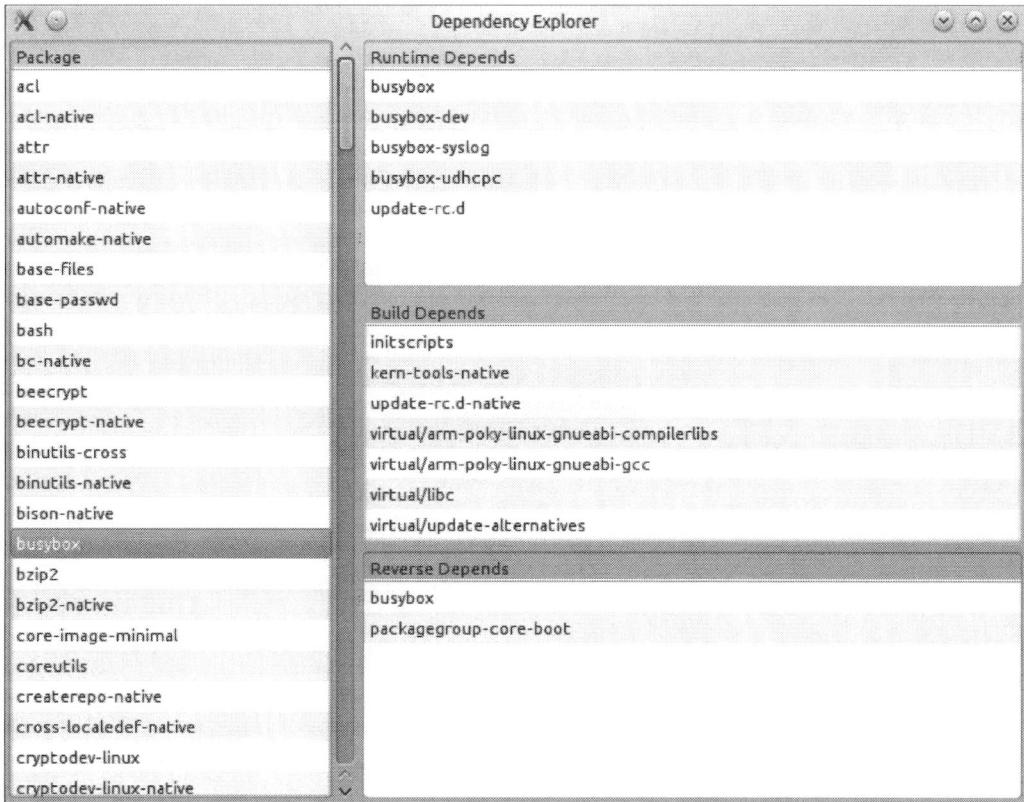

Debugging BitBake

It is not common to have to debug BitBake itself, but you may find a bug in BitBake and want to explore it by yourself before reporting it to the BitBake community. For such cases, you can ask BitBake to output the debug information at three different levels with the `-D` flag. To display all the debug information, run the following command:

```
$ bitbake -DDD <target>
```

Error reporting tool

Sometimes, you will find a build error on a Yocto recipe that you have not modified. The first place to check for errors is the community itself, but before launching your mail client, head to `http://errors.yoctoproject.org`.

This is a central database of user-reported errors. Here, you may check whether someone else is experiencing the same problem.

You can submit your own build failure to the database to help the community debug the problem. To do so, you may use the `report-error` class. Add the following to your `conf/local.conf` file:

```
INHERIT += "report-error"
```

By default, the error information is stored under `tmp/log/error-report` under the `build` directory, but you can set a specific location with the `ERR_REPORT_DIR` variable.

When the error reporting tool is activated, a build error will be captured in a file in the `error-report` folder. The build output will also print a command to send the error log to the server:

```
$ send-error-report ${LOG_DIR}/error-report/error-report_${TSTAMP}
```

When this command is executed, it will report back with a link to the upstream error.

You can set up a local error server, and use that instead by passing a server argument. The error server code and setting up details can be found at `http://git.yoctoproject.org/cgit/cgit.cgi/error-report-web/tree/README`.

There's more...

Although you can use Linux utilities to parse Yocto's metadata and build output, BitBake lacks a command base UI for common tasks. One project that aims to provide it is `bb`, which is available at `https://github.com/kergoth/bb`.

To use it, you need to clone the repository locally by executing the following command:

```
$ cd /opt/yocto/fsl-community-bsp/sources
$ git clone https://github.com/kergoth/bb.git
```

Then run the `bb/bin/bb init` command, which prompts you to add a bash command to your `~/.bash_profile` file.

You can either do that or execute it in your current shell as follows:

```
$ eval "$(/opt/yocto/fsl-community-bsp/sources/bb/bin/bb init -)"
```

You will first need to set up your environment as usual:

```
$ cd /opt/yocto/fsl-community-bsp
$ source setup-environment wandboard-quad
```

> Some of the commands only work with a populated work directory, so you may need to remove the `rm_work` class if you want to use `bb`.

Some of the tasks that are made easier by the `bb` utility are:

- Exploring the contents of a package:

  ```
  $ bb contents <target>
  ```

- Searching for a pattern in the recipes:

  ```
  $ bb search <pattern>
  ```

- Displaying either the global BitBake environment or the environment for a specific package and grepping for a specific variable:

  ```
  $ bb show -r <recipe> <variable>
  ```

2
The BSP Layer

In this chapter, we will cover the following recipes:

- ▶ Creating a custom BSP layer
- ▶ Introducing system development workflows
- ▶ Adding a custom kernel and bootloader
- ▶ Building the U-Boot bootloader
- ▶ Explaining Yocto's Linux kernel support
- ▶ Describing Linux's build system
- ▶ Configuring the Linux kernel
- ▶ Building the Linux source
- ▶ Building external kernel modules
- ▶ Debugging the Linux kernel and modules
- ▶ Debugging the Linux kernel booting process
- ▶ Using the kernel tracing system
- ▶ Managing the device tree
- ▶ Debugging device tree issues

Introduction

Once we have our build environment ready with the Yocto project, it's time to think about beginning development work on our embedded Linux project.

Most of the embedded Linux projects require both custom hardware and software. An early task in the development process is to test different hardware reference boards and the selection of one to base our design on. We have chosen the Wandboard, a Freescale i.MX6-based platform, as it is an affordable and open board, which makes it perfect for our needs.

On an embedded project, it is usually a good idea to start working on the software as soon as possible, probably before the hardware prototypes are ready, so that it is possible to start working directly with the reference design.

But at some point, the hardware prototypes will be ready and changes will need to be introduced into Yocto to support the new hardware.

This chapter will explain how to create a BSP layer to contain those hardware-specific changes, as well as show how to work with the U-Boot bootloader and the Linux kernel, components which are likely to take most of the customization work.

Creating a custom BSP layer

These custom changes are kept on a separate Yocto layer, called a **Board Support Package** (**BSP**) layer. This separation is best for future updates and patches to the system. A BSP layer can support any number of new machines and any new software feature that is linked to the hardware itself.

How to do it...

By convention, Yocto layer names start with `meta`, short for metadata. A BSP layer may then add a `bsp` keyword, and finally a unique name. We will call our layer `meta-bsp-custom`.

There are several ways to create a new layer:

▶ Manually, once you know what is required

▶ By copying the `meta-skeleton` layer included in Poky

▶ By using the `yocto-layer` command-line tool

You can have a look at the `meta-skeleton` layer in Poky and see that it includes the following elements:

▶ A `layer.conf` file, where the layer configuration variables are set

▶ A `COPYING.MIT` license file

▶ Several directories named with the `recipes` prefix with example recipes for BusyBox, the Linux kernel and an example module, an example service recipe, an example user management recipe, and a multilib example.

How it works...

We will cover some of the use cases that appear in the available examples in the next few recipes, so for our needs, we will use the `yocto-layer` tool, which allows us to create a minimal layer.

Open a new terminal and change to the `fsl-community-bsp` directory. Then set up the environment as follows:

```
$ source setup-environment wandboard-quad
```

> Note that once the `build` directory has been created, the `MACHINE` variable has already been configured in the `conf/local.conf` file and can be omitted from the command line.

Change to the `sources` directory and run:

```
$ yocto-layer create bsp-custom
```

Note that the `yocto-layer` tool will add the `meta` prefix to your layer, so you don't need to. It will prompt a few questions:

▶ The layer priority which is used to decide the layer precedence in cases where the same recipe (with the same name) exists in several layers simultaneously. It is also used to decide in what order `bbappends` are applied if several layers append the same recipe. Leave the default value of 6. This will be stored in the layer's `conf/layer.conf` file as `BBFILE_PRIORITY`.

▶ Whether to create example recipes and append files. Let's leave the default *no* for the time being.

Our new layer has the following structure:

```
meta-bsp-custom/
    conf/layer.conf
    COPYING.MIT
    README
```

There's more...

The first thing to do is to add this new layer to your project's `conf/bblayer.conf` file. It is a good idea to add it to your template conf directory's `bblayers.conf.sample` file too, so that it is correctly appended when creating new projects. The highlighted line in the following code shows the addition of the layer to the `conf/bblayers.conf` file:

```
LCONF_VERSION = "6"

BBPATH = "${TOPDIR}"
BSPDIR := "${@os.path.abspath(os.path.dirname(d.getVar('FILE',
  True)) + '/../..')}"

BBFILES ?= ""
BBLAYERS = " \
  ${BSPDIR}/sources/poky/meta \
  ${BSPDIR}/sources/poky/meta-yocto \
  \
  ${BSPDIR}/sources/meta-openembedded/meta-oe \
  ${BSPDIR}/sources/meta-openembedded/meta-multimedia \
  \
  ${BSPDIR}/sources/meta-fsl-arm \
  ${BSPDIR}/sources/meta-fsl-arm-extra \
  ${BSPDIR}/sources/meta-fsl-demos \
  ${BSPDIR}/sources/meta-bsp-custom \
"
```

Now, BitBake will parse the `bblayers.conf` file and find the `conf/layers.conf` file from your layer. In it, we find the following line:

```
BBFILES += "${LAYERDIR}/recipes-*/*/*.bb \
        ${LAYERDIR}/recipes-*/*/*.bbappend"
```

It tells BitBake which directories to parse for recipes and append files. You need to make sure your directory and file hierarchy in this new layer matches the given pattern, or you will need to modify it.

BitBake will also find the following:

```
BBPATH .= ":${LAYERDIR}"
```

The `BBPATH` variable is used to locate the `bbclass` files and the configuration and files included with the `include` and `require` directives. The search finishes with the first match, so it is best to keep filenames unique.

Some other variables we might consider defining in our `conf/layer.conf` file are:

```
LAYERDEPENDS_bsp-custom = "fsl-arm"
LAYERVERSION_bsp-custom = "1"
```

The `LAYERDEPENDS` literal is a space-separated list of other layers your layer depends on, and the `LAYERVERSION` literal specifies the version of your layer in case other layers want to add a dependency to a specific version.

The `COPYING.MIT` file specifies the license for the metadata contained in the layer. The Yocto project is licensed under the *MIT* license, which is also compatible with the **General Public License** (**GPL**). This license applies only to the metadata, as every package included in your build will have its own license.

The `README` file will need to be modified for your specific layer. It is usual to describe the layer and provide any other layer dependencies and usage instructions.

Adding a new machine

When customizing your BSP, it is usually a good idea to introduce a new machine for your hardware. These are kept under the `conf/machine` directory in your BSP layer. The usual thing to do is to base it on the reference design. For example, `wandboard-quad` has the following machine configuration file:

```
include include/wandboard.inc

SOC_FAMILY = "mx6:mx6q:wandboard"

UBOOT_MACHINE = "wandboard_quad_config"

KERNEL_DEVICETREE = "imx6q-wandboard.dtb"

MACHINE_FEATURES += "bluetooth wifi"

MACHINE_EXTRA_RRECOMMENDS += " \
```

```
    bcm4329-nvram-config \
    bcm4330-nvram-config \
"
```

A machine based on the Wandboard design could define its own machine configuration file, `wandboard-quad-custom.conf`, as follows:

```
include conf/machine/include/wandboard.inc

SOC_FAMILY = "mx6:mx6q:wandboard"

UBOOT_MACHINE = "wandboard_quad_custom_config"

KERNEL_DEVICETREE = "imx6q-wandboard-custom.dtb"

MACHINE_FEATURES += "wifi"
```

The `wandboard.inc` file now resides on a different layer, so in order for BitBake to find it, we need to specify the full path from the `BBPATH` variable in the corresponding layer. This machine defines its own U-Boot configuration file and Linux kernel device tree in addition to defining its own set of machine features.

Adding a custom device tree to the Linux kernel

To add this device tree file to the Linux kernel, we need to add the device tree file to the `arch/arm/boot/dts` directory under the Linux kernel source and also modify the Linux build system's `arch/arm/boot/dts/Makefile` file to build it as follows:

```
dtb-$(CONFIG_ARCH_MXC) += \
+imx6q-wandboard-custom.dtb \
```

This code uses diff formatting, where the lines with a minus prefix are removed, the ones with a plus sign are added, and the ones without a prefix are left as reference.

Once the patch is prepared, it can be added to the `meta-bsp-custom/recipes-kernel/linux/linux-wandboard-3.10.17/` directory and the Linux kernel recipe appended adding a `meta-bsp-custom/recipes-kernel/linux/linux-wandboard_3.10.17.bbappend` file with the following content:

```
SRC_URI_append = " file://0001-ARM-dts-Add-wandboard-custom-dts-
    file.patch"
```

An example patch that adds a custom device tree to the Linux kernel can be found in the source code that accompanies the book.

Adding a custom U-Boot machine

In the same way, the U-Boot source may be patched to add a new custom machine. Bootloader modifications are not as likely to be needed as kernel modifications though, and most custom platforms will leave the bootloader unchanged. The patch would be added to the `meta-bsp-custom/recipes-bsp/u-boot/u-boot-fslc-v2014.10/` directory and the U-Boot recipe appended with a `meta-bsp-custom/recipes-bsp/u-boot/u-boot-fslc_2014.10.bbappend` file with the following content:

```
SRC_URI_append = " file://0001-boards-Add-wandboard-custom.patch"
```

An example patch that adds a custom machine to U-Boot can be found in the source code that accompanies the book.

Adding a custom formfactor file

Custom platforms can also define their own `formfactor` file with information that the build system cannot obtain from other sources, such as defining whether a touchscreen is available or defining the screen orientation. These are defined in the `recipes-bsp/formfactor/` directory in our `meta-bsp-custom` layer. For our new machine, we could define a `meta-bsp-custom/recipes-bsp/formfactor/formfactor_0.0.bbappend` file to include a `formfactor` file as follows:

```
FILESEXTRAPATHS_prepend := "${THISDIR}/${PN}:"
```

And the machine-specific `meta-bsp-custom/recipes-bsp/formfactor/formfactor/wandboard-quadcustom/machconfig` file would be as follows:

```
HAVE_TOUCHSCREEN=1
```

Introducing system development workflows

When customizing the software, there are some system development workflows that are commonly used, and we will introduce them in this recipe.

How to do it...

We will see an overview of the following development workflows:

- External development
- Working directory development
- External source development

They are all used under different scenarios.

How it works...

Let's understand what the use of each of these development workflows is individually.

External development

In this workflow, we don't use the Yocto build system to build our packages, just a Yocto toolchain and the package's own build system.

The resulting source can be integrated into Yocto in the following ways:

- ▶ With a recipe that fetches a released tarball.
- ▶ With a recipe that fetches directly from a source-controlled repository.

External development is usually the preferred method for U-Boot and Linux kernel development, as they can be easily cross-compiled. Third-party packages in Yocto are also developed in this way.

However, third-party packages can be tricky to cross-compile, and that is just what the Yocto build system makes easy. So, if we are not the main developers of the package and we only want to introduce some fixes or modifications, we can use Yocto to help us. The two workflows explained in the following sections use the Yocto build system.

Working directory development

In this workflow, we use the working directory inside the `build` directory, `tmp/work`. As we know, when Yocto builds a package, it uses the working directory to extract, patch, configure, build, and package the source. We can directly modify the source in this directory and use the Yocto system to build it.

This methodology is commonly used when sporadically debugging third-party packages.

The workflow is as follows:

1. Remove the package's `build` directory to start from scratch:

   ```
   $ bitbake -c cleanall <target>
   ```

2. Tell BitBake to fetch, unpack, and patch the package, but stop there:

   ```
   $ bitbake -c patch <target>
   ```

3. Enter the package's source directory and modify the source. Usually, we would create a temporary local Git directory to help us with our development and to extract the patches easily.

   ```
   $ bitbake -c devshell <target>
   ```

4. Build it without losing our changes:

   ```
   $ bitbake -C compile <target>
   ```

Note the capital C. This instructs BitBake to run the compile task and all the tasks that follow it. This is the same as running:

```
$ bitbake -c compile <target>
$ bitbake <target>
```

5. Test it by copying the package to a running system and installing it with the target's package management system. When you run your system from an NFS root filesystem, it's as easy as to copy it there and run the following command (assuming the default RPM package format):

```
$ rpm -i <package>
```

Optionally, you can also use a package feed as we saw in the *Setting up a package feed* recipe in *Chapter 1, The Build System*, in which case you would rebuild the index with the following:

```
$ bitbake package-index
```

And then use the smart package management utility on the target to install the package as previously shown.

6. Extract the patches and add them to the recipe's bbappend file.

External source development

In this workflow, we will use the Yocto build system to build an external directory containing the source. This external directory is usually source controlled to help us in our development.

This is the usual methodology to follow for extensive package development once the source has already been integrated with the Yocto build system.

The workflow is as follows:

1. We perform our development on this external-version-controlled directory and commit our changes locally.

2. We configure the Yocto build system to use a directory in our host system to fetch the source from, and optionally also to build in. This guarantees that our changes cannot be lost by any action of the Yocto build system. We will see some examples of this later on.

3. Build it using Yocto:

```
$ bitbake <target>
```

4. Test it by copying the package to a running system and installing it with the target's package management system.

5. Extract the patches and add them to the recipe's bbappend file.

Adding a custom kernel and bootloader

Development in U-Boot and the Linux kernel is usually done externally to Yocto, as they are easy to build using a toolchain, like the one provided by Yocto.

The development work is then integrated into Yocto in one of two ways:

- ▶ With patches added to the kernel and U-Boot bbappend files. This method will build the same source as the reference design board we are using as base, and apply our changes over it.

- ▶ Using a different Git repository, forked from the Linux kernel and U-Boot Git repositories being used by the reference design, and using a bbappend file to point the recipe to it. This way, we can directly commit the changes to the repository and the Yocto build system will build them.

Usually a forked Git repository is only needed when the hardware changes are substantial and the work in the Linux kernel and bootloader is going to be extensive. The recommendation is to start with patches, and only use a forked repository when they become difficult to manage.

Getting Ready

The first question when starting work on the Linux kernel and U-Boot modifications is how do you find which of the several available recipes are being used for your build.

Finding the Linux kernel source

To find the Linux kernel source, we might use several methods. As we are aware we are building for a wandboard-quad machine, the first thing to do is find a machine configuration file:

```
$ cd /opt/yocto/fsl-community-bsp/sources
$ find -name wandboard-quad.conf
./meta-fsl-arm-extra/conf/machine/wandboard-quad.conf
```

The machine configuration file above in turn includes a wandboard.inc file:

```
include conf/machine/include/imx-base.inc
include conf/machine/include/tune-cortexa9.inc

PREFERRED_PROVIDER_virtual/kernel ?= "linux-wandboard"
PREFERRED_VERSION_linux-wandboard ?= "3.10.17"
```

Here we find a Linux kernel recipe being specified as the preferred provider for virtual/kernel. Virtual packages like this are used when a feature or element is provided by more than one recipe. It allows us to choose which of all those recipes will finally be used. Virtual packages will be further explained in the *Selecting a specific package versions and providers* recipe in *Chapter 3, The Software Layer.*

We could check the actual output from our previous `core-image-minimal` build:

```
$ find tmp/work -name "*linux-wandboard*"
tmp/work/wandboard_quad-poky-linux-gnueabi/linux-wandboard
```

As the `linux-wanboard` directory exists in our `work` folder, we can be sure the recipe has been used.

We can check what the available Linux recipes are with:

```
$ find -name "*linux*.bb"
```

We have lots of options, but we can use some of our acquired knowledge to filter them out. Let's exclude the `poky` and `meta-openembedded` directories, as we know the BSP support is included in the Freescale community BSP layers:

```
$ find -path ./poky -prune -o -path ./meta-openembedded -prune -o -name "*linux*.bb"
```

Finally, we can also use the `bitbake-layers` script included in Poky:

```
$ cd /opt/yocto/fsl-community-bsp/
$ source setup-environment wandboard-quad
$ bitbake-layers show-recipes 'linux*'
```

Not all those kernels support the Wandboard machine completely, but they all support Freescale ARM machines, so they are useful for comparisons.

Finding the U-Boot source

If we continue to pull the include chain, we have `imx-base.inc`, which itself includes `fsl-default-providers.inc`, where we find:

```
PREFERRED_PROVIDER_u-boot ??= "u-boot-fslc"
PREFERRED_PROVIDER_virtual/bootloader ??= "u-boot-fslc"
```

So `u-boot-fslc` is the U-Boot recipe we are looking for.

Developing using a Git repository fork

We will show how to append a recipe to use a forked repository to work from it. We will use the Linux kernel as an example, but the concept works just as well for U-Boot or any other package, although the specifics will change.

We will fork or branch the repository used in the reference design and use it to specify SRC_URI for the recipe.

How to do it...

For this example, I have forked the repository to `https://github.com/yoctocookbook/linux`, so my `recipes-kernel/linux/linux-wandboard_3.10.17.bbappend` file would have the following changes:

```
# Copyright Packt Publishing 2015
WANDBOARD_GITHUB_MIRROR = "git://github.com/yoctocookbook/linux.git"
SRCBRANCH = "wandboard_imx_3.10.17_1.0.2_ga-dev"
SRCREV = "${AUTOREV}"
```

> Note how the URL needs to start with `git://`. This is so that BitBake can recognize it as a Git source. Now we can clean and build the Linux kernel and the source will be fetched from the forked repository.

How it works...

Let's have a look at the `linux-wandboard_3.10.17.bb` recipe:

```
include linux-wandboard.inc
require recipes-kernel/linux/linux-dtb.inc

DEPENDS += "lzop-native bc-native"

# Wandboard branch - based on 3.10.17_1.0.2_ga from Freescale git
SRCBRANCH = "wandboard_imx_3.10.17_1.0.2_ga"
SRCREV = "be8d6872b5eb4c94c15dac36b028ce7f60472409"
LOCALVERSION = "-1.0.2-wandboard"

COMPATIBLE_MACHINE = "(wandboard)"
```

The first interesting thing is the inclusion of both `linux-wandboard.inc` and `linux-dtb.inc`. We will look at the first later on, and the other is a class that allows us to compile Linux kernel device trees. We will discuss device trees in the *Managing the device tree* recipe later in this chapter.

Then it declares two package dependencies, `lzop-native` and `bc-native`. The `native` part tells us that these are used in the host system, so they are used during the Linux kernel build process. The `lzop` tool is used to create the `cpio` compressed files needed in the `initramfs` system, which is a system that boots from a memory-based root filesystem, and `bc` was introduced to avoid a Perl kernel dependency when generating certain kernel files.

Then it sets the branch and revision, and finally it sets `COMPATIBLE_MACHINE` to `wandboard`. We will speak about machine compatibility in the *Adding new packages* recipe of *Chapter 3*, *The Software Layer*.

Let's now have a look at the `linux-wandboard.inc` include file:

```
SUMMARY = "Linux kernel for Wandboard"
LICENSE = "GPLv2"
LIC_FILES_CHKSUM =
    "file://COPYING;md5=d7810fab7487fb0aad327b76f1be7cd7"


require recipes-kernel/linux/linux-imx.inc


# Put a local version until we have a true SRCREV to point to
SCMVERSION ?= "y"


SRCBRANCH ??= "master"
LOCALVERSION ?= "-${SRCBRANCH}"


# Allow override of WANDBOARD_GITHUB_MIRROR to make use of
# local repository easier
WANDBOARD_GITHUB_MIRROR ?= "git://github.com/wandboard-
    org/linux.git"


# SRC_URI for wandboard kernel
SRC_URI = "${WANDBOARD_GITHUB_MIRROR};branch=${SRCBRANCH} \
          file://defconfig \
    "
```

This is actually the file we were looking for. Initially, it specifies the license for the kernel source and points to it, sets a default branch and local version kernel string, and sets up the `SCR_URI` variable, which is the place where the source code is fetched from.

It then offers the `WANDBOARD_GITHUB_MIRROR` variable, which we can modify in our `bbappend` file.

So the logical setup would be to create a GitHub account and fork the provided `wandboard-org` Linux repository.

Once the fork is in place, we need to modify the `WANDBOARD_GITHUB_MIRROR` variable. But as we saw before, the recipe configures a specific revision and branch. We want to develop here, so we want to change this to a new development branch we have created. Let's call it `wandboard_imx_3.10.17_1.0.2_ga-dev` and set the revision to automatically fetch the newest point in the branch.

Building the U-Boot bootloader

In this recipe, we will go through the several development workflows described previously using the U-Boot bootloader as an example.

How to do it...

We will see how the following development workflows are applied to U-Boot:

- ▶ External development
- ▶ External source development
- ▶ Working directory development

How it works...

Let's explain the three workflows, previously mentioned, in detail.

External development

We will use a Yocto toolchain to build the U-Boot source externally from the Yocto build system.

1. Download and install a Yocto project cross-compilation toolchain for your host by going to the following:

   `http://downloads.yoctoproject.org/releases/yocto/yocto-1.7.1/toolchain/`

> Choose either the 32- or 64-bit version and execute the installation script, accepting the default installation location. It is recommended not to change the default location to avoid relocation issues.

2. Find the upstream Git repository:

```
$ bitbake -e u-boot-fslc | grep ^SRC_URI=
SRC_URI="git://github.com/Freescale/u-boot-
    imx.git;branch=patches-2014.10"
```

3. Clone the U-Boot's source from its upstream repository:

```
$ cd /opt/yocto/
$ git clone git://github.com/Freescale/u-boot-imx.git
$ cd u-boot-imx
```

The default branch should be `patches-2014.10`, but if it's not, you can change it with the following:

```
$ git checkout -b patches-2014.10 origin/patches-2014.10
```

4. Set up the environment using the script provided with the toolchain:

```
$ source /opt/poky/1.7.1/environment-setup-armv7a-vfp-neon-
    poky-linux-gnueabi
```

5. Configure U-Boot for `wandboard-quad`:

```
$ make wandboard_quad_config
```

6. If you try to build U-Boot, it will fail. This is because the default Yocto environment setup does not cater to U-Boot's needs. A quick look at the U-Boot recipe shows that it clears some flags before building, so let's do that:

```
$ unset LDFLAGS CFLAGS CPPFLAGS
```

7. Now we are ready to build. The U-Boot recipe also passes `CC` to the `make` utility in the `EXTRA_OEMAKE` flags as U-Boot does not read it from the environment, so we also need to run:

```
$ make CC="${CC}"
```

> You can optionally pass a `-jN` argument for multithreaded compilation. Here, `N` is the number of CPU cores.

How it works...

The U-Boot `Makefile` looks for `libgcc` using the following command:

```
PLATFORM_LIBGCC := -L $(shell dirname `$(CC) $(CFLAGS) -print-libgcc-
    file-name`) -lgcc
```

If we don't define CC, the expression does not correctly expand to the location of the libgcc library in the toolchain, as the sysroot option is not passed to the compiler.

> Newer versions of U-Boot have already fixed this issue, but we decided to leave the instruction as the following:
>
> ```
> $ make CC="${CC}"
> ```
>
> That works for older versions of U-Boot too.

Another way to avoid the problem would be to define the USE_PRIVATE_LIBGCC U-Boot configuration variable, but that would use an internal libgcc library to U-Boot, which may not be what we want.

We would then need to copy the image to the target to test our changes, as we will see soon.

External source development

We will use the Yocto build system from a local directory by cloning a local copy of the source used in the reference design and configuring our project to use it as an external source. We will then develop from it, extract the patches, and add them to a bbappend file on our BSP layer.

We will use the U-Boot source cloned in the example beforehand.

To configure our conf/local.conf file to work from the cloned source, modify it as follows:

```
INHERIT += "externalsrc"
EXTERNALSRC_pn-u-boot-fslc = "/opt/yocto/u-boot-imx"
EXTERNALSRC_BUILD_pn-u-boot-fslc = "/opt/yocto/u-boot-imx"
```

The EXTERNALSRC variable defines the source location (S), while the EXTERNALSRC_BUILD variable defines the build location (B). This code will also build on the external source location as the u-boot-fslc recipe does not currently support the separation of the source and build directories.

> Remember to remove the aforementioned configuration when trying the working directory development methodology explained next in this recipe.

Now we can build on a new shell with:

```
$ cd /opt/yocto/fsl-community-bsp/
$ source setup-environment wandboard-quad
$ bitbake u-boot-fslc
```

When building from an external source, the expansion of SRCPV fails with an error. Recipes need to be temporarily modified to use static versioning while the external source compilation is enabled. In the case of U-Boot, we would make the following change in the `meta-fsl-arm/recipes-bsp/u-boot/u-boot-fslc_2014.10.bb` file:

```
- PV = "v2014.10+git${SRCPV}"
+ PV = "v2014.10"
```

This uses diff formatting, where the lines with a minus prefix are removed and the ones with a plus sign are added.

An example patch to U-Boot that allows us to perform external source development can be found in the source code that accompanies the book.

Development work can now be committed in the local Git repository, and patches can be generated with `git format-patch`. For example, we could change the board information for the Wandboard with the `0001-wandboard-Change-board-info.patch` file:

```
diff --git a/board/wandboard/wandboard.c
  b/board/wandboard/wandboard.c
index 3c8b7a5d2d0a..a466d4c74b8f 100644
--- a/board/wandboard/wandboard.c
+++ b/board/wandboard/wandboard.c
@@ -404,7 +404,7 @@ int board_init(void)

 int checkboard(void)
 {
-        puts("Board: Wandboard\n");
+        puts("Board: Wandboard custom\n");

         return 0;
 }
```

To add this patch to Yocto's U-Boot recipe, we create a `meta-bsp-custom/recipes-bsp/u-boot/u-boot-fslc_2014.10.bbappend` file with the following content:

```
# Copyright Packt Publishing 2015
FILESEXTRAPATHS_prepend := "${THISDIR}/${PN}-${PV}:"
SRC_URI_append = " file://0001-wandboard-Change-board-info.patch"
```

The patch needs to be placed under `meta-bsp-custom/recipes-bsp/u-boot/u-boot-fslc-v2014.10/`, as specified in the FILESEXTRAPATHS variable.

Files added to the SRC_URI variable that end in the patch or diff prefixes will be applied in the order they are found. You can also force a file to be treated as patch by specifying an apply=yes property to it in SRC_URI.

Working directory development

A typical workflow when working on a small modification would be:

1. Start the U-Boot package compilation from scratch:

    ```
    $ bitbake -c cleanall virtual/bootloader
    ```

    This will erase the build folder, shared state cache, and downloaded package source.

2. Start a development shell:

    ```
    $ bitbake -c devshell virtual/bootloader
    ```

    This will fetch, unpack, and patch the U-Boot sources and spawn a new shell with the environment ready for U-Boot compilation. The new shell will change to the U-Boot build directory, which contains a local Git repository.

3. Perform your modifications on the local Git repository.

4. Leave the devshell open and use a different terminal to compile the source without erasing our modifications:

    ```
    $ bitbake -C compile virtual/bootloader
    ```

    Note the capital C. This invokes the compile task but also all the tasks that follow it.

    The newly compiled U-Boot image is available under tmp/deploy/images/wandboard-quad.

5. Test your changes. Typically, this means that we need to reprogram the bootloader into the microSD card (as is the case with the Wandboard) or the internal emmc (if available) at the correct offset. We can do it both from the target or from your host computer.

    From the host computer, we would use dd to copy the new U-Boot image to an offset of 0x400, which is where the i.MX6 bootrom expects to find it.

    ```
    sudo dd if=u-boot.imx of=/dev/sdN bs=512 seek=2 && sync
    ```

    This writes with an offset of 2 blocks, which, given a 512-byte block size, is 0x400 (1024) bytes.

> Be careful when running the dd command, as it could harm your machine. You need to be absolutely sure that the sdN device corresponds to your microSD card and not a drive on your development machine.

From the device itself, we can use U-Boot's `mmc` command as follows:

> ❑ Load the U-Boot image to memory:

```
> setenv ipaddr <target_ip>
> setenv serverip <host_ip>
> tftp ${loadaddr} u-boot.imx
```

The hexadecimal file size of the TFTP transfer is kept in the filesize environment variable, which we will use later on.

> ❑ Select the MMC device to operate on. You can use the `mmc` part to discover which is the correct device.

```
> mmc dev 0
> mmc part

Partition Map for MMC device 0  --   Partition Type: DOS

Part    Start Sector    Num Sectors    UUID          Type
  1     8192            16384          0003b9dd-01   0c
  2     24576           131072         0003b9dd-02   83
```

We can see that partition `1` starts at sector `8192`, leaving enough space to program U-Boot.

> ❑ With a 512-byte block size, we calculate the number of blocks as follows:

```
> setexpr filesizeblks $filesize / 0x200
> setexpr filesizeblks $filesizeblks + 1
```

> ❑ We then write to an offset of two blocks with the numbers of blocks occupied by our image.

```
> mmc write ${loadaddr} 0x2 ${filesizeblks}
```

6. Go back to the devshell and commit your change to the local Git repository.

```
$ git add --all .
$ git commit -s -m "Well thought commit message"
```

7. Generate a patch into the U-Boot recipe patch directory as follows:

```
$ git format-patch -1 -o /opt/yocto/fsl-community-
  bsp/sources/meta-bsp-custom/recipes-bsp/u-boot/u-boot-fslc-
  v2014.10/
```

8. Finally, add the patch to the U-Boot recipe as explained before.

Explaining Yocto's Linux kernel support

The Yocto project offers a kernel framework that allows us to work with the Linux kernel in different ways:

- Fetching the source from a Git repository and applying patches to it. This is the path taken by the Freescale community BSP-supported kernels, as we saw previously.

- The `linux-yocto` style kernels that generate the kernel source from a set of Git branches and leafs. Specific features are developed in branches, and a leaf is followed for a complete set of features.

In this recipe, we will show how to work with a `linux-yocto` style kernel.

How to do it...

To use a `linux-yocto` style kernel, the kernel recipe inherits the `linux-yocto.inc` file. A Git repository for a `linux-yocto` style kernel contains metadata either in the recipe or inside the kernel Git tree, in branches named with the `meta` prefix.

The `linux-yocto` style kernel recipes are all named `linux-yocto` and follow the upstream kernel development, rooted in the `kernel.org` repository. Once a new Yocto release cycle starts, a recent upstream kernel version is chosen, and the kernel version from the previous Yocto release is maintained. Older versions are updated inline with the **Long Term Support Initiative** (**LTSI**) releases. There is also a `linux-yocto-dev` package, which always follows the latest upstream kernel development.

Yocto kernels are maintained separately from the upstream kernel sources, and add features and BSPs to cater to embedded system developers.

Although the Freescale community BSP does not include `linux-yocto` style kernels, some other BSP layers do.

Metadata variables that are used to define the build include:

- `KMACHINE`: This is usually the same as the `MACHINE` variable, but not always. It defines the kernel's machine type.

- `KBRANCH`: This explicitly sets the kernel branch to build. It is optional.

- `KBRANCH_DEFAULT`: This is the default value for KBRANCH, initially `master`.

- `KERNEL_FEATURES`: This adds additional metadata that is used to specify configuration and patches. It appears above the defined `KMACHINE` and `KBRANCH`. It is defined in **Series Configuration Control** (**SCC**) files as described soon.

▶ LINUX_KERNEL_TYPE: This defaults to standard, but may also be tiny or preempt-rt. It is defined in its own SCC description files, or explicitly defined using the KTYPE variable in the SCC files.

How it works...

The metadata included in the Linux kernel manages the configuration and source selection to support multiple BSPs and kernel types. The tools that manage this metadata are built in the kern-tools package.

The metadata can be set either in recipes, for small changes or if you are using a kernel repository you do not have access to, or most usually inside the kernel Git repository in meta branches. The meta branch that is to be used defaults to a meta directory in the same repository branch as the sources, but can be specified using the KMETA variable in your kernel recipe. If it does not reside in the same branch as the kernel source, it is kept in an orphan branch; that is, a branch with its own history. To create an orphan branch, use the following commands:

```
$ git checkout --orphan meta
$ git rm -rf .
$ git commit --allow-empty -m "Meta branch"
```

Your recipe must then include SRCREV_meta to point to the revision of the meta branch to use.

The metadata is described in SCC files, which can include a series of commands:

▶ kconf: This command applies a configuration fragment to the kernel configuration.

▶ patch: This command applies the specified patch.

▶ define: This introduces the variable definitions.

▶ include: This includes another SCC file.

▶ git merge: This merges the specified branch into the current branch.

▶ branch: This creates a new branch relative to the current branch, usually KTYPE or as specified.

SCC files are broadly divided into the following logical groupings:

▶ **configuration** (cfg): This contains one or more kernel configuration fragments and an SCC file to describe them. For example:

```
cfg/spidev.scc:
        define KFEATURE_DESCRIPTION "Enable SPI device
    support"
```

```
kconf hardware spidev.cfg
```

```
cfg/spidev.cfg:
        CONFIG_SPI_SPIDEV=y
```

▶ **patches**: This contains one or more kernel patches and an SCC file to describe them. For example:

```
patches/fix.scc:
        patch fix.patch
```

```
patches/fix.patch
```

▶ **features**: This contains mix configurations and patches to define complex features. It can also include other description files. For example:

```
features/feature.scc
        define KFEATURE_DESCRIPTION "Enable feature"

        patch 0001-feature.patch

        include cfg/feature_dependency.scc
        kconf non-hardware feature.cfg
```

▶ **kernel types**: This contains features that define a high-level kernel policy. By default, three kernel types are defined in SCC files:

- ❑ **standard**: This is a generic kernel definition policy

- ❑ **tiny**: This is a bare minimum kernel definition policy and is independent of the standard type

- ❑ **preempt-rt**: This inherits from the standard type to define a real-time kernel where the PREEMTP-RT patches are applied

Other kernel types can be defined by using the KTYPE variable on an SCC file.

▶ **Board Support Packages** (**BSP**): A combination of kernel types and hardware features. BSP types should include KMACHINE for the kernel machine and KARCH for the kernel architecture.

See also

▶ Detailed information regarding linux-yocto style kernels can be found in the *Yocto Project Linux Kernel Development Manual* at http://www.yoctoproject.org/docs/1.7.1/kernel-dev/kernel-dev.html

Describing Linux's build system

The Linux kernel is a monolithic kernel and as such shares the same address space. Although it has the ability to load modules at runtime, the kernel must contain all the symbols the module uses at compilation time. Once the module is loaded, it will share the kernel's address space.

The kernel build system, or **kbuild**, uses conditional compilation to decide which parts of the kernel are compiled. The kernel build system is independent of the Yocto build system.

In this recipe, we will explain how the kernel's build system works.

How to do it...

The kernel configuration is stored in a `.config` text file in the kernel root directory. The kbuild system reads this configuration to build the kernel. The `.config` file is referred to as the kernel configuration file. There are multiple ways to define a kernel configuration file:

- Manually editing the `.config` file, although this is not recommended.
- Using one of the user interfaces the kernel offers (type the make help command for other options):
    - `menuconfig`: An ncurses menu-based interface (`make menuconfig`)
    - `xconfig`: A Qt-based interface (`make xconfig`)
    - `gconfig`: A GTK-based interface (`make gconfig`)

> Note that to build and use these interfaces, your Linux host needs to have the appropriate dependencies.

- Automatically via a build system such as Yocto.

Each machine also defines a default configuration in the kernel tree. For ARM platforms, these are stored in the `arch/arm/configs` directory. To configure an ARM kernel, that is, to produce a `.config` file from a default configuration, you run:

```
$ make ARCH=arm <platform>_defconfig
```

For example we can build a default configuration for Freescale i.MX6 processors by running:

```
$ make ARCH=arm imx_v6_v7_defconfig
```

How it works...

Kbuild uses `Makefile` and `Kconfig` files to build the kernel source. Kconfig files define configuration symbols and attributes, and `Makefile` file match configuration symbols to source files.

The kbuild system options and targets can be seen by running:

```
$ make ARCH=arm help
```

There's more...

In recent kernels, a default configuration contains all the information needed to expand to a full configuration file. It is a minimal kernel configuration file where all dependencies are removed. To create a default configuration file from a current `.config` file, you run:

```
$ make ARCH=arm savedefconfig
```

This creates a `defconfig` file in the current kernel directory. This `make` target can be seen as the opposite of the `<platform>_defconfig` target explained before. The former creates a configuration file from a minimal configuration, and the other expands the minimal configuration into a full configuration file.

Configuring the Linux kernel

In this recipe, we will explain how to configure a Linux kernel using the Yocto build system.

Getting ready

Before configuring the kernel, we need to provide a default configuration for our machine, which is the one the Yocto project uses to configure a kernel. When defining a new machine in your BSP layer, you need to provide a `defconfig` file.

The Wandboard's `defconfig` file is stored under `sources/meta-fsl-arm-extra/recipes-kernel/linux/linux-wandboard-3.10.17/defconfig`.

This would be the base `defconfig` file for our custom hardware, so we copy it to our BSP layer:

```
$ cd /opt/yocto/fsl-community-bsp/sources
$ mkdir -p meta-bsp-custom/recipes-kernel/linux/linux-wandboard-
  3.10.17/
$ cp meta-fsl-arm-extra/recipes-kernel/linux/linux-wandboard-
  3.10.17/defconfig meta-bsp-custom/recipes-kernel/linux/linux-
  wandboard-3.10.17/
```

We then add it to our kernel using `meta-bsp-custom/recipes-kernel/linux/linux-wandboard_3.10.17.bbappend` as follows:

```
# Copyright Packt Publishing 2015
FILESEXTRAPATHS_prepend := "${THISDIR}/${PN}-${PV}:"
SRC_URI_append = " file://defconfig"
```

Kernel configuration changes to your platform can be made directly in this `defconfig` file.

How to do it...

To create a `.config` file from the machine `defconfig` file, execute the following command:

```
$ bitbake -c configure virtual/kernel
```

This will also run the oldconfig kernel `make` target to validate the configuration against the Linux source.

We can then configure the Linux kernel from the BitBake command line using the following:

```
$ bitbake -c menuconfig virtual/kernel
```

The menuconfig user interface, as well as other kernel configuration user interfaces, has a search functionality that allows you to locate configuration variables by name. Have a look at the following screenshot:

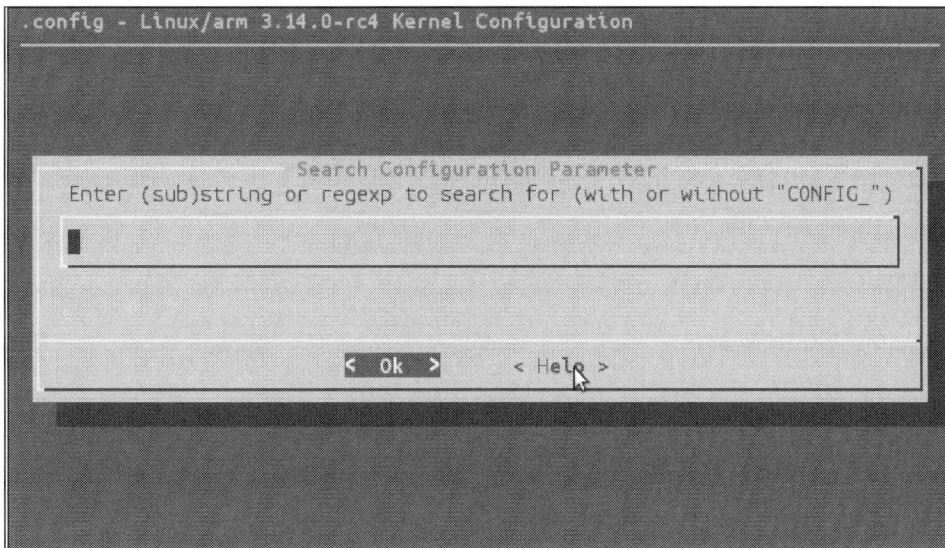

> In the following chapters, we will mention specific kernel configuration variables, like CONFIG_PRINTK, without specifying the whole path to the configuration variable. The search interface of the different UIs can be used to locate the configuration variable path.

When you save your changes, a new .config file is created on the kernel's build directory, which you can find using the following command:

```
$ bitbake -e virtual/kernel | grep ^B=
```

You can also modify the configuration using a graphical UI, but not from the BitBake command line. This is because graphical UIs need host dependencies, which are not natively built by Yocto.

To make sure your Ubuntu system has the needed dependencies, execute the following command:

```
$ sudo apt-get install git-core libncurses5 libncurses5-dev libelf-
  dev asciidoc binutils-dev qt3-dev-tools libqt3-mt-dev libncurses5
  libncurses5-dev fakeroot build-essential crash kexec-tools
  makedumpfile libgtk2.0-dev libglib2.0-dev libglade2-dev
```

Then change to the kernel build directory, which you found before, with:

```
$ cd /opt/yocto/fsl-community-bsp/wandboard-
  quad/tmp/work/wandboard_quad-poky-linux-gnueabi/linux-
  wandboard/3.10.17-r0/git
```

Next, run the following:

```
$ make ARCH=arm xconfig
```

> If you encounter compilation errors, attempt to run from a new terminal that has not had the environment configured with the setup-environment script.

A new window will open with the graphical configuration user interface shown in the next screenshot:

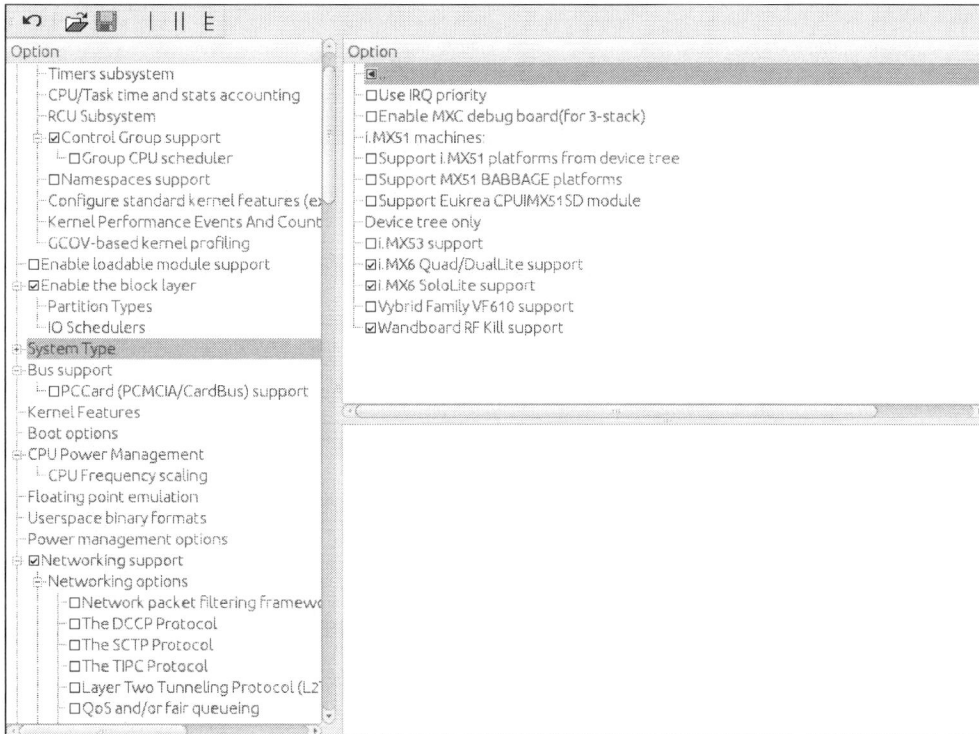

When you save your changes, the `.config` file will be updated.

To use an updated configuration, you need to take care that BitBake does not revert your changes when building. Refer to the *Building the Linux kernel* recipe in this chapter for additional details.

There's more...

You can make your kernel changes permanent with the following steps:

1. Create a default configuration from your `.config` file from the kernel source directory and a clean environment (not configured with the `setup-environment` script) by running:

   ```
   $ make ARCH=arm savedefconfig
   ```

2. Copy the `defconfig` file from your kernel `build` folder to your kernel recipe's `defconfig` file as follows:

```
$ cp defconfig /opt/yocto/fsl-community-bsp/sources/meta-bsp-
    custom/recipes-kernel/linux/linux-wandboard-3.10.17
```

Alternatively, you may use BitBake from the `build` directory as follows:

```
$ cd /opt/yocto/fsl-community-bsp/
$ source setup-environment wandboard-quad
$ bitbake -c savedefconfig virtual/kernel
```

This also creates a `defconfig` file in the Linux kernel's source directory, which needs to be copied to your recipe.

Using configuration fragments

The `linux-yocto` style kernels can also apply isolated kernel configuration changes defined in the kernel configuration fragments; for example:

```
spidev.cfg:
  CONFIG_SPI_SPIDEV=y
```

Kernel configuration fragments are appended to `SRC_URI` in the same way, and are applied over the `defconfig` file.

The `linux-yocto` style kernels (not the one for the Wandboard though) also provide a set of tools to manage kernel configuration:

▶ To configure the kernel from the `defconfig` file and the supplied configuration fragments, execute:

```
$ bitbake -f -c kernel_configme linux-yocto
```

▶ To create a configuration fragment with your changes, execute:

```
$ bitbake -c diffconfig linux-yocto
```

▶ To validate the kernel configuration, you may run:

```
$ bitbake -f -c kernel_configcheck linux-yocto
```

Building the Linux kernel

In this recipe, we will go through the development workflows described earlier using the Linux kernel as an example.

How to do it...

We will see how the following development workflows are applied to the Linux kernel:

- ▸ External development
- ▸ Working directory development
- ▸ External source development

How it works...

Let's explain the three methodologies listed previously in detail.

External development

When compiling outside of the Yocto build environment, we can still use the Yocto-provided toolchain to build. The process is as follows:

1. We will use the Yocto project cross-compilation toolchain already installed in your host.

2. Clone the `wandboard-org linux-wandboard` repository locally:

   ```
   $ cd /opt/yocto
   $ git clone https://github.com/wandboard-org/linux.git linux-wandboard
   $ cd linux-wandboard
   ```

3. Go to the branch specified in the `linux-wandboard_3.10.17.bb` recipe:

   ```
   $ git checkout -b wandboard_imx_3.10.17_1.0.2_ga
     origin/wandboard_imx_3.10.17_1.0.2_ga
   ```

4. Compile the kernel source as follows:

   ❑ Prepare the environment as follows:

   ```
   $ source /opt/poky/1.7.1/environment-setup-armv7a-vfp-neon-
     poky-linux-gnueabi
   ```

   ❑ Configure the kernel with the default machine configuration:

   ```
   $ cp /opt/yocto/fsl-community-bsp/sources/meta-bsp-custom/recipes-
   kernel/linux/linux-wandboard-3.10.17/defconfig arch/arm/configs/
   wandboard-quad_defconfig
   $ make wandboard-quad_defconfig
   ```

   ❑ Compile the kernel image, modules, and the device tree file with:

   ```
   $ make
   ```

You can optionally pass a `-jN` argument to make to build multithreaded.

This will build the kernel's zImage, modules, and device tree files.

> Older Yocto environment setup scripts set the `LD` variable to use `gcc`, but the Linux kernel uses `ld` instead. If your compilation is failing, try the following before running `make`:
>
> `$ unset LDFLAGS`

To build only modules, you may run:

`$ make modules`

And to build only device tree files, you may run:

`$ make dtbs`

  ❑ Copy the kernel image and device tree file to the TFTP root to test using network booting:

`$ cp arch/arm/boot/zImage arch/arm/boot/dts/imx6q-wandboard.dtb /var/lib/tftpboot`

Some other embedded Linux targets might need to compile a uImage if the U-Boot bootloader is not compiled with zImage booting support:

`$ make LOADADDR=0x10800000 uImage`

> The `mkimage` tool is part of the Yocto toolchain when built with the FSL community BSP. We will see how to build and install an SDK in the *Preparing and using an SDK* recipe in *Chapter 4, Application Development*.
>
> If it is not included in your toolchain, you can install the tool in your host using the following command:
>
> `$ sudo apt-get install u-boot-tools`

`LOADADDR` is the U-Boot entry point; that is, the address where U-Boot will place the kernel in memory. It is defined in the `meta-fsl-arm imx-base.inc` file:

```
UBOOT_ENTRYPOINT_mx6   = "0x10008000"
```

External source development

As we did with U-Boot before, we will use the Yocto build system, pointing it to a local directory with a clone of the Linux source repository. We will use the local Git repository cloned in the earlier section.

We configure for external development in our `conf/local.conf` file using the following code:

```
INHERIT += "externalsrc"
EXTERNALSRC_pn-linux-wandboard = "/opt/yocto/linux-wandboard"
EXTERNALSRC_BUILD_pn-linux-wandboard = "/opt/yocto/linux-
  wandboard"
```

> Remember to remove this configuration when using the working directory development methodology explained next in this recipe.

But, just as before, the compilation fails with U-Boot. In this case, the linux-wandboard recipe, not being a `linux-yocto` style recipe, is not prepared for external source compilation and it fails in the configuration task.

Kernel developers prefer to compile the kernel externally as we saw earlier, so this scenario is not likely to be fixed soon.

Working directory development

Typically we work with patches and use this development workflow when we have a small amount of changes or we don't own the source repository.

A typical workflow when working on a modification would be:

1. Start the kernel package compilation from scratch:

   ```
   $ cd /opt/yocto/fsl-community-bsp/
   $ source setup-environment wandboard-quad
   $ bitbake -c cleanall virtual/kernel
   ```

   This will erase the `build` folder, shared state cache, and downloaded package source.

2. Configure the kernel as follows:

   ```
   $ bitbake -c configure virtual/kernel
   ```

   This will convert the machine `defconfig` file into a `.config` file and call `oldconfig` to validate the configuration with the kernel source.

   You can optionally add your own configuration changes with:

   ```
   $ bitbake -c menuconfig virtual/kernel
   ```

3. Start a development shell on the kernel:

```
$ bitbake -c devshell virtual/kernel
```

This will fetch, unpack, and patch the kernel sources and spawn a new shell with the environment ready for kernel compilation. The new shell will change to the kernel `build` directory which contains a local Git repository.

4. Perform our modifications, including kernel configuration changes.

5. Leave the devshell open and go back to the terminal with the sourced Yocto environment to compile the source without erasing our modifications as follows:

```
$ bitbake -C compile virtual/kernel
```

Note the capital C. This invokes the compile task but also all the tasks that follow it.

The newly compiled kernel image is available under `tmp/deploy/images/wandboard-quad`.

6. Test your changes. Typically, we would work from a network-booted system, so we would copy the kernel image and the device tree file to the TFTP server root and boot the target with them using the following command:

```
$ cd tmp/deploy/images/wandboard-quad/
$ cp zImage-wandboard-quad.bin zImage-imx6q-wandboard.dtb
  /var/lib/tftpboot
```

Refer to the *Configuring network booting for a development setup* recipe in *Chapter 1, The Build System* for details.

Alternatively, the U-Boot bootloader can boot a Linux zImage kernel from memory with its corresponding device tree using the following syntax:

```
> bootz <kernel_addr> - <dtb_addr>
```

For example, we can fetch images from TFTP and boot the Wandboard images as follows:

```
> tftp ${loadaddr} ${image}
> tftp ${fdt_addr} ${fdt_file}
> bootz ${loadaddr} - ${fdt_addr}
```

If we were using an initramdisk, we would pass it as the second argument. Since we aren't, we use a dash instead.

The command to boot a uImage Linux kernel image from memory would use `bootm` instead, as in:

```
> bootm <kernel_addr> - <dtb_addr>
```

7. Go back to the devshell and commit your change to the local Git repository:

```
$ git add --all .
$ git commit -s -m "Well thought commit message"
```

8. Generate a patch into the kernel recipe patch directory:

```
$ git format-patch -1 -o /opt/yocto/fsl-community-
    bsp/sources/meta-bsp-custom/recipes-kernel/linux/linux-
    wandboard-3.10.17
```

9. Finally, add the patch to the kernel recipe as previously described.

Building external kernel modules

The Linux kernel has the ability to load modules at runtime that extend the kernel functionality. Kernel modules share the kernel's address space and have to be linked against the kernel they are going to be loaded onto. Most device drivers in the Linux kernel can either be compiled into the kernel itself (built-in) or as loadable kernel modules that need to be placed in the root filesystem under the `/lib/modules` directory.

The recommended approach to develop and distribute a kernel module is to do it with the kernel source. A module in the kernel tree uses the kernel's kbuild system to build itself, so as long as it is selected as module in the kernel configuration and the kernel has module support enabled, Yocto will build it.

However, it is not always possible to develop a module in the kernel. Common examples are hardware manufacturers who provide Linux drivers for a wide variety of kernel versions and have an internal development process separated from the kernel community. The internal development work is usually released first as an external out-of-tree module, although it is common for some or all of these internal developments to finish up in the mainstream kernel eventually. However, upstreaming is a slow process and hardware companies will therefore prefer to develop internally first.

It's worth remembering that the Linux kernel is covered under a GPLv2 license, so Linux kernel modules should be released with a compatible license. We will cover licenses in more detail in the following chapters.

Getting ready

To compile an external kernel module with Yocto, we first need to know how we would link the module source with the kernel itself. An external kernel module is also built using the kbuild system of the Linux kernel it is going to be linked against, so the first thing we need is a `Makefile`:

```
obj-m:= hello_world.o
SRC := $(shell pwd)
```

```
all:
        $(MAKE) -C $(KERNEL_SRC) M=$(SRC)

modules_install:
        $(MAKE) -C $(KERNEL_SRC) M=$(SRC) modules_install

clean:
        rm -f *.o *~ core .depend .*.cmd *.ko *.mod.c
        rm -f Module.markers Module.symvers modules.order
        rm -rf .tmp_versions Modules.symvers
```

The `Makefile` file just wraps the `make` command used to compile a module on a Linux system:

```
make -C $(KERNEL_SRC) M=$(SRC)
```

Here, `make` is instructed to build in the location of the kernel source, and the `M` argument tells kbuild it is building a module at the specified location.

And then we code the source of the module itself (`hello_world.c`):

```
/ *
 * This program is free software; you can redistribute it and/or
   modify
 * it under the terms of the GNU General Public License as
   published by
 * the Free Software Foundation; either version 2 of the License,
   or
 * (at your option) any later version.
 *
 * This program is distributed in the hope that it will be useful,
 * but WITHOUT ANY WARRANTY; without even the implied warranty of
 * MERCHANTABILITY or FITNESS FOR A PARTICULAR PURPOSE. See the
 * GNU General Public License for more details.
 *
 * You should have received a copy of the GNU General Public
   License
 * along with this program. If not, see
   <http://www.gnu.org/licenses/>.
 */

#include <linux/module.h>

static int hello_world_init(void)
{
        printk("Hello world\n");
```

```
        return 0;
}

static void hello_world_exit(void)
{
        printk("Bye world\n");
}
module_init(hello_world_init);
module_exit(hello_world_exit);

MODULE_LICENSE("GPL v2");
```

It's worth remembering that we need to compile against a kernel source that has already been built. Use the following steps for compilation:

1. We prepare the environment using the Yocto toolchain environment setup script:

   ```
   $ source /opt/poky/1.7.1/environment-setup-armv7a-vfp-neon-
     poky-linux-gnueabi
   ```

2. Next we build the module. We execute the following from the module source directory:

   ```
   $ KERNEL_SRC=/opt/yocto/linux-wandboard make
   ```

How to do it...

Once we know how to compile the module externally, we are ready to prepare a Linux kernel module Yocto recipe for it.

We place the module source file and `Makefile` in `recipes-kernel/hello-world/ files/` inside our `meta-bsp-custom` layer. We then create a `recipes-kernel/hello-world/hello-world.bb` file with the following content:

```
# Copyright (C) 2015 Packt Publishing.

SUMMARY = "Simplest hello world kernel module."
LICENSE = "GPLv2"
LIC_FILES_CHKSUM = "file://${COMMON_LICENSE_DIR}/GPL-
   2.0;md5=801f80980d171dd6425610833a22dbe6"

inherit module

SRC_URI = " \
```

```
        file://hello_world.c \
        file://Makefile \
    "

    S = "${WORKDIR}"

    COMPATIBLE_MACHINE = "(wandboard)"
```

The recipe defines the source directory and the two module files after inheriting the `module` class, which takes care of everything. The `KERNEL_SRC` argument in our `Makefile` is set by the module class to `STAGING_KERNEL_DIR`, the location where the kernel class places the Linux kernel headers needed for external module compilation.

We build it with the following command:

$ bitbake hello-world

The resulting module is called `hello_world.ko`, with the `kernel-module` prefix being added to the package name by the module `bbclass` automatically.

There's more...

The previous instructions will build the module but will not install it in the root filesystem. For that, we need to add a dependency to the root filesystem. This is usually done in machine configuration files using `MACHINE_ESSENTIAL` (for modules that are needed to boot) or `MACHINE_EXTRA` (if they are not essential for boot but needed otherwise), variables.

- The dependencies that are essential to boot are:
    - `MACHINE_ESSENTIAL_EXTRA_RDEPENDS`: The build will fail if they can't be found
    - `MACHINE_ESSENTIAL_EXTRA_RRECOMMENDS`: The build will not fail if they can't be found
- The dependencies that are not essential to boot are:
    - `MACHINE_EXTRA_RDEPENDS`: The build will fail if they can't be found
    - `MACHINE_ESSENTIAL_EXTRA_RRECOMMENDS`: The build will not fail if they can't be found

Debugging the Linux kernel and modules

We will highlight some of the most common methods employed by kernel developers to debug kernel issues.

How to do it...

Above all, debugging the Linux kernel remains a manual process, and the most important developer tool is the ability to print debug messages.

The kernel uses the `printk` function, which is very similar syntactically to the `printf` function call from standard C libraries, with the addition of an optional log level. The allowed formats are documented in the kernel source under `Documentation/printk-formats.txt`.

The `printk` functionality needs to be compiled into the kernel with the `CONFIG_PRINTK` configuration variable. You can also configure the Linux kernel to prepend a precise timestamp to every message with the `CONFIG_PRINTK_TIME` configuration variable, or even better, with the `printk.time` kernel command-line argument or through sysfs under `/sys/module/printk/parameters`. Usually all kernels contain `printk` support, and the Wandboard kernel does too, although it is commonly removed on production kernels for small embedded systems.

The `printk` function can be used in any context, interrupt, **non-maskable interrupt** (**NMI**), or scheduler. Note that using it inside interrupt context is not recommended.

A useful debug statement to be used during development could be:

```
printk(KERN_INFO "[%s:%d] %pf -> var1: %d var2: %d\n",
    __FUNCTION__, __LINE__, __builtin_return_address(0), var1,
    var2);
```

The first thing to note is that there is no comma between the log level macro and the print format. We then print the function and line where the debug statement is placed and then the parent function. Finally, we print the variables we are actually interested in.

How it works...

The available log levels in `printk` are presented in the following table:

Type	Symbol	Description
Emergency	KERN_EMERG	System is unstable and about to crash
Alert	KERN_ALERT	Immediate action is needed
Critical	KERN_CRIT	Critical software or hardware failure
Error	KERN_ERR	Error condition
Warning	KERN_WARNING	Nothing serious, but might indicate a problem
Notice	KERN_NOTICE	Nothing serious, but user should take note
Information	KERN_INFO	System information

Type	Symbol	Description
Debug	KERN_DEBUG	Debug messages

If no log level is specified, the default log message as configured in the kernel configuration is used. By default, this is KERN_WARNING.

All printk statements go to the kernel log buffer, which may wrap around, except debug statements, which only appear if the DEBUG symbol is defined. We will see how to enable kernel debug messages soon. The printk log buffer must be a power of two, and its size should be set in the CONFIG_LOG_BUF_SHIFT kernel configuration variable. You may modify it with the log_buf_len kernel command-line parameter.

We print the kernel log buffer with the dmesg command. Also, a Yocto user space will have a kernel log daemon running that will log kernel messages to disk under /var/log/messages.

Messages above the current console log level will also appear on the console immediately. The ignore_loglevel kernel command-line argument, also available under /sys/module/printk/parameters, may be used to print all kernel messages to the console independently of the log level.

You can also change the log level at runtime via the proc filesystem. The /proc/sys/kernel/printk file contains the current, default, minimum, and boot time default log levels. To change the current log level to the maximum, execute:

```
$ echo 8 > /proc/sys/kernel/printk
```

You can also set the console log level with the dmesg tool as follows:

```
$ dmesg -n 8
```

To make the change persistent, you can pass a log level command-line parameter to the kernel, or on some Yocto root filesystem images, you could also use a /etc/sysctl.conf file (those that install the procps package).

There's more...

Linux drivers do not use the `printk` function directly. They use, in order of preference, subsystem-specific messages (such as `netdev` or `v4l`) or the `dev_*` and `pr_*` family of functions. The latter are described in the following table:

Device message	Generic message	Printk symbol
dev_emerg	pr_emerg	KERN_EMERG
dev_alert	pr_alert	KERN_ALERT
dev_crit	pr_crit	KERN_CRIT
dev_err	pr_err	KERN_ERR
dev_warn	pr_warn	KERN_WARNING
dev_notice	pr_notice	KERN_NOTICE
dev_info	pr_info	KERN_INFO
dev_dbg	pr_debug	KERN_DEBUG

To enable the debug messages within a driver, you may do either of these:

▸ Define DEBUG in a macro before any other header file in your driver source, as follows:

```
#define DEBUG
```

▸ Use the dynamic debug kernel feature. You can then enable/disable all `dev_dbg` and `pr_debug` debug messages with granularity through `debugfs`.

Using dynamic debug

To use the dynamic debug functionality in the Linux kernel, follow these steps:

1. Make sure your kernel is compiled with dynamic debugging (CONFIG_DYNAMIC_ DEBUG).

2. Mount the debug filesystem if it hasn't already been mounted:

```
$ mount -t debugfs nodev /sys/kernel/debug
```

3. Configure the debug though the `dynamic_debug/control` folder. It accepts a whitespace-separated sequence of words:

   ❑ func <function name>

   ❑ file <filename>

   ❑ module <module name>

   ❑ format <pattern>

   ❑ line <line or line range>

❏   + `<flag>`: This adds the specified flag

❏   - `<flag>`: This one removes the specified flag

❏   = `<flag>`: This sets the specified flag

The flags are defined as follows:

❏   `f`: This flag includes the function name in the message

❏   `l`: This flag includes the line number in the message

❏   `m`: This flag includes the module name in the message

❏   `p`: This flag enables the debug message

❏   `t`: This flag includes the thread ID in non-interrupt context messages

4. By default all debug messages are disabled. The control file contains all the available debug points, and by default they have no flags enabled (marked as `=_`).

5. Now we will enable the debug as follows:

   ❏   Enable all debug statements in a file:

```
echo -n 'file <filename> +p' >
    /sys/kernel/debug/dynamic_debug/control
```

   ❏   Optionally, you could run a specific debug statement:

```
$ echo -n 'file <filename> line nnnn +p' >
    /sys/kernel/debug/dynamic_debug/control
```

6. To list all enabled debug statements, we use the following command:

```
$ awk '$3 != "=_"' /sys/kernel/debug/dynamic_debug/control
```

To make the debug changes persistent, we can pass `dyndbg="<query>"` or `module.dyndbg="<query>"` to the kernel in the command-line arguments.

Note that the query string needs to be passed surrounded by quotes so that it is correctly parsed. You can concatenate more than one query in the command-line argument by using a semicolon to separate them; for example, `dyndbg="file mxc_v4l2_capture.c +pfl; file ipu_bg_overlay_sdc.c +pfl"`

Rate-limiting debug messages

There are rate-limiting and one-shot extensions to the `dev_*`, `pr_*`, and `printk` family of functions:

▸   `printk_ratelimited()`, `pr_*_ratelimited()`, and `dev_*_ratelimited()` print no more than 10 times in a 5 * HZ interval

▸ `printk_once()`, `pr_*_once()`, and `dev_*_once()` will print only once.

And you also have utility functions to dump a buffer in hexadecimal; for example, `print_hex_dump_bytes()`.

See also

▸ The dynamic debug is documented in the Linux kernel source under `Documentation/dynamic-debug-howto.txt`

Debugging the Linux kernel booting process

We have seen the most general techniques for debugging the Linux kernel. However, some special scenarios require the use of different methods. One of the most common scenarios in embedded Linux development is the debugging of the booting process. This recipe will explain some of the techniques used to debug the kernel's booting process.

How to do it...

A kernel crashing on boot usually provides no output whatsoever on the console. As daunting as that may seem, there are techniques we can use to extract debug information. Early crashes usually happen before the serial console has been initialized, so even if there were log messages, we would not see them. The first thing we will show is how to enable early log messages that do not need the serial driver.

In case that is not enough, we will also show techniques to access the log buffer in memory.

How it works...

Debugging booting problems have two distinctive phases, before and after the serial console is initialized. After the serial is initialized and we can see serial output from the kernel, debugging can use the techniques described earlier.

Before the serial is initialized, however, there is a basic **UART** support in ARM kernels that allows you to use the serial from early boot. This support is compiled in with the `CONFIG_DEBUG_LL` configuration variable.

This adds supports for a debug-only series of assembly functions that allow you to output data to a UART. The low-level support is platform specific, and for the i.MX6, it can be found under `arch/arm/include/debug/imx.S`. The code allows for this low-level UART to be configured through the `CONFIG_DEBUG_IMX_UART_PORT` configuration variable.

We can use this support directly by using the `printascii` function as follows:

```
extern void printascii(const char *);
printascii("Literal string\n");
```

However, much more preferred would be to use the `early_print` function, which makes use of the function explained previously and accepts formatted input in `printf` style; for example:

```
early_print("%08x\t%s\n", p->nr, p->name);
```

Dumping the kernel's printk buffer from the bootloader

Another useful technique to debug Linux kernel crashes at boot is to analyze the kernel log after the crash. This is only possible if the RAM memory is persistent across reboots and does not get initialized by the bootloader.

As U-Boot keeps the memory intact, we can use this method to peek at the kernel login memory in search of clues.

Looking at the kernel source, we can see how the log ring buffer is set up in `kernel/printk/printk.c` and also note that it is stored in `__log_buf`.

To find the location of the kernel buffer, we will use the `System.map` file created by the Linux build process, which maps symbols with virtual addresses using the following command:

```
$grep __log_buf System.map
80f450c0 b __log_buf
```

To convert the virtual address to physical address, we look at how `__virt_to_phys()` is defined for ARM:

```
x - PAGE_OFFSET + PHYS_OFFSET
```

The `PAGE_OFFSET` variable is defined in the kernel configuration as:

```
config PAGE_OFFSET
        hex
        default 0x40000000 if VMSPLIT_1G
        default 0x80000000 if VMSPLIT_2G
        default 0xC0000000
```

Some of the ARM platforms, like the i.MX6, will dynamically patch the `__virt_to_phys()` translation at runtime, so `PHYS_OFFSET` will depend on where the kernel is loaded into memory. As this can vary, the calculation we just saw is platform specific.

For the Wandboard, the physical address for 0x80f450c0 is 0x10f450c0.

We can then force a reboot using a magic *SysRq* key, which needs to be enabled in the kernel configuration with `CONFIG_MAGIC_SYSRQ`, but is enabled in the Wandboard by default:

```
$ echo b > /proc/sysrq-trigger
```

We then dump that memory address from U-Boot as follows:

```
> md.l 0x10f450c0
10f450c0: 00000000 00000000 00210038 c6000000    ........8.!.....
10f450d0: 746f6f42 20676e69 756e694c 6e6f2078    Booting Linux on
10f450e0: 79687020 61636973 5043206c 78302055     physical CPU 0x
10f450f0: 00000030 00000000 00000000 00000000    0...............
10f45100: 009600a8 a6000000 756e694c 65762078    ........Linux ve
10f45110: 6f697372 2e33206e 312e3031 2e312d37    rsion 3.10.17-1.
10f45120: 2d322e30 646e6177 72616f62 62672b64    0.2-wandboard+gb
10f45130: 36643865 62323738 20626535 656c6128    e8d6872b5eb (ale
10f45140: 6f6c4078 696c2d67 2d78756e 612d7068    x@log-linux-hp-a
10f45150: 7a6e6f67 20296c61 63636728 72657620    gonzal) (gcc ver
10f45160: 6e6f6973 392e3420 2820312e 29434347    sion 4.9.1 (GCC)
10f45170: 23202920 4d532031 52502050 504d4545    ) #1 SMP PREEMP
10f45180: 75532054 6546206e 35312062 3a323120    T Sun Feb 15 12:
10f45190: 333a3733 45432037 30322054 00003531    37:37 CET 2015..
10f451a0: 00000000 00000000 00400050 82000000    ........P.@.....
10f451b0: 3a555043 4d524120 50203776 65636f72    CPU: ARMv7 Proce
```

There's more...

Another method is to store the kernel log messages and kernel panics or oops into persistent storage. The Linux kernel's persistent store support (`CONFIG_PSTORE`) allows you to log in to the persistent memory kept across reboots.

To log panic and oops messages into persistent memory, we need to configure the kernel with the `CONFIG_PSTORE_RAM` configuration variable, and to log kernel messages, we need to configure the kernel with `CONFIG_PSTORE_CONSOLE`.

We then need to configure the location of the persistent storage on an unused memory location, but keep the last 1 MB of memory free. For example, we could pass the following kernel command-line arguments to reserve a 128 KB region starting at 0x30000000:

```
ramoops.mem_address=0x30000000 ramoops.mem_size=0x200000
```

We would then mount the persistent storage by adding it to /etc/fstab so that it is available on the next boot as well:

```
/etc/fstab:
pstore   /pstore   pstore   defaults   0   0
```

We then mount it as follows:

```
# mkdir /pstore
# mount /pstore
```

Next, we force a reboot with the magic *SysRq* key:

```
# echo b > /proc/sysrq-trigger
```

On reboot, we will see a file inside /pstore:

```
-r--r--r--   1 root root 4084 Sep 16 16:24 console-ramoops
```

This will have contents such as the following:

```
SysRq : Resetting
CPU3: stopping
CPU: 3 PID: 0 Comm: swapper/3 Not tainted 3.14.0-rc4-1.0.0-wandboard-37774-g1eae
[<80014a30>]  (unwind_backtrace) from [<800116cc>]  (show_stack+0x10/0x14)
[<800116cc>]  (show_stack) from [<806091f4>]  (dump_stack+0x7c/0xbc)
[<806091f4>]  (dump_stack) from [<80013990>]  (handle_IPI+0x144/0x158)
[<80013990>]  (handle_IPI) from [<800085c4>]  (gic_handle_irq+0x58/0x5c)
[<800085c4>]  (gic_handle_irq) from [<80012200>]  (__irq_svc+0x40/0x70)
Exception stack(0xee4c1f50 to 0xee4c1f98)
```

We should move it out of /pstore or remove it completely so that it doesn't occupy memory.

Using the kernel function tracing system

Recent versions of the Linux kernel contain a set of tracers that, by instrumenting the kernel, allow you to analyze different areas like:

- ▸ Interrupt latency
- ▸ Preemption latency
- ▸ Scheduling latency

- ▶ Process context switches
- ▶ Event tracing
- ▶ Syscalls
- ▶ Maximum stack
- ▶ Block layer
- ▶ Functions

The tracers have no performance overhead when not enabled.

Getting ready...

The tracing system can be used in a wide variety of debugging scenarios, but one of the most common tracers used is the function tracer. It instruments every kernel function with a NOP call that is replaced and used to trace the kernel functions when a trace point is enabled.

To enable the function tracer in the kernel, use the `CONFIG_FUNCTION_TRACER` and `CONFIG_FUNCTION_GRAPH_TRACER` configuration variables.

The kernel tracing system is controlled via a `tracing` file in the `debug` filesystem, which is mounted by default on Yocto's default images. If not, you can mount it with:

```
$ mount -t debugfs nodev /sys/kernel/debug
```

We can list the available tracers in our kernel by executing:

```
$ cat /sys/kernel/debug/tracing/available_tracers
function_graph function nop
```

How to do it...

You can enable a tracer by echoing its name to the `current_tracer` file. No tracers are enabled by default:

```
$ cat /sys/kernel/debug/tracing/current_tracer
nop
```

You can disable all tracers by executing the following command:

```
$ echo -n nop > /sys/kernel/debug/tracing/current_tracer
```

We use `echo -n` to avoid the trailing newline when echoing to files in `sysfs`.

To enable the function tracer, you would execute:

```
$ echo -n function > /sys/kernel/debug/tracing/current_tracer
```

A prettier graph can be obtained by using the function graph tracer as follows:

```
$ echo -n function_graph > /sys/kernel/debug/tracing/current_tracer
```

How it works...

You can look at the captured trace in human-readable format via the `trace` and `trace_pipe` files, with the latter blocking on `read` and consuming the data.

The function tracer provides the following output:

```
$ cat  /sys/kernel/debug/tracing/trace_pipe
root@wandboard-quad:~# cat /sys/kernel/debug/tracing/trace_pipe
            sh-394     [003] ...1      46.205203: mutex_unlock <-
tracing_set_tracer
            sh-394     [003] ...1      46.205215: __fsnotify_parent <-
vfs_write
            sh-394     [003] ...1      46.205218: fsnotify <-vfs_write
            sh-394     [003] ...1      46.205220: __srcu_read_lock <-
fsnotify
            sh-394     [003] ...1      46.205223: preempt_count_add <-
__srcu_read_lock
            sh-394     [003] ...2      46.205226: preempt_count_sub <-
__srcu_read_lock
            sh-394     [003] ...1      46.205229: __srcu_read_unlock <-
fsnotify
            sh-394     [003] ...1      46.205232: __sb_end_write <-
vfs_write
            sh-394     [003] ...1      46.205235: preempt_count_add <-
__percpu_counter_add
            sh-394     [003] ...2      46.205238: preempt_count_sub <-
__percpu_counter_add
            sh-394     [003] d..1      46.205247: gic_handle_irq <-
__irq_usr
          <idle>-0     [002] d..2      46.205247: ktime_get <-
cpuidle_enter_state
```

The format for the function tracer output is:

```
task-PID [cpu-nr] irqs-off need-resched hard/softirq preempt-depth
    delay-timestamp function
```

The graphical function tracer output is as follows:

```
$ cat /sys/kernel/debug/tracing/trace_pipe
 3)    =========> |
 3)               |  gic_handle_irq() {
 2)    =========> |
 2)               |  gic_handle_irq() {
 3)    0.637 us   |    irq_find_mapping();
 2)    0.712 us   |    irq_find_mapping();
 3)               |    handle_IRQ() {
 2)               |    handle_IRQ() {
 3)               |      irq_enter() {
 2)               |      irq_enter() {
 3)    0.652 us   |        rcu_irq_enter();
 2)    0.666 us   |        rcu_irq_enter();
 3)    0.591 us   |        preempt_count_add();
 2)    0.606 us   |        preempt_count_add();
```

The format for the grapical function tracer output is:

```
cpu-nr) timestamp | functions
```

There's more...

The kernel tracing system allows us to insert traces in the code by using the `trace_printk` function call. It has the same syntax as `printk` and can be used in the same scenarios, interrupts, NMI, or scheduler contexts.

Its advantage is that as it prints to the tracing buffer in memory and not to the console, it has much lower delays than `printk`, so it is useful to debug scenarios where `printk` is affecting the system's behavior; for example, when masking a timing bug.

Tracing is enabled once a tracer is configured, but whether the trace writes to the ring buffer or not can be controlled. To disable the writing to the buffer, use the following command:

```
$ echo 0 > /sys/kernel/debug/tracing/tracing_on
```

And to re-enable it, use the following command:

```
$ echo 1 > /sys/kernel/debug/tracing/tracing_on
```

You can also enable and disable the tracing from kernel space by using the `tracing_on` and `tracing_off` functions.

Inserted traces will appear in any tracer, including the `function` tracer, in which case it will appear as a comment.

Filtering function traces

You can get finer granularity in the functions being traced by using the dynamic tracer, which can be enabled with the `CONFIG_DYNAMIC_FTRACE` configuration variable. This is enabled with the tracing functionality by default. This adds two more files, `set_ftrace_filter` and `set_ftrace_notrace`. Adding functions to `set_ftrace_filter` will trace only those functions, and adding them to `set_ftrace_notrace` will not trace them, even if they are also added to `set_ftrace_filter`.

The set of available function names that can be filtered may be obtained by executing the following command:

```
$ cat /sys/kernel/debug/tracing/available_filter_functions
```

Functions can be added with:

```
$ echo -n <function_name> >>
  /sys/kernel/debug/tracing/set_ftrace_filter
```

Note that we use the concatenation operator (`>>`) so that the new function is appended to the existing ones.

And functions can also be removed with:

```
$ echo -n '!<function>' >>  /sys/kernel/debug/tracing/set_ftrace_filter
```

To remove all functions, just echo a blank line into the file:

```
$ echo >  /sys/kernel/debug/tracing/set_ftrace_filter
```

There is a special syntax that adds extra flexibility to the filtering: `<function>:<command>:[<parameter>]`

Let's explain each of the components individually:

- ▶ `function`: This specifies the function name. Wildcards are allowed.
- ▶ `command`: This has the following attributes:
  - ❑ `mod`: This enables the given function name only in the module specified in the parameter
  - ❑ `traceon/traceoff`: This enables or disables tracing when the specified function is hit the numbers of times given in the parameter, or always if no parameter is given.
  - ❑ `dump`: Dump the contents of the tracing buffer when the given function is hit.

Here are some examples:

```
$ echo -n 'ipu_*:mod:ipu' >
  /sys/kernel/debug/tracing/set_ftrace_filter
$ echo -n 'suspend_enter:dump' >
  /sys/kernel/debug/tracing/set_ftrace_filter
$ echo -n 'suspend_enter:traceon' >
  /sys/kernel/debug/tracing/set_ftrace_filter
```

Enabling trace options

Traces have a set of options that can be individually enabled in the `/sys/kernel/debug/tracing/options` directory. Some of the most useful options include:

- ▶ `print-parent`: This option displays the caller function too
- ▶ `trace_printk`: This option disables `trace_printk` writing

Using the function tracer on oops

Another alternative to log the kernel messages on oops or panic is to configure the function tracer to dump its buffer contents to the console so that the events leading up to the crash can be analyzed. Use the following command:

```
$ echo 1 > /proc/sys/kernel/ftrace_dump_on_oops
```

The `sysrq-z` combination will also dump the contents of the tracing buffer to the console, as does calling `ftrace_dump()` from the kernel code.

Getting a stack trace for a given function

The tracing code can create a backtrace for every function called. However, this is a dangerous feature and should only be used with a filtered selection of functions. Have a look at the following commands:

```
$ echo -n <function_name> > /sys/kernel/debug/tracing/set_ftrace_filter
$ echo -n function > /sys/kernel/debug/tracing/current_tracer
$ echo 1 > /sys/kernel/debug/tracing/options/func_stack_trace
$ cat /sys/kernel/debug/tracing/trace
$ echo 0 > /sys/kernel/debug/tracing/options/func_stack_trace
$ echo > /sys/kernel/debug/tracing/set_ftrace_filter
```

Configuring the function tracer at boot

The function tracer can be configured in the kernel command-line arguments and started as early as possible in the boot process. For example, to configure the graphic function tracer and filter some functions, we would pass the following arguments from the U-Boot bootloader to the kernel:

```
ftrace=function_graph ftrace_filter=mxc_hdmi*,fb_show*
```

See also

> ▶ More details can be found in the kernel source documentation folder at `Documentation/trace/ftrace.txt`

Managing the device tree

The device tree is a data structure that is passed to the Linux kernel to describe the physical devices in a system.

In this recipe, we will explain how to work with device trees.

Getting ready

Devices that cannot be discovered by the CPU are handled by the platform devices API on the Linux kernel. The device tree replaces the legacy platform data where hardware characteristics were hardcoded in the kernel source so that platform devices can be instantiated. Before device trees came into use, the bootloader (for example, U-Boot) had to tell the kernel what machine type it was booting. Moreover, it had to pass other information such as memory size and location, kernel command line, and more.

The device tree should not be confused with the Linux kernel configuration. The device tree specifies what devices are available and how they are accessed, not whether the hardware is used.

The device tree was first used by the PowerPC architecture and was adopted later on by ARM and all others, except x86. It was defined by the Open Firmware specification, which defined the flattened device tree format in **Power.org Standard for Embedded Power Architecture Platform Requirements** (**ePAPR**), which describes an interface between a boot program and a client.

Platform customization changes will usually happen in the device tree without the need to modify the kernel source.

How to do it...

A device tree is defined in a human-readable device tree syntax (.dts) text file. Every board has one or several DTS files that correspond to different hardware configurations.

These DTS files are compiled into **Device Tree Binary** (**DTB**) blobs, which have the following properties:

▸ They are relocatable, so pointers are never used internally

▸ They allow for dynamic node insertion and removal

▸ They are small in size

Device tree blobs can either be attached to the kernel binary (for legacy compatibility) or, as is more commonly done, passed to the kernel by a bootloader like U-Boot.

To compile them, we use a **Device Tree Compiler** (**DTC**), which is included in the kernel source inside scripts/dtc and is compiled along with the kernel itself, or we could alternatively install it as part of your distribution. It is recommended to use the DTC compiler included in the kernel tree.

The device trees can be compiled independently or with the Linux kernel kbuild system, as we saw previously. However, when compiling independently, modern device trees will need to be preprocessed by the C preprocessor first.

It's important to note that the DTC currently performs syntax checking but no binding checking, so invalid DTS files may be compiled, and the resulting DTB file may result in a non-booting kernel. Invalid DTB files usually hang the Linux kernel very early on so there will be no serial output.

The bootloader might also modify the device tree before passing it to the kernel.

How it works...

The DTS file for the `wandboard-quad` variant is under `arch/arm/boot/dts/imx6q-wandboard.dts` and looks as follows:

```
#include "imx6q.dtsi"
#include "imx6qdl-wandboard.dtsi"

/ {
    model = "Wandboard i.MX6 Quad Board";
    compatible = "wand,imx6q-wandboard", "fsl,imx6q";

    memory {
        reg = <0x10000000 0x80000000>;
    };
};
```

What we see here is the device tree root node that has no parents. The rest of the nodes will have a parent. The structure of a node can be represented as follows:

```
node@0{
  an-empty-property;
  a-string-property = "a string";
  a-string-list-property = "first string", "second string";
  a-cell-property = <1>;
  a-cell-property = <0x1 0x2>;
  a-byte-data-property = [0x1 0x2 0x3 0x4];
  a-phandle-property = <&node1>;
}
```

The node properties can be:

▶ Empty

▶ Contain one or more strings

▶ Contain one or more unsigned 32-bit numbers, called **cells**

▶ Contain a binary byte stream

▶ Be a reference to another node, called a **phandle**

The device tree is initially parsed by the C preprocessor and it can include other DTS files. These `include` files have the same syntax and are usually appended with the `dtsi` suffix. File inclusion can also be performed with the device tree `/include/` operator, although `#include` is recommended, and they should not be mixed. In this case, both `imx6q.dtsi` and `imx6qdl-wandboard.dtsi` are overlaid with the contents of `imx6q-wandboard.dts`.

Device tree nodes are documented in bindings contained in the `Documentation/devicetree/bindings/` directory of the kernel source. New nodes must include the corresponding bindings, and these must be reviewed and accepted by the device tree maintainers. Theoretically, all bindings need to be maintained, although it is likely this will be relaxed in the future.

The compatible property

The most important property in a device tree node is the `compatible` property. In the root node, it defines the machine types the device tree is compatible with. The DTS file we just saw is compatible in order of precedence with the `wand,imx6q-wandboard` and `fsl,imx6q` machine types.

On a non-root node, it will define the driver match for the device tree node, binding a device with the driver. For example, a platform driver that binds with a node that defines a property that is compatible with `fsl,imx6q-tempmon` would contain the following excerpt:

```
static const struct of_device_id of_imx_thermal_match[] = {
    { .compatible = "fsl,imx6q-tempmon", },
    { /* end */ }
};
MODULE_DEVICE_TABLE(of, of_imx_thermal_match);

static struct platform_driver imx_thermal = {
    .driver = {
        .name    = "imx_thermal",
        .owner   = THIS_MODULE,
        .of_match_table = of_imx_thermal_match,
    },
    .probe      = imx_thermal_probe,
    .remove     = imx_thermal_remove,
};
module_platform_driver(imx_thermal);
```

The Wandboard device tree file

Usually, the first DTSI file to be included is `skeleton.dtsi`, which is the minimum device tree needed to boot, once a compatible property is added.

```
/ {
    #address-cells = <1>;
    #size-cells = <1>;
    chosen { };
    aliases { };
    memory { device_type = "memory"; reg = <0 0>; };
};
```

Here are the other common top nodes:

- ▶ **chosen**: This node defines fixed parameters set at boot, such as the Linux kernel command line or the initramfs memory location. It replaces the information traditionally passed in ARM tags (ATAGS).

- ▶ **memory**: This node is used to define the location and size of RAM. This is usually filled in by the bootloader.

- ▶ **aliases**: This defines shortcuts to other nodes.

- ▶ **address-cells** and **size-cells**: These are used for memory addressability and will be discussed later on.

A summary representation of the imx6q-wandboard.dts file showing only the selected buses and devices follows:

```
#include "skeleton.dtsi"

/ {
    model = "Wandboard i.MX6 Quad Board";
    compatible = "wand,imx6q-wandboard", "fsl,imx6q";

    memory {};

    aliases {};

    intc: interrupt-controller@00a01000 {};

    soc {
        compatible = "simple-bus";

        dma_apbh: dma-apbh@00110000 {};

        timer@00a00600 {};

        L2: l2-cache@00a02000 {};

        pcie: pcie@0x01000000 {};

        aips-bus@02000000 { /* AIPS1 */
            compatible = "fsl,aips-bus", "simple-bus";

            spba-bus@02000000 {
                compatible = "fsl,spba-bus", "simple-bus";
```

```
        };

        aipstz@0207c000 {};

        clks: ccm@020c4000 {};

        iomuxc: iomuxc@020e0000 {};
    };

    aips-bus@02100000 {
        compatible = "fsl,aips-bus", "simple-bus";
    };
    };
};
```

On this DTS, we can find several nodes defining **system on chip** (**SoC**) buses and several other nodes defining on-board devices.

Defining buses and memory-addressable devices

Buses are typically defined by the `compatible` property or the `simple-bus` property (to define a memory-mapped bus with no specific driver binding) or both. The `simple-bus` property is needed so that children nodes to the bus are registered as platform devices.

For example, the `soc` node is defined as follows:

```
soc {
    compatible = "simple-bus";
    #address-cells = <1>;
    #size-cells = <1>;
    ranges;

    aips-bus@02000000 { /* AIPS1 */
        compatible = "fsl,aips-bus", "simple-bus";
        reg = <0x02000000 0x100000>;
    }
}
```

The properties on the `soc` node are used to specify the memory addressability of the children nodes.

▶ `address-cells`: This property indicates how many base address cells are needed in the `reg` property.

▶ `size-cells`: This property indicates how many size cells are needed in the `reg` property.

▶ `ranges`: This one describes an address translation between parent and child buses. In here, there is no translation and parent and child addressing is identical.

In this case, any child of `soc` needs to define its memory addressing with a `reg` property that contains one cell for the address and one cell for the size. The `aips-bus` node does that with the following property:

```
reg = <0x02000000 0x100000>;
```

There's more...

When the device tree binary blob is loaded in memory by the Linux kernel, it is expanded into a flattened device tree that is accessed by offset. The `fdt_*` kernel functions are used to access the flattened device tree. This `fdt` is then parsed and transformed into a tree memory structure that can be efficiently accessed with the `of_*` family of functions (the prefix comes from Open Firmware).

Modifying and compiling the device tree in Yocto

To modify the device tree in the Yocto build system, we execute the following set of commands:

```
$ cd /opt/yocto/fsl-community-bsp/
$ source setup-environment wandboard-quad
$ bitbake -c devshell virtual/kernel
```

We then edit `arch/arm/boot/dts/imx6q-wandboard.dts` and compile the changes with:

```
$ make dtbs
```

If we want to create a device tree with extra space, let's say 1024 bytes (for example, to add nodes dynamically as explained in the next recipe), we need to specify it with a DTC flag as follows:

```
    DTC_FLAGS="-p 1024" make dtbs
```

To deploy it, we exit the devshell and build the kernel from the project's `build` directory:

```
$ bitbake -c deploy -f virtual/kernel
```

See also

▶ More information regarding device trees can be found at `http://www.devicetree.org`

Debugging device tree issues

This recipe will show some techniques to debug common problems with the device tree.

How to do it...

As mentioned before, problems with the syntax of device tree files usually result in the kernel crashing early in the boot process. Other type of problems are more subtle and usually appear once a driver is making use of the information provided by the device tree. For both types of problems, it is helpful to be able to look not only at the device tree syntax file, but also at the device tree blob, as it is read by both U-Boot and the Linux kernel. It may also be helpful to modify the device tree on the fly using the tools that U-Boot offers.

How it works...

Looking at the device tree from U-Boot

The U-Boot bootloader offers the `fdt` command to interact with a device tree blob. On the Wandboard's default environment, there are two variables related to the device tree:

- `fdt_file`: This variable contains the name of the device tree file used
- `fdt_addr`: This variable contains the location in memory to load the device tree

To fetch the Wandboard's device tree from the TFTP server location and place it in memory, we use the following command:

```
> tftp ${fdt_addr} ${fdt_file}
```

Once we have the device tree blob in memory, we tell U-Boot where it is located:

```
> fdt addr ${fdt_addr}
```

And then we can inspect nodes from the device tree using the full path to them from the root node. To inspect the selected levels, we use the `list` command, and to print complete subtrees, we use the `print` command:

```
> fdt list /cpus
cpus {
        #address-cells = <0x00000001>;
        #size-cells = <0x00000000>;
        cpu@0 {
        };
};
```

```
> fdt print /cpus
cpus {
        #address-cells = <0x00000001>;
        #size-cells = <0x00000000>;
        cpu@0 {
                compatible = "arm,cortex-a9";
                device_type = "cpu";
                reg = <0x00000000>;
                next-level-cache = <0x0000001d>;
                [omitted]
        };
};
```

U-Boot can also attach new nodes to the tree assuming there is extra space in the device tree:

```
> fdt mknode / new-node
> fdt list /new-node
new-node {
};
```

It can also create or remove properties:

```
> fdt set /new-node testprop testvalue
> fdt print /new-node
new-node {
        testprop = "testvalue";
};
> fdt rm /new-node testprop
> fdt print /new-node
new-node {
};
```

For example, it can be useful to modify the kernel command line through the chosen node.

Looking at the device tree from the Linux kernel

Once the Linux kernel is booted, it can be useful to expose the device tree to user space so that it can be explored. You can do this by configuring the Linux kernel with the `CONFIG_PROC_DEVICETREE` configuration variable. The Wandboard Linux kernel comes preconfigured to expose the device tree in `/proc/device-tree` as follows:

```
# ls /proc/device-tree/cpus/
#address-cells   cpu@0          cpu@2          name
#size-cells      cpu@1          cpu@3
```

3
The Software Layer

In this chapter, we will cover the following recipes:

- Exploring an image's contents
- Adding a new software layer
- Selecting a specific package versions and providers
- Adding supported packages
- Adding new packages
- Adding data, scripts, or configuration files
- Managing users and groups
- Using the sysvinit initialization system
- Using the systemd initialization system
- Installing package-installation scripts
- Reducing the Linux kernel image size
- Reducing the root filesystem image size
- Releasing software
- Analyzing your system for compliance
- Working with open source and proprietary code

Introduction

With hardware-specific changes on their way, the next step is customizing the target root filesystem; that is, the software that runs under the Linux kernel, also called the Linux user space.

The usual approach to this is to start with one of the available core images and both optimize and customize it as per the needs of your embedded project. Usually, the images chosen as a starting point are either `core-image-minimal` or `core-image-sato`, but any of them will do.

This chapter will show you how to add a software layer to contain those changes, and will explain some of the common customizations made, such as size optimization. It will also show you how to add new packages to your root filesystem, including licensing considerations.

Exploring an image's contents

We have already seen how to use the build history feature to obtain a list of packages and files included in our image. In this recipe, we will explain how the root filesystem is built so that we are able to track its components.

Getting ready

When packages are built, they are classified inside the working directory of your project (`tmp/work`) according to their architecture. For example, on a `wandboard-quad` build, we find the following directories:

* `all-poky-linux`: This is used for architecture-independent packages
* `cortexa9hf-vfp-neon-poky-linux-gnueabi`: This is used for cortexa9, hard floating point packages
* `wandboard_quad-poky-linux-gnueabi`: This is used for machine-specific packages; in this case, `wandboard-quad`
* `x86_64-linux`: This is used for the packages that form the host `sysroot`

BitBake will build all the packages included in its dependency list inside its own directory.

How to do it...

To find the `build` directory for a given package, we can execute the following command:

```
$ bitbake -e <package> | grep ^WORKDIR=
```

Inside the `build` directory, we find some subdirectories (assuming `rm_work` is not used) that the build system uses in the packaging task. These subdirectories include the following:

* `deploy-rpms`: This is the directory where the final packages are stored. We look here for individual packages that can be locally copied to a target and installed. These packages are copied to the `tmp/deploy` directory and are also used when Yocto builds the root filesystem image.

▶ `image`: This is the default destination directory where the `do_install` task installs components. It can be modified by the recipe with the `D` configuration variable.

▶ `package`: This one contains the actual package contents.

▶ `package-split`: This is where the contents are categorized in subdirectories named after their final packages. Recipes can split the package contents into several final packages, as specified by the `PACKAGES` variable. The default packages besides the default package name are:

  ❑ `dbg`: This installs components used in debugging

  ❑ `dev`: This installs components used in development, such as headers and libraries

  ❑ `staticdev`: This installs libraries and headers used in static compilation

  ❑ `doc`: This is where the documentation is placed

  ❑ `locale`: This installs localization components

The components to be installed in each package are selected using the `FILES` variable. For example, to add to the default package, you could execute the following command:

```
FILES_${PN} += "${bindir}/file.bin"
```

And to add to the development package, you could use the following:

```
FILES_${PN}-dev += "${libdir}/lib.so"
```

How it works...

Once the Yocto build system has built all the individual packages in its dependency list, it runs the `do_rootfs` task, which populates the `sysroot` and builds the root filesystem before creating the final package images. You can find the location of the root filesystem by executing:

```
$ bitbake -e core-image-minimal | grep ^IMAGE_ROOTFS=
```

Note that the `IMAGE_ROOTFS` variable is not configurable and should not be changed.

The contents of this directory will later be prepared into an image according to what image types are configured in the `IMAGE_FSTYPES` configuration variable. If something has been installed in this directory, it will then be installed in the final image.

Adding a new software layer

Root filesystem customization involves adding or modifying content to the base image. Metadata for this content goes into one or more software layers, depending on the amount of customization needed.

A typical embedded project will have just one software layer containing all non-hardware-specific customizations. But it is also possible to have extra layers for graphical frameworks or system-wide elements.

Getting ready

Before starting work on a new layer, it is good practice to check whether someone else provides a similar layer. Also, if you are trying to integrate an open source project, check whether a layer for it already exists. There is an index of available layers at `http://layers.openembedded.org/`.

How to do it...

We can then create a new `meta-custom` layer using the `yocto-layer` command as we learned in the *Creating a custom BSP layer* recipe in *Chapter 2, The BSP Layer*. From the `sources` directory, execute the following command:

```
$ yocto-layer create custom
```

Don't forget to add the layer to your project's `conf/bblayers.conf` file and to your template's `conf` directory to make it available for all new projects.

The default `conf/layer.conf` configuration file is as follows:

```
# We have a conf and classes directory, add to BBPATH
BBPATH .= ":${LAYERDIR}"

# We have recipes-* directories, add to BBFILES
BBFILES += "${LAYERDIR}/recipes-*/*/*.bb \
            ${LAYERDIR}/recipes-*/*/*.bbappend"

BBFILE_COLLECTIONS += "custom"
BBFILE_PATTERN_custom = "^${LAYERDIR}/"
BBFILE_PRIORITY_custom = "6"
```

We have discussed all the relevant variables in this snippet in the *Creating a custom BSP layer* recipe in *Chapter 2, The BSP Layer*.

How it works...

When adding content to a new software layer, we need to keep in mind that our layer needs to play well with other layers in the Yocto project. To this end, when customizing recipes, we will always use append files, and will only override existing recipes if we are completely sure there is no way to add the customization required through an append file.

To help us manage the content across several layers, we can use the following `bitbake-layers` command-line utilities:

- ▶ `$ bitbake-layers show-layers`: This will display the configured layers as BitBake sees them. It is helpful to detect errors on your `conf/bblayer.conf` file.

- ▶ `$ bitbake-layers show-recipes`: This command will display all the available recipes and the layers that provide them. It can be used to verify that BitBake is seeing your newly created recipe. If it does not appear, verify that the filesystem hierarchy corresponds to the one defined in your layer's `BBFILES` variable in `conf/layer.conf`.

- ▶ `$ bitbake-layers show-overlayed`: This command will show all the recipes that are overlayed by another recipe with the same name but in a higher priority layer. It helps detect recipe clashes.

- ▶ `$ bitbake-layers show-appends`: This command will list all available append files and the recipe files they apply to. It can be used to verify that BitBake is seeing your append files. Also, as before with recipes, if they don't appear, you will need to check the filesystem hierarchy and your layer's `BBFILES` variable.

- ▶ `$ bitbake-layers flatten <output_dir>`: This command will create a directory with the contents of all configured layers without overlayed recipes and with all the append files applied. This is how BitBake will see the metadata. This flattened directory is useful to discover conflicts with your layer's metadata.

There's more...

We will sometimes add customizations that are specific to one board or machine. These are not always hardware-related, so they could be found both in a BSP or software layer.

When doing so, we will try to keep our customizations as specific as possible. One typical example is customizing for a specific machine or machine family. If you need to add a patch for the `wandboard-quad` machine, you would use the following line of code:

```
SRC_URI_append_wandboard-quad = " file://mypatch.patch"
```

And, if the patch is applicable to all i.MX6-based boards, you can use the following:

```
SRC_URI_append_mx6 = " file://mypatch.patch"
```

To be able to use machine families overrides, the machine configuration files need to include a `SOC_FAMILY` variable, such as the one for the `wandboard-quad` in `meta-fsl-arm-extra`. Refer to the following line of code:

```
conf/machine/wandboard-quad.conf:SOC_FAMILY = "mx6:mx6q:wandboard"
```

And for it to appear in the MACHINEOVERRIDES variable, the soc-family.inc file needs to be included, as it is in meta-fsl-arm. Here is the relevant code excerpt from the conf/machine/include/imx-base.inc file:

```
include conf/machine/include/soc-family.inc
MACHINEOVERRIDES =. "${@['', '${SOC_FAMILY}:']['${SOC_FAMILY}' != 
  '']}"
```

BitBake will search a predefined path, looking for files inside the package's working directory, defined in the FILESPATH variable as a colon-separated list. Specifically:

```
${PN}-${PV}/${DISTRO}
${PN}/${DISTRO}
files/${DISTRO}

${PN}-${PV}/${MACHINE}
${PN}/${MACHINE}
files/${MACHINE}

${PN}-${PV}/${SOC_FAMILY}
${PN}/${SOC_FAMILY}
files/${SOC_FAMILY}

${PN}-${PV}/${TARGET_ARCH}
${PN}/${TARGET_ARCH}
files/${TARGET_ARCH}

${PN}-${PV}/
${PN}/
files/
```

In the specific case of the wandboard-quad, this translates to the following:

```
${PN}-${PV}/poky
${PN}/poky
files/poky
${PN}-${PV}/wandboard-quad
${PN}/wandboard-quad
files/wandboard-quad
${PN}-${PV}/wandboard
${PN}/wandboard
files/wandboard
${PN}-${PV}/mx6q
${PN}/mx6q
files/mx6q
${PN}-${PV}/mx6
${PN}/mx6
```

```
files/mx6
${PN}-${PV}/armv7a
${PN}/armv7a
files/armv7a
${PN}-${PV}/arm
${PN}/arm
files/arm
${PN}-${PV}/
${PN}/
files/
```

Here, PN is the package name and PV is the package version.

It is best to place patches in the most specific of these, so wandboard-quad, followed by wandboard, mx6q, mx6, armv7a, arm, and finally the generic PN-PV, PN, and files.

Note that the search path refers to the location of the BitBake recipe, so append files need to always add the path when adding content. Our append files can add extra folders to this search path if needed by appending or prepending to the FILESEXTRAPATHS variable as follows:

```
FILESEXTRAPATHS_prepend := "${THISDIR}/folder:"
```

> Note the immediate operator (:=) that expands THISDIR immediately, and the prepend that places your added path before any other path so that your patches and files are found first in the search.
>
> Also, we have seen the += and =+ style of operators in configuration files, but they should be avoided in recipe files and the append and prepend operators should be given preference, as seen in the example code explained previously to avoid ordering issues.

Selecting a specific package version and providers

Our layers can provide recipes for different versions of the same package. For example, the meta-fsl-arm layer contains several different types of Linux sources:

- linux-imx: This corresponds to the Freescale BSP kernel image fetched from http://git.freescale.com/git/cgit.cgi/imx/linux-2.6-imx.git/

- linux-fslc: This is the mainline Linux kernel and fetched from https://github.com/Freescale/linux-fslc

- linux-timesys: This is a kernel with Vybrid platform support fetched from https://github.com/Timesys/linux-timesys

As we mentioned before, all recipes provide the package name (for example, `linux-imx` or `linux-fslc`) by default, but all Linux recipes must also provide the `virtual/kernel` virtual package. The build system will resolve `virtual/kernel` to the most appropriate Linux recipe name, taking into account the requirements of the build, such as the machine it is building for.

And within those recipes, `linux-imx`, for example, has both 2.6.35.3 and 3.10.17 recipe versions.

In this recipe, we will show how to tell the Yocto build system which specific package and version to build.

How to do it...

To specify the exact package we want to build, the build system allows us to specify what provider and version to use.

How do we select which provider to use?

We can tell BitBake which recipe to use by using the `PREFERRED_PROVIDER` variable. To set a preferred provider for the `virtual/kernel` virtual package on our Wandboard machine, we would add the following to its machine configuration file:

```
PREFERRED_PROVIDER_virtual/kernel = "linux-imx"
```

How do we select which version to use?

Within a specific provider, we can also tell BitBake which version to use with the `PREFERRED_VERSION` variable. For example, to set a specific `linux-imx` version for all i.MX6-based machines, we would add the following to our `conf/local.conf` file:

```
PREFERRED_VERSION_linux-imx_mx6 = "3.10.17"
```

The `%` wildcard is accepted to match any character, as we see here:

```
PREFERRED_VERSION_linux-imx_mx6 = "3.10%"
```

It is, however, more common to see this type of configuration done in machine configuration files, in which case we would not use the `_mx6` append.

How do we select which version not to use?

We can use the `DEFAULT_PREFERENCE` variable set to `-1` to specify that a version is not to be used unless explicitly set by a `PREFERRED_VERSION` variable. This is commonly used in development versions of packages.

```
DEFAULT_PREFERENCE = "-1"
```

Adding supported packages

It is common to want to add new packages to an image that already has an available recipe in one of the included Yocto layers.

When the target image desired is very different from the supplied core images, it is recommended to define a new image rather than to customize an existing one.

This recipe will show how to customize an existing image by adding supported packages to it, but also to create a completely new image recipe if needed.

Getting ready

To discover whether a package we require is included in our configured layers, and what specific versions are supported, we can use `bitbake-layers` from our build directory as we saw previously:

```
$ bitbake-layers show-recipes | grep -A 1 htop
htop:
  meta-oe                1.0.3
```

Alternatively, we can also use BitBake as follows:

```
$ bitbake -s | grep htop
htop                                           :1.0.3-r0
```

Or we can use the `find` Linux command in our `sources` directory:

```
$ find . -type f -name "htop*.bb"
./meta-openembedded/meta-oe/recipes-support/htop/htop_1.0.3.bb
```

Once we know what packages we want to include in our final images, let's see how we can add them to the image.

How to do it...

While developing, we will use our project's `conf/local.conf` file to add customizations. To add packages to all images, we can use the following line of code:

```
IMAGE_INSTALL_append = " htop"
```

> Note that there is a space after the first quote to separate the new package from the existing ones, as the append operator does not add a space.

We could also limit the addition to a specific image with:

```
IMAGE_INSTALL_append_pn-core-image-minimal = " htop"
```

Another way to easily customize is by making use of **features**. A feature is a logical grouping of packages. For example, we could create a new feature called `debug-utils`, which will add a whole set of debugging utilities. We could define our feature in a configuration file or class as follows:

```
FEATURE_PACKAGES_debug-utils = "strace perf"
```

We could then add this feature to our image by adding an `EXTRA_IMAGE_FEATURES` variable to our `conf/local.conf` file as follows:

```
EXTRA_IMAGE_FEATURES += "debug-utils"
```

If you were to add it to an image recipe, you would use the `IMAGE_FEATURES` variable instead.

Usually, features get added as a `packagegroup` recipe instead of being listed as packages individually. Let's show how to define a `packagegroup` recipe in the `recipes-core/packagegroups/packagegroup-debug-utils.bb` file:

```
SUMMARY = "Debug applications packagegroup"
LICENSE = "GPLv2"
LIC_FILES_CHKSUM = "file://${COREBASE}/LICENSE;md5=3f40d7994397109285e
c7b81fdeb3b58"

inherit packagegroup

RDEPENDS_${PN} = "\
    strace \
    perf \
"
```

And you would then add it to the `FEATURE_PACKAGES` variable as follows:

```
FEATURE_PACKAGES_debug-utils = "packagegroup-debug-utils"
```

We can use `packagegroups` to create more complex examples. Refer to the *Yocto Project Development Manual* at `http://www.yoctoproject.org/docs/1.7.1/dev-manual/dev-manual.html` for details.

How it works...

The best approach to customize images is to create our own images using an existing image as template. We could use `core-image-minimal.bb`, which contains the following code:

```
SUMMARY = "A small image just capable of allowing a device to
    boot."

IMAGE_INSTALL = "packagegroup-core-boot
    ${ROOTFS_PKGMANAGE_BOOTSTRAP} ${CORE_IMAGE_EXTRA_INSTALL}"

IMAGE_LINGUAS = " "

LICENSE = "MIT"

inherit core-image

IMAGE_ROOTFS_SIZE ?= "8192"
```

And extend it to your own version that allows for the customization of `IMAGE_FEATURES`, by adding the following `meta-custom/recipes-core/images/custom-image.bb` image file:

```
require recipes-core/images/core-image-minimal.bb
IMAGE_FEATURES += "ssh-server-dropbear package-management"
```

Of course, we can also define a new image from scratch using one of the available images as a template.

There's more...

A final way to customize images is by adding shell functions that get executed once the image has been created. You do this by adding the following to your image recipe or `conf/local.conf` file:

```
ROOTFS_POSTPROCESS_COMMAND += "function1;...;functionN"
```

You can use the path to the root filesystem in your command with the `IMAGE_ROOTFS` variable.

Classes would use the `IMAGE_POSTPROCESS_COMMAND` variable instead of `ROOTFS_POSTPROCESS_COMMAND`.

One example of usage can be found in the `debug-tweaks` feature in `image.bbclass`, when images are tweaked to allow passwordless root logins. This method is also commonly used to customize the root password of a target image.

Configuring packages

As we saw in the *Configuring the Linux kernel* recipe in *Chapter 2, The BSP Layer*, some packages, like the Linux kernel, provide a configuration menu and can be configured with the `menuconfig` BitBake command.

Another package worth mentioning with a configuration interface is BusyBox. We will show how to configure BusyBox, for example to add `pgrep`, a tool that looks up process's IDs by name. To do so follow the next steps:

1. Configure BusyBox:

   ```
   $ bitbake -c menuconfig busybox
   ```

2. In **Process utilities** choose `pgrep`.

3. Compile BusyBox:

   ```
   $ bitbake -C compile busybox
   ```

4. Copy the RPM package into the target:

   ```
   $ bitbake -e busybox | grep ^WORKDIR=
   ```

   ```
   $ scp ${WORKDIR}/deploy-rpms/cortexa9hf_vfp_neon/busybox-
     1.22.1-r32.cortexa9hf_vfp_neon.rpm root@<target_ip>:/tmp
   ```

5. Install the RPM package on the target:

   ```
   # rpm --force -U /tmp/busybox-1.22.1-
     r32.cortexa9hf_vfp_neon.rpm
   ```

   Note that we are forcing the update as the package version has not increased with the configuration change.

Adding new packages

We have seen how to customize our image so that we can add supported packages to it. When we can't find an existing recipe or we need to integrate some new software we have developed, we will need to create a new Yocto recipe.

Getting ready

There are some questions we need to ask ourselves before starting to write a new recipe:

- ▸ Where is the source code stored?
- ▸ Is it source-controlled or released as a tarball?
- ▸ What is the source code license?
- ▸ What build system is it using?

- ▸ Does it need configuration?

- ▸ Can we cross-compile it as is or does it need to be patched?

- ▸ What are the files that need to be deployed to the root filesystem, and where do they go?

- ▸ Are there any system changes that need to happen, such as new users or `init` scripts?

- ▸ Are there any dependencies that need to be installed into `sysroot` beforehand?

Once we know the answers to these questions, we are ready to start writing our recipe.

How to do it...

It is best to start from a blank template like the one that follows than to start from a similar recipe and modify it, as the result will be cleaner and contain only the strictly needed instructions.

A good starting base for a minimal recipe addition is:

```
SUMMARY = "The package description for the package management
    system"

LICENSE = "The package's licenses typically from
    meta/files/common-licenses/"
LIC_FILES_CHKSUM = "License checksum used to track open license
    changes"
DEPENDS = "Package list of build time dependencies"

SRC_URI = "Local or remote file or repository to fetch"
SRC_URI[md5sum] = "md5 checksums for all remote fetched files (not
    for repositories)"
SRC_URI[sha256sum] = "sha256 checksum for all remote fetched files
    (not for repositories)"

S = "Location of the source in the working directory, by default
    ${WORKDIR}/${PN}-${PV}."

inherit <class needed for some functionality>

# Task overrides, like do_configure, do_compile and do_install, or
    nothing.

# Package splitting (if needed).

# Machine selection variables (if needed).
```

How it works...

We will explain each one of the recipe sections in more detail in the following sections.

Package licensing

Every recipe needs to contain a `LICENSE` variable. The `LICENSE` variable allows you to specify multiple, alternative, and per-package type licenses, as seen in the following examples:

- For MIT or GPLv2 alternative licenses, we will use:

  ```
  LICENSE = "GPL-2.0 | MIT"
  ```

- For both ISC and MIT licenses, we will use:

  ```
  LICENSE = "ISC & MIT"
  ```

- For split packages, all of them GPLv2 except the documentation that is covered under the Creative Commons, we will use:

  ```
  LICENSE_${PN} = "GPLv2"
  LICENSE_${PN}-dev = "GPLv2"
  LICENSE_${PN}-dbg = "GPLv2"
  LICENSE_${PN}-doc = "CC-BY-2.0"
  ```

Open source packages usually have the license included with the source code in `README`, `COPYING`, or `LICENSE` files, and even the source code header files.

For open source licenses, we also need to specify `LIC_FILES_CHECKSUM` for all licenses so that the build system can notify us when the licenses change. To add it, we locate the file or file portion that contains the license and provide its relative path from the directory containing the source and a MD5 checksum for it. For example:

```
LIC_FILES_CHKSUM = "file://${COREBASE}/meta/files/common-
    licenses/GPL-2.0;md5=801f80980d171dd6425610833a22dbe6"
LIC_FILES_CHKSUM =
    "file://COPYING;md5=f7bdc0c63080175d1667091b864cb12c"
LIC_FILES_CHKSUM =
    "file://usr/include/head.h;endline=7;md5=861ebad4adc7236f8d1905338
    abd7eb2"
LIC_FILES_CHKSUM =
    "file://src/file.c;beginline=5;endline=13;md5=6c7486b21a8524b1879f
    a159578da31e"
```

Proprietary code should have the license set as `CLOSED`, and no `LIC_FILES_CHECKSUM` is needed for it.

Fetching package contents

The `SRC_URI` variable lists the files to fetch. The build system will use different fetchers depending on the file prefix. These can be:

- Local files included with the metadata (`file://`). If the local file is a patch, the `SRC_URI` variable can be extended with patch-specific arguments such as:
    - `striplevel`: The default patch strip level is 1 but it can be modified with this argument
    - `patchdir`: This specifies the directory location to apply the patch to, with the default being the source directory
    - `apply`: This argument controls whether to apply the patch or not, with the default being to apply it
- Files stored in remote servers (typically, `http(s)://`, `ftp://`, or `ssh://`).
- Files stored in remote repositories (typically, `git://`, `svn://`, `hg://`, or `bzr://`). These also need a `SRCREV` variable to specify the revision.

Files stored in remote servers (not local files or remote repositories) need to specify two checksums. If there are several files, they can be distinguished with a `name` argument; for example:

```
SRCREV = "04024dea2674861fcf13582a77b58130c67fccd8"
SRC_URI = "git://repo.com/git/ \
           file://fix.patch;name=patch \
           http://example.org/archive.data;name=archive"
SRC_URI[archive.md5sum] = "aaf32bde135cf3815aa3221726bad71e"
SRC_URI[archive.sha256sum] =
   "65be91591546ef6fdfec93a71979b2b108eee25edbc20c53190caafc9a92d4e7"
```

The source directory folder, `S`, specifies the location of the source files. The repository will be checked out here, or the tarball decompressed in this location. If the tarball decompresses in the standard `${PN}-${PV}` location, it can be omitted as it is the default. For repositories, it needs to always be specified; for example:

```
S = "${WORKDIR}/git"
```

Specifying task overrides

All recipes inherit the `base.bbclass` class, which defines the following tasks:

- `do_fetch`: This method fetches the source code, selecting the fetcher using the `SRC_URI` variable.
- `do_unpack`: This method unpacks the code in the working directory to a location specified by the `S` variable.
- `do_configure`: This method configures the source code if needed. It does nothing by default.

- ▶ do_compile: This method compiles the source and runs the GNU make target by default.

- ▶ do_install: This method copies the results of the build from the build directory B to the destination directory D. It does nothing by default.

- ▶ do_package: This method splits the deliverables into several packages. It does nothing by default.

Usually, only the configuration, compilation, and installation tasks are overridden, and this is mostly done implicitly by inheriting a class like autotools.

For a custom recipe that does not use a build system, you need to provide the required instructions for configuration (if any), compilation, and installation in their corresponding do_configure, do_compile, and do_install overrides. As an example of this type of recipe, meta-custom/recipes-example/helloworld/helloworld_1.0.bb, may be seen here:

```
DESCRIPTION = "Simple helloworld application"
SECTION = "examples"
LICENSE = "MIT"
LIC_FILES_CHKSUM =
   "file://${COMMON_LICENSE_DIR}/MIT;md5=0835ade698e0bcf8506ecda2f7b4
   f302"

SRC_URI = "file://helloworld.c"

S = "${WORKDIR}"

do_compile() {
             ${CC} helloworld.c -o helloworld
}

do_install() {
             install -d ${D}${bindir}
             install -m 0755 helloworld ${D}${bindir}
}
```

With the meta-custom/recipes-example/helloworld/helloworld-1.0/ helloworld.c source file being the following:

```
#include <stdio.h>

int main(void)
{
    return printf("Hello World");
}
```

We will see example recipes that use the most common build systems in the next chapter.

Configuring packages

The Yocto build system provides the `PACKAGECONFIG` variable to help in the configuration of packages by defining a number of features. Your recipe defines the individual features as follows:

```
PACKAGECONFIG ??= "feature"
PACKAGECONFIG[feature] = "--with-feature,--without-feature,build-
   deps-feature,rt-deps-feature"
```

The `PACKAGECONFIG` variable contains a space-separated list of feature names, and it can be extended or overridden in `bbappend` files; have a look at the following example:

```
PACKAGECONFIG_append = " feature1 feature2"
```

To extend or override it from a distribution or local configuration file, you would use the following syntax:

```
PACKAGECONFIG_pn-<package_name> = "feature1 feature2"
PACKAGECONFIG_append_pn-<package_name> = " feature1 feature2"
```

Following that, we characterize each feature with four ordered arguments:

- Extra configuration arguments (for `EXTRA_OECONF`) when the feature is enabled
- Extra configuration arguments (for `EXTRA_OECONF`) when the feature is disabled
- Extra build dependencies (for `DEPENDS`) when the feature is enabled
- Extra runtime dependencies (for `RDEPENDS`) when the feature is enabled

The four arguments are optional, but the ordering needs to be maintained by leaving the surrounding commas.

For example, the `wpa-supplicant` recipe defines two features, `gnutls` and `openssl`, but only enables `gnutls` by default, as seen here:

```
PACKAGECONFIG ??= "gnutls"
PACKAGECONFIG[gnutls] = ",,gnutls"
PACKAGECONFIG[openssl] = ",,openssl"
```

Splitting into several packages

It is common to separate the recipe contents into different packages that serve different needs. Typical examples are to include documentation in a `doc` package, and header and/or libraries in a `dev` package. We can do this using the `FILES` variable as follows:

```
FILES_${PN} += "List of files to include in the main package"
FILES_${PN}-dbg += "Optional list of files to include in the debug
   package"
FILES_${PN}-dev += "Optional list of files to include in the
   development package"
FILES_${PN}-doc += "Optional list of files to include in the
   documentation package"
```

Setting machine-specific variables

Each recipe has a PACKAGE_ARCH variable that categorizes the recipe into a package feed, as we saw in the *Exploring an image's contents* recipe. Most of the times, they are automatically sorted out by the Yocto build system. For example, if the recipe is a kernel, a kernel module recipe, or an image recipe, or even if it is cross-compiling or building native applications, the Yocto build system will set the package architecture accordingly.

BitBake will also look at the SRC_URI machine overrides and adjust the package architecture, and if your recipe is using the allarch class, it will set the package architecture to all.

So when working on a recipe that only applies to a machine or machine family, or that contains changes that are specific to a machine or machine family, we need to check whether the package is categorized in the appropriate package feed, and if not, specify the package architecture explicitly in the recipe itself by using the following line of code:

```
PACKAGE_ARCH = "${MACHINE_ARCH}"
```

Also, when a recipe is only to be parsed for specific machine types, we specify it with the COMPATIBLE_MACHINE variable. For example, to make it compatible only with the mxs, mx5 and mx6 SoC families, we would use the following:

```
COMPATIBLE_MACHINE = "(mxs|mx5|mx6)"
```

Adding data, scripts, or configuration files

All recipes inherit the base class with the default set of tasks to run. After inheriting the base class, a recipe knows how to do things like fetching and compiling.

As most recipes are meant to install some sort of executable, the base class knows how to build it. But sometimes all we want is to install data, scripts, or configuration files into the filesystem.

If the data or configuration is related to an application, the most logical thing to do is to package it together with the application's recipe itself, and if we think it is better to be installed separately, we could even split it into its own package.

But some other times, the data or configuration is unrelated to an application, maybe it applies to the whole system or we just want to provide a separate recipe for it. Optionally, we could even want to install some Perl or Python scripts that don't need to be compiled.

How to do it...

In those cases, our recipe should inherit the allarch class that is inherited by recipes that do not produce architecture-specific output.

An example of this type of recipe, `meta-custom/recipes-example/example-data/example-data_1.0.bb`, may be seen here:

```
DESCRIPTION = "Example of data or configuration recipe"
SECTION = "examples"

LICENSE = "GPLv2"
LIC_FILES_CHKSUM = "file://${COREBASE}/meta/files/common-licenses/GPL-
2.0;md5=801f80980d171dd6425610833a22dbe6"

SRCREV = "${AUTOREV}"
SRC_URI = "git://github.com/yoctocookbook/examples.git \
           file://example.data"

S = "${WORKDIR}/git"

inherit allarch

do_compile() {
}

do_install() {
        install -d ${D}${sysconfdir}
        install -d ${D}${sbindir}
        install -m 0755 ${WORKDIR}/example.data ${D}/${sysconfdir}/
        install -m 0755 ${S}/python-scripts/* ${D}/${sbindir}
}
```

It assumes that the fictitious `examples.git` repository contains a `python-scripts` folder, which we want to include in our root filesystem.

A working recipe example can be found in the source that accompanies the book.

Managing users and groups

It is also common to need to add or modify users and groups to our filesystem. This recipe explains how it is done.

Getting ready

The user information is stored in the `/etc/passwd` file, a text file that is used as a database for the system user's information. The `passwd` file is human-readable.

Each line on it corresponds to one user in the system, and it has the following format:

```
<username>:<password>:<uid>:<gid>:<comment>:<home
  directory>:<login shell>
```

Let's see each of the parameters of this format:

- ▸ `username`: A unique string that identifies the user at login
- ▸ `uid`: User ID, a number that Linux uses to identify the user
- ▸ `gid`: Group ID, a number that Linux uses to identify the user's primary group
- ▸ `comment`: Comma-separated values that describe the account, typically the user's contact details
- ▸ `home directory`: Path to the user's home directory
- ▸ `login shell`: Shell that is started for interactive logins

The default `passwd` file is stored with the `base-passwd` package and looks as follows:

```
root::0:0:root:/root:/bin/sh
daemon:*:1:1:daemon:/usr/sbin:/bin/sh
bin:*:2:2:bin:/bin:/bin/sh
sys:*:3:3:sys:/dev:/bin/sh
sync:*:4:65534:sync:/bin:/bin/sync
games:*:5:60:games:/usr/games:/bin/sh
man:*:6:12:man:/var/cache/man:/bin/sh
lp:*:7:7:lp:/var/spool/lpd:/bin/sh
mail:*:8:8:mail:/var/mail:/bin/sh
news:*:9:9:news:/var/spool/news:/bin/sh
uucp:*:10:10:uucp:/var/spool/uucp:/bin/sh
proxy:*:13:13:proxy:/bin:/bin/sh
www-data:*:33:33:www-data:/var/www:/bin/sh
backup:*:34:34:backup:/var/backups:/bin/sh
list:*:38:38:Mailing List Manager:/var/list:/bin/sh
irc:*:39:39:ircd:/var/run/ircd:/bin/sh
gnats:*:41:41:Gnats Bug-Reporting System (admin):/var/lib/gnats:/bin/
sh
nobody:*:65534:65534:nobody:/nonexistent:/bin/sh
```

All accounts have disabled direct logins, indicated by an asterisk on the password field, except for root, which has no password. This is because, by default, the image is built with the `debug-tweaks` feature that enables passwordless login for the root user, among other things. If the root password was enabled, we would see the encrypted root password.

> Do not forget to remove the `debug-tweaks` feature from production images.

There is a corresponding /etc/group file that is installed at the same time with the information for the system groups.

The core-image-minimal image does not include shadow password protection, but other images, such as core-image-full-cmdline, do. When enabled, all password fields contain an x, and the encrypted passwords are kept on a /etc/shadow file, which is only accessible to the super user.

Any user that is needed by the system but not included in the list we saw earlier needs to be created.

How to do it...

The standard way for a recipe to add or modify system users or groups is to use the useradd class, which uses the following variables:

- ▶ USERADD_PACKAGES: This variable specifies the individual packages in the recipe that require users or groups to be added. For the main package, you would use the following:

  USERADD_PACKAGES = "${PN}"

- ▶ USERADD_PARAM: This variable corresponds to the arguments passed to the Linux useradd command, to add new users to the system.

- ▶ GROUPADD_PARAM: This variable corresponds to the arguments passed to the Linux groupadd command, to add new groups to the system.

- ▶ GROUPMEMS_PARAM: This variable corresponds to the arguments passed to the Linux groupmems command, which administers members of the user's primary group.

An example snippet of a recipe using the useradd class follows:

```
inherit useradd

PASSWORD ?= "miDBHFo2hJSAA"
USERADD_PACKAGES = "${PN}"
USERADD_PARAM_${PN} = "--system --create-home \
                       --groups tty \
                       --password ${PASSWORD} \
                       --user-group ${PN}"
```

The password can be generated on your host using the mkpasswd Linux command-line utility, installed with the whois Ubuntu package.

There's more...

When generating users and groups using the `useradd` class, the `uid` and `gid` values are assigned dynamically during package installation. If this is not desired, there is a way to assign system-wide static `uid` and `gid` values by providing your own `passwd` and group files.

To do this, you need to define the `USERADDEXTENSION` variable in your `conf/local.conf` file as follows:

```
USERADDEXTENSION = "useradd-staticids"
```

The build system will then search the `BBPATH` variable for `files/passwd` and `files/group` files to obtain the `uid` and `gid` values. The files have the standard `passwd` layout as defined previously, with the password field ignored.

The default filenames can be overridden by using the `USERADD_UID_TABLES` and `USERADD_GID_TABLES` variables.

You also need to define the following:

```
USERADD_ERROR_DYNAMIC = "1"
```

This is done so that the build system produces an error if the required `uid` and `gid` values are not found in the provided files.

> Note that if you use the `useradd` class in a project that is already built, you will need to remove the `tmp` directory and rebuild from the `sstate-cache` directory or you will get build errors.

There is also a way to add user and group information that is not tied to a specific recipe but to an image – by using the `extrausers` class. It is configured by the `EXTRA_USERS_PARAMS` variable in an image recipe and used as follows:

```
inherit extrausers

EXTRA_USERS_PARAMS = "\
  useradd -P password root; \
  "
```

This sets the root password to `password`.

Using the sysvinit initialization manager

The initialization manager is an important part of the root filesystem. It is the first thing the kernel executes, and it has the responsibility to start the rest of the system.

This recipe will introduce the `sysvinit` initialization manager.

Getting ready

This is the default initialization manager in Yocto and it has been used in Linux since the operating system's origin. The kernel is passed an `init` command-line argument, typically `/sbin/init`, which is then launched. This `init` process has PID 1 and is the parent of all processes. The `init` process can either be implemented by BusyBox or be an independent program installed with the `sysvinit` package. Both of them work in the same way, based on the concept of **runlevel**, a machine state that defines which processes to run.

The `init` process will read an `inittab` file and look for a default runlevel. The default `inittab` file is installed with the `sysvinit-inittab` package and is as follows:

```
# /etc/inittab: init(8) configuration.
# $Id: inittab,v 1.91 2002/01/25 13:35:21 miquels Exp $

# The default runlevel.
id:5:initdefault:

# Boot-time system configuration/initialization script.
# This is run first except when booting in emergency (-b) mode.
si::sysinit:/etc/init.d/rcS

# What to do in single-user mode.
~~:S:wait:/sbin/sulogin

# /etc/init.d executes the S and K scripts upon change
# of runlevel.
#
# Runlevel 0 is halt.
# Runlevel 1 is single-user.
# Runlevels 2-5 are multi-user.
# Runlevel 6 is reboot.

l0:0:wait:/etc/init.d/rc 0
l1:1:wait:/etc/init.d/rc 1
l2:2:wait:/etc/init.d/rc 2
l3:3:wait:/etc/init.d/rc 3
```

```
14:4:wait:/etc/init.d/rc 4
15:5:wait:/etc/init.d/rc 5
16:6:wait:/etc/init.d/rc 6
# Normally not reached, but fallthrough in case of emergency.
z6:6:respawn:/sbin/sulogin
```

Then, `init` runs all scripts starting with `S` in the `/etc/rcS.d` directory, followed by all the scripts starting with `S` in the `/etc/rcN.d` directory, where `N` is the runlevel value.

So the `init` process just performs the initialization and forgets about the processes. If something goes wrong and the processes are killed, no one will care. The system watchdog will reboot the system if it becomes unresponsive, but applications built with more than one process usually need some type of process monitor that can react to the health of the system, but `sysvinit` does not offer these types of mechanisms.

However, `sysvinit` is a well-understood and reliable initialization manager and the recommendation is to keep it unless you need some extra feature.

How to do it...

When using `sysvinit` as the initialization manager, Yocto offers the `update-rc.d` class as a helper to install initialization scripts so that they are started and stopped when needed.

When using this class, you need to specify the `INITSCRIPT_NAME` variable with the name of the script to install and `INITSCRIPT_PARAMS` with the options to pass to the `update-rc.d` utility. You can optionally use the `INITSCRIPT_PACKAGES` variable to list the packages to contain the initialization scripts. By default, this contains the main package only, and if multiple packages are provided, the `INITSCRIPT_NAME` and `INITSCRIPT_PARAMS` need to be specified for each using overrides. An example snippet follows:

```
INITSCRIPT_PACKAGES = "${PN}-httpd ${PN}-ftpd"
INITSCRIPT_NAME_${PN}-httpd = "httpd.sh"
INITSCRIPT_NAME_${PN}-ftpd = "ftpd.sh"
INITSCRIPT_PARAMS_${PN}-httpd = "defaults"
INITSCRIPT_PARAMS_${PN}-ftpd = "start 99 5 2 . stop 20 0 1 6 ."
```

When an initialization script is not tied to a particular recipe, we can add a specific recipe for it. For example, the following recipe will run a `mount.sh` script in the `recipes-example/sysvinit-mount/sysvinit-mount_1.0.bb` file.

```
DESCRIPTION = "Initscripts for mounting filesystems"
LICENSE = "MIT"

LIC_FILES_CHKSUM =
   "file://${COMMON_LICENSE_DIR}/MIT;md5=0835ade698e0bcf8506ecda2f7b4
   f302"
```

```
SRC_URI = "file://mount.sh"

INITSCRIPT_NAME = "mount.sh"
INITSCRIPT_PARAMS = "start 09 S ."

inherit update-rc.d

S = "${WORKDIR}"

do_install () {
    install -d ${D}${sysconfdir}/init.d/
    install -c -m 755 ${WORKDIR}/${INITSCRIPT_NAME}
  ${D}${sysconfdir}/init.d/${INITSCRIPT_NAME}
}
```

Using the systemd initialization manager

As an alternative to `sysvinit`, you can configure your project to use `systemd` as an initialization manager, although `systemd` packs many more features.

Getting ready

The `systemd` initialization manager is replacing `sysvinit` and other initialization managers in most Linux distributions. It is based on the concepts of units, an abstraction of all elements that are relevant for system startup and maintenance, and targets, which group units and can be viewed as a runlevel equivalent. Some of the units `systemd` defines are:

- Services
- Sockets
- Devices
- Mount points
- Snapshots
- Timers
- Paths

The default targets and their runlevel equivalents are defined in the following table:

Sysvinit	Runlevel	Systemd target	Notes
0	runlevel0.target	poweroff.target	Halt the system.
1, s, single	runlevel1.target	rescue.target	Single user mode.

Sysvinit	Runlevel	Systemd target	Notes
2, 4	`runlevel2. target, runlevel4. target`	`multi-user. target`	User-defined/site-specific runlevels. By default, identical to 3.
3	`runlevel3. target`	`multi-user. target`	Multiuser, non-graphical. Users can usually log in via multiple consoles or via the network.
5	`runlevel5. target`	`graphical. target`	Multiuser, graphical. Usually has all the services of runlevel 3 plus a graphical login.
6	`runlevel6. target`	`reboot.target`	Reboot the system.

The `systemd` initialization manager is designed to be compatible with `sysvinit`, including using `sysvinit init` scripts.

Some of the features of `systemd` are:

 ▶ Parallelization capabilities that allow for faster boot times

 ▶ Service initialization via sockets and D-Bus so that services are only started when needed

 ▶ Process monitoring that allows for process failure recovery

 ▶ System state snapshots and restoration

 ▶ Mount point management

 ▶ Transactional-dependency-based unit control, where units establish dependencies between them

How to do it...

To configure your system to use `systemd`, you need to add the `systemd` distribution feature to your project by adding the following to your distribution's configuration file, under `sources/poky/meta-yocto/conf/distro/poky.conf` for the default `poky` distribution, or locally on your project's `conf/local.conf` file:

```
DISTRO_FEATURES_append = " systemd"
```

> Note the space required after the starting quote.

```
VIRTUAL-RUNTIME_init_manager = "systemd"
```

This configuration example allows you to define a main image with `systemd` and a rescue image with `sysvinit`, providing it does not use the `VIRTUAL-RUNTIME_init_manager` variable. Hence, the rescue image cannot use the `packagegroup-core-boot` or `packagegroup-core-full-cmdline` recipes. As an example, the recipe where the image size has been reduced, which we will introduce in the *Reducing the root filesystem image size* recipe in this chapter, could be used as the basis for a rescue image.

To remove `sysvinit` completely from your system, you would do the following:

```
DISTRO_FEATURES_BACKFILL_CONSIDERED = "sysvinit"
VIRTUAL-RUNTIME_initscripts = ""
```

Feature backfilling is the automatic extension of machine and distribution features to keep backwards compatibility. The `sysvinit` distribution feature is automatically filled in, so to remove it, we need to blacklist it by adding it to the `DISTRO_FEATURES_BACKFILL_CONSIDERED` variable as shown earlier.

> Note that if you are using an existing project and you change the `DISTRO_FEATURES` variable as explained earlier, you will need to remove the `tmp` directory and build with `sstate-cache` or the build will fail.

There's more...

Not only does the root filesystem needs to be configured, but the Linux kernel also needs to be specifically configured with all the features required by `systemd`. There is an extensive list of kernel configuration variables in the `systemd` source README file. As an example, to extend the minimal kernel configuration that we will introduce in the *Reducing the Linux kernel image size* recipe later on this chapter, for the Wandboard to support `systemd`, we would need to add the following configuration changes in the `arch/arm/configs/wandboard-quad_minimal_defconfig` file:

```
+CONFIG_FHANDLE=y
+CONFIG_CGROUPS=y
+CONFIG_SECCOMP=y
+CONFIG_NET=y
+CONFIG_UNIX=y
+CONFIG_INET=y
+CONFIG_AUTOFS4_FS=y
+CONFIG_TMPFS=y
+CONFIG_TMPFS_POSIX_ACL=y
+CONFIG_SCHEDSTATS=y
```

The default kernel configuration provided for the Wandboard will launch a `core-image-minimal` image of `systemd` just fine.

Installing systemd unit files

Yocto offers the `systemd` class as a helper to install unit files. By default, unit files are installed on the `${systemd_unitdir}/system` path on the destination directory.

When using this class, you need to specify the `SYSTEMD_SERVICE_${PN}` variable with the name of the unit file to install. You can optionally use the `SYSTEMD_PACKAGES` variable to list the packages to contain the unit files. By default, this is the main package only, and if multiple packages are provided, the `SYSTEMD_SERVICE` variable needs to be specified using overrides.

Services are configured to launch at boot by default, but this can be changed with the `SYSTEMD_AUTO_ENABLE` variable.

An example snippet follows:

```
SYSTEMD_PACKAGES = "${PN}-syslog"
SYSTEMD_SERVICE_${PN}-syslog = "busybox-syslog.service"
SYSTEMD_AUTO_ENABLE = "disabled"
```

Installing package-installation scripts

The supported package formats, RPM, ipk, and deb, support the addition of installation scripts that can be run at different times during a package installation process. In this recipe, we will see how to install them.

Getting ready

There are different types of installation scripts:

▶ **Preinstallation scripts** (`pkg_preinst`): These are called before the package is unpacked

▶ **Postinstallation scripts** (`pkg_postinst`): These are called after the package is unpacked, and dependencies will be configured

▶ **Preremoval scripts** (`pkg_prerm`): These are called with installed or at least partially installed packages

▶ **Postremoval scripts** (`pkg_postrm`): These are called after the package's files have been removed or replaced

How to do it...

An example snippet of the installation of a preinstallation script in a recipe is as follows:

```
pkg_preinst_${PN} () {
    # Shell commands
}
```

All installation scripts work in the same way, with the exception that the postinstallation scripts may be run either on the host at root filesystem image creation time, on the target (for those actions that cannot be performed on the host), or when a package is directly installed on the target. Have a look at the following code:

```
pkg_postinst_${PN} () {
    if [ x"$D" = "x" ]; then
        # Commands to execute on device
    else
        # Commands to execute on host
    fi
}
```

If the postinstallation script succeeds, the package is marked as installed. If the script fails, the package is marked as unpacked and the script is executed when the image boots again.

How it works...

Once the recipe defines an installation script, the class for the specific package type will install it while following the packaging rules of the specific format.

For postinstallation scripts, when running on the host, D is set to the destination directory, so the comparison test will fail. But D will be empty when running on the target.

> It is recommended to perform postinstallation scripts on the host if possible, as we need to take into account that some root filesystems will be read only and hence it would not be possible to perform some operations on the target.

Reducing the Linux kernel image size

Before or in parallel with the root filesystem customization, embedded projects usually require an image size optimization that will reduce the boot time and memory usage.

Smaller images mean less storage space, less transmission time, and less programming time, which saves money both in manufacturing and field updates.

By default, the compressed Linux kernel image (**zImage**) for the wandboard-quad is around 5.2 MB. This recipe will show how we can reduce that.

How to do it...

An example of a minimal kernel configuration for a Wandboard that is able to boot from a microSD card root filesystem is the `arch/arm/configs/wandboard-quad_minimal_defconfig` file that follows:

```
CONFIG_KERNEL_XZ=y
CONFIG_NO_HZ=y
CONFIG_HIGH_RES_TIMERS=y
CONFIG_BLK_DEV_INITRD=y
CONFIG_CC_OPTIMIZE_FOR_SIZE=y
CONFIG_EMBEDDED=y
CONFIG_SLOB=y
CONFIG_ARCH_MXC=y
CONFIG_SOC_IMX6Q=y
CONFIG_SOC_IMX6SL=y
CONFIG_SMP=y
CONFIG_VMSPLIT_2G=y
CONFIG_AEABI=y
CONFIG_CPU_FREQ=y
CONFIG_ARM_IMX6_CPUFREQ=y
CONFIG_CPU_IDLE=y
CONFIG_VFP=y
CONFIG_NEON=y
CONFIG_DEVTMPFS=y
CONFIG_DEVTMPFS_MOUNT=y
CONFIG_PROC_DEVICETREE=y
CONFIG_SERIAL_IMX=y
CONFIG_SERIAL_IMX_CONSOLE=y
CONFIG_REGULATOR=y
CONFIG_REGULATOR_ANATOP=y
CONFIG_MMC=y
CONFIG_MMC_SDHCI=y
CONFIG_MMC_SDHCI_PLTFM=y
CONFIG_MMC_SDHCI_ESDHC_IMX=y
CONFIG_DMADEVICES=y
CONFIG_IMX_SDMA=y
CONFIG_EXT3_FS=y
```

This configuration builds an 886 K compressed Linux kernel image (zImage).

How it works...

Apart from hardware design considerations (such as running the Linux kernel from a NOR flash and **execute in place** (**XIP**) to avoid loading the image to memory), the first step in kernel size optimization is to review the kernel configuration and remove all superfluous features.

To analyze the sizes of kernel blocks, we may use:

```
$ size vmlinux */built-in.o
text      data     bss      dec       hex filename
8746205   356560   394484   9497249   90eaa1 vmlinux
117253    2418     1224     120895    1d83f block/built-in.o
243859    11158    20       255037    3e43d crypto/built-in.o
2541356   163465   34404    2739225   29cc19 drivers/built-in.o
1956      0        0        1956      7a4 firmware/built-in.o
1728762   18672    10544    1757978   1ad31a fs/built-in.o
20361     14701    100      35162     895a init/built-in.o
29628     760      8        30396     76bc ipc/built-in.o
576593    20644    285052   882289    d7671 kernel/built-in.o
106256    24847    2344     133447    20947 lib/built-in.o
291768    14901    3736     310405    4bc85 mm/built-in.o
1722683   39947    50928    1813558   1bac36 net/built-in.o
34638     848      316      35802     8bda security/built-in.o
276979    19748    1332     298059    48c4b sound/built-in.o
138       0        0        138       8a usr/built-in.o
```

Here, `vmlinux` is the Linux kernel ELF image, which can be found in the Linux `build` directory.

Some of the usual things to exclude are:

▸ Remove IPv6 (`CONFIG_IPV6`) and other superfluous networking features
▸ Remove block devices (`CONFIG_BLOCK`) if not needed
▸ Remove cryptographic features (`CONFIG_CRYPTO`) if unused
▸ Review the supported filesystem types and remove the unneeded ones, such as flash filesystems on flashless devices
▸ Avoid modules and remove the module support (`CONFIG_MODULES`) from the kernel if possible

A good strategy is to start with a minimal kernel and add the essential stuff until you get a working system. Start with the `allnoconfig` GNU make target and review the configuration items under `CONFIG_EXPERT` and `CONFIG_EMBEDDED` as they are not included in the `allnoconfig` setting.

Some configuration changes that might not be obvious but reduce the image size considerably without feature removal are listed here:

▶ Change the default compression method from **Lempel–Ziv–Oberhumer** (**LZO**) to XZ (`CONFIG_KERNEL_XZ`). The decompression speed will be a bit lower though.

▶ Change the allocator from SLUB to **Simple List Of Blocks** (**SLOB**) (`CONFIG_SLOB`) for small embedded systems with little memory.

▶ Use no high memory (`CONFIG_HIGHMEM`) unless you have 4 GB or more memory.

You may also want to have a different configuration for production and development systems, so you may remove the following from your production images:

▶ `printk` support (`CONFIG_PRINTK`)

▶ `tracing` support (`CONFIG_FTRACE`)

In the compilation side of things, optimize for size using `CONFIG_CC_OPTIMIZE_FOR_SIZE`.

Once the basics are covered, we would need to analyze the kernel functions to identify further reduction areas. You can print a sorted list of kernel symbols with the following:

```
$ nm --size-sort --print-size -r vmlinux | head
        808bde04 00040000 B __log_buf
        8060f1c0 00004f15 r kernel_config_data
        80454190 000041f0 T hidinput_connect
        80642510 00003d40 r drm_dmt_modes
        8065cbbc 00003414 R v4l2_dv_timings_presets
        800fbe44 000032c0 T __blockdev_direct_IO
        80646290 00003100 r edid_cea_modes
        80835970 00003058 t imx6q_clocks_init
        8016458c 00002e74 t ext4_fill_super
        8056a814 00002aa4 T hci_event_packet
```

You would then need to look into the kernel source to find optimizations.

The actual space used by the uncompressed kernel in memory can be obtained from a running Wandboard kernel log as follows:

```
$ dmesg | grep -A 3 "text"
      .text : 0x80008000 - 0x80a20538   (10338 kB)
      .init : 0x80a21000 - 0x80aae240   ( 565 kB)
      .data : 0x80ab0000 - 0x80b13644   ( 398 kB)
      .bss  : 0x80b13644 - 0x80b973fc   ( 528 kB)
```

From here, the .text section contains code and constant data, the .data section contains the initialization data for variables, and the .bss sections contains all uninitialized data. The .init section contains global variables used during Linux initialization only, which are freed afterwards as can be seen from the following Linux kernel boot message:

```
Freeing unused kernel memory: 564K (80a21000 - 80aae000)
```

There are ongoing efforts to reduce the size of the Linux kernel, so it is expected that newer kernel versions will be smaller and will allow for better customization for use in embedded systems.

Reducing the root filesystem image size

By default, the core-image-minimal size for the wandboard-quad unpacked tarball is around 45 MB, and core-image-sato is around 150 MB. This recipe will explore methods to reduce their size.

How to do it...

An example of a small image, core-image-small, that does not include the packagegroup-core-boot recipe and can be used as the base for a root filesystem image with reduced size, recipes-core/images/core-image-small.bb, is shown next:

```
DESCRIPTION = "Minimal console image."

IMAGE_INSTALL= "\
       base-files \
       base-passwd \
       busybox \
       sysvinit \
       initscripts \
       ${ROOTFS_PKGMANAGE_BOOTSTRAP} \
       ${CORE_IMAGE_EXTRA_INSTALL} \
"
```

```
IMAGE_LINGUAS = " "

LICENSE = "MIT"

inherit core-image

IMAGE_ROOTFS_SIZE ?= "8192"
```

This recipe produces an image of about 6.4 MB. You can go even smaller if you use the `poky-tiny` distribution by adding the following to your `conf/local.conf` file:

```
DISTRO = "poky-tiny"
```

The `poky-tiny` distribution makes a series of size optimizations that may restrict the set of packages you can include in your image. To successfully build this image, you have to skip one of the sanity checks that the Yocto build system performs, by adding the following:

```
INSANE_SKIP_glibc-locale = "installed-vs-shipped"
```

With `poky-tiny`, the size of the image is further reduced to around 4 MB.

There are further reductions that can be done to the image; for example, we could replace `sysvinit` with `tiny-init`, but that is left as an exercise for the reader.

Images with reduced sizes are also used alongside production images for tasks such as rescue systems and manufacturing test processes. They are also ideal to be built as `initramfs` images; that is, images that the Linux kernel mounts from memory, and can even be bundled into a single Linux kernel image binary.

How it works...

Start with an appropriate image like `core-image-minimal` and analyze the dependencies as shown in the *Debugging the build system* recipe in *Chapter 1, The Build System*, and decide which of them are not needed. You could also use the file sizes listed in the image's build history, as seen in the *Using build history* recipe, also in *Chapter 1, The Build System*, to detect the biggest files in the filesystem and review them. To sort the file sizes, which appear in the fourth column of the `files-in-image.txt` file, in reverse order, we could execute:

```
$ sort -r -g  -k 4,4 files-in-image.txt -o sorted-files-in-image.txt
sorted-files-in-image.txt:
-rwxr-xr-x root        root          1238640 ./lib/libc-2.19.so
-rwxr-xr-x root        root           613804 ./sbin/ldconfig
-rwxr-xr-x root        root           539860 ./bin/busybox.nosuid
-rwxr-xr-x root        root           427556 ./lib/libm-2.19.so
```

```
-rwxr-xr-x root         root              130304 ./lib/ld-2.19.so
-rwxr-xr-x root         root               88548 ./lib/libpthread-2.19.so
-rwxr-xr-x root         root               71572 ./lib/libnsl-2.19.so
-rwxr-xr-x root         root               71488 ./lib/libresolv-2.19.so
-rwsr-xr-x root         root               51944 ./bin/busybox.suid
-rwxr-xr-x root         root               42668 ./lib/libnss_files-
   2.19.so
-rwxr-xr-x root         root               30536 ./lib/libnss_compat-
   2.19.so
-rwxr-xr-x root         root               30244 ./lib/libcrypt-2.19.so
-rwxr-xr-x root         root               28664 ./sbin/init.sysvinit
-rwxr-xr-x root         root               26624 ./lib/librt-2.19.so
```

From this, we observe that `glic` is the biggest contributor to the filesystem size. Some other places where some space on a console-only system can be saved are:

▶ Use the IPK package manager, as it is the lightest, or better yet, remove the `package-management` feature from your production root filesystem altogether.

▶ Use BusyBox's `mdev` device manager instead of `udev` by specifying it in your `conf/local.conf` file as follows:

```
VIRTUAL-RUNTIME_dev_manager = "mdev"
```

Note that this will only work with core images that include `packagegroup-core-boot`.

▶ If we are running the root filesystem on a block device, use ext2 instead of ext3 or ext4 without the journal.

▶ Configure BusyBox with only the essential applets by providing your own configuration file in `bbappend`.

▶ Review the `glibc` configuration, which can be changed via the `DISTRO_FEATURES_LIBC` distribution configuration variable. An example of its usage can be found in the `poky-tiny` distribution, which is included in the `poky` source. The `poky-tiny` distribution can be used as a template for the distribution customization of small systems.

▶ Consider switching to a lighter `C` library than the default `glibc`. For a while, `uclibc` was being used as an alternative, but the library seems to be unmaintained for the last couple of years, and the `core-image-minimal` image for the Wandboard does not currently build using it.

> Recently, there has been some activity with **musl** (`http://www.musl-libc.org/`), a new MIT-licensed C library. To enable it, you would add the following to your `conf/local.conf` file:
>
> TCLIBC = "musl"
>
> And you would need to add the `meta-musl` layer (`https://github.com/kraj/meta-musl`) to your `conf/bblayers.conf` file.
>
> It currently builds `core-image-minimal` for QEMU targets, but there is still work to be done to use it on real hardware like the Wandboard.

▶ Compile your applications with `-Os` to optimize for size.

Releasing software

When releasing a product based on the Yocto project, we have to consider that we are building on top of a multitude of different open source projects, each with different licensing requirements.

At the minimum, your embedded product will contain a bootloader (probably U-Boot), the Linux kernel, and a root filesystem with one or more applications. Both U-Boot and the Linux kernel are licensed under the **General Public License version 2** (**GPLv2**). And the root filesystem could contain a variety of programs with different licenses.

All open source licenses allow you to sell a commercial product with a mixture of proprietary and open licenses as long as they are independent and the product complies with all the open source licenses. We will discuss open source and proprietary cohabiting in the *Working with open source and proprietary code* recipe later on.

It is important to understand all the licensing implications before releasing your product to the public. The Yocto project provides tools to make handling licensing requirements an easier job.

Getting ready

We first need to specify what requirements we need to comply with to distribute a product built with the Yocto project. For the most restrictive open source licenses, this usually means:

▶ Source code distribution, including modifications

▶ License texts distributions

▶ Distribution of the tools used to build and run the software

How to do it...

We can use the `archiver` class to provide the deliverables that need to be distributed to comply with the licenses. We can configure it to:

- Provide the original unpatched source as tarballs
- Provide the patches to apply to the original source
- Provide the recipes used to build the source
- Provide the license text that must sometimes accompany the binary (according to some licenses)

To use the `archiver` class as specified earlier, we add the following to our `conf/local.conf` file:

```
INHERIT += "archiver"
ARCHIVER_MODE[src] = "original"
ARCHIVER_MODE[diff] = "1"
ARCHIVER_MODE[recipe] = "1"
COPY_LIC_MANIFEST = "1"
COPY_LIC_DIRS = "1"
```

The sources will be provided in the `tmp/deploy/sources` directory under a license subdirectory hierarchy.

For the `wandboard-quad`, we find the following directories under `tmp/deploy/sources`:

- `allarch-poky-linux`
- `arm-poky-linux-gnueabi`

And looking for what's distributed for the Linux kernel source, a GPLv2 package, we find under `tmp/deploy/sources/arm-poky-linux-gnueabi/linux-wandboard-3.10.17-r0`:

- `defconfig`
- `github.com.wandboard-org.linux.git.tar.gz`
- `linux-wandboard-3.10.17-r0-recipe.tar.gz`

So we have the kernel configuration, the source tarball, and the recipes used to build it, which include:

- `linux-wandboard_3.10.17.bb`
- `linux-dtb.inc`
- `linux-wandboard.inc`

And the license text for the root filesystem packages will also be included in the root filesystem under `/usr/share/common-licenses`, in a package directory hierarchy.

This configuration will provide deliverables for all build packages, but what we really want to do is provide them only for those whose licenses require us to.

For sure, we don't want to blindly distribute all the contents of the `sources` directory as is, as it will also contain our proprietary source, which we most likely don't want to distribute.

We can configure the `archiver` class only to provide the source for GPL and LGPL packages with the following:

```
COPYLEFT_LICENSE_INCLUDE = "GPL* LGPL*"
COPYLEFT_LICENSE_EXCLUDE = "CLOSED Proprietary"
```

And also, for an embedded product, we are usually only concerned with the software that ships in the product itself, so we can limit the recipe type to be archived to target images with the following:

```
COPYLEFT_RECIPE_TYPES = "target"
```

We should obtain legal advice to decide which packages have licenses that make source distribution a requirement.

Other configuration options exist, such as providing the patched or configured source instead of the separated original source and patches, or source `rpms` instead of source tarballs. See the `archiver` class for more details.

There's more...

We can also choose to distribute the whole of our build environment. The best way to do this is usually to publish our BSP and software layers on a public Git repository. Our software layer can then provide `bblayers.conf.sample` and `local.conf.sample`, which can be used to set up ready-to-use `build` directories.

See also

> ▶ There are other requirements that haven't been discussed here, such as the mechanism chosen for distribution. It is recommended to get legal advice before releasing a product to ensure all the license obligations have been met.

Analyzing your system for compliance

The Yocto build system makes it easy to provide auditing information to our legal advisers. This recipe will explain how.

How to do it...

Under `tmp/deploy/licenses`, we find a directory list of packages (including their corresponding licenses) and an `image` folder with a package and license manifest.

For the example image provided before, `core-image-small`, we have the following:

```
tmp/deploy/licenses/core-image-small-wandboard-quad-<timestamp>/
package.manifest
base-files
base-passwd
busybox
busybox-syslog
busybox-udhcpc
initscripts
initscripts-functions
libc6
run-postinsts
sysvinit
sysvinit-inittab
sysvinit-pidof
update-alternatives-opkg
update-rc.d
```

And the corresponding `tmp/deploy/licenses/core-image-small-wandboard-quad-<timestamp>/license.manifest` file excerpt is as follows:

```
PACKAGE NAME: base-files
PACKAGE VERSION: 3.0.14
RECIPE NAME: base-files
LICENSE: GPLv2

PACKAGE NAME: base-passwd
PACKAGE VERSION: 3.5.29
RECIPE NAME: base-passwd
LICENSE: GPLv2+
```

These files can be used to analyze all the different packages that form our root filesystem. We can also audit them to make sure we comply with the licenses when releasing our product to the public.

There's more

You can instruct the Yocto build system to specifically avoid certain licenses by using the `INCOMPATIBLE_LICENSE` configuration variable. The usual way to use it is to avoid GPLv3-type licenses by adding the following to your `conf/local.conf` file:

```
INCOMPATIBLE_LICENSE = "GPL-3.0 LGPL-3.0 AGPL-3.0"
```

This will build `core-image-minimal` and `core-image-base` images as long as no extra image features are included.

Working with open source and proprietary code

It is common for an embedded product to be built upon an open source system like the one built by Yocto, and to include proprietary software that adds value and specializes the product. This proprietary part usually is intellectual property and needs to be protected, and it's important to understand how it can coexist with open source.

This recipe will discuss some examples of open source packages commonly found on embedded products and will briefly explain how to use proprietary software with them.

How to do it...

Open source licenses can be broadly divided into two categories based on whether they are:

- ▶ **Permissive**: These are similar to **Internet Software Consortium** (**ISC**), MIT, and BSD licenses. They have few requirements attached to them and just require us to preserve copyright notices.

- ▶ **Restrictive**: These are similar to the GPL, which bind us to not only distribute the source code and modifications, either with the binary itself or at a later date, but also to distribute tools to build, install, and run the source.

However, some licenses might "pollute" modifications and derivative work with their own conditions, commonly referred to as *viral licenses*, while others will not. For example, if you link your application to GPL-licensed code, your application will be bound by the GPL too.

The virulent nature of the GPL has made some people wary of using GPL-licensed software, but it's important to note that proprietary software can run alongside GPL software as long as the license terms are understood and respected.

For example, violating the GPLv2 license would mean losing the right to distribute the GPLv2 code in the future, even if further distribution is GPLv2 compliant. In this case, the only way to be able to distribute the code again would be to ask the copyright holder for permission.

How it works...

Next, we will provide guidance regarding licensing requirements for some open source packages commonly used in embedded products. It does not constitute legal advice, and as stated before, proper legal auditing of your product should be done before public release.

The U-Boot bootloader

U-Boot is licensed under the GPLv2, but any program launched by it does not inherit its license. So you are free to use U-Boot to launch a proprietary operating system, for example. However, your final product must comply with the GPLv2 with regards to U-Boot, so U-Boot source code and modifications must be provided.

The Linux kernel

The Linux kernel is also licensed under the GPLv2. Any application that runs in the Linux kernel user space does not inherit its license, so you can run your proprietary software in Linux freely. However, Linux kernel modules are part of the Linux kernel and as such must comply with the GPLv2. Also, your final product must release the Linux kernel source and modifications, including external modules that run in your product.

Glibc

The GNU C library is licensed under the **Lesser General Public License** (**LGPL**), which allows dynamic linking without license inheritance. So your proprietary code can dynamically link with `glibc`, but of course you still have to comply with the LGPL with regards to `glibc`. Note, however, that statically linking your application would pollute it with the LGPL.

BusyBox

BusyBox is also licensed under the GPLv2. The license allows for non-related software to run alongside it, so your proprietary software can run alongside BusyBox freely. As before, you have to comply with the GPLv2 with regards to BusyBox and distribute its source and modifications.

The Qt framework

Qt is licensed under three different licenses, which is common for open source projects. You can choose whether you want a commercial license (in which case, your proprietary application is protected), a LGPL license (which, as discussed before, would also protect your proprietary software by allowing the dynamic linking of your application as long as you complied with the LGPL for the Qt framework itself), or the GPLv3 (which would be inherited by your application).

The X Windows system

The `X.Org` source is licensed under permissive MIT-style licenses. As such, your proprietary software is free to make any use of it as long as its use is stated and copyright notices are preserved.

There's more...

Let's see how to integrate our proprietary-licensed code into the Yocto build system. When preparing the recipe for our application, we can take several approaches to licensing:

- Mark `LICENSE` as closed. This is the usual case for a proprietary application. We use the following:

  ```
  LICENSE = "CLOSED"
  ```

- Mark `LICENSE` as proprietary and include some type of license agreement. This is commonly done when releasing binaries with some sort of end user agreement that is referenced in the recipe. For example, `meta-fsl-arm` uses this type of license to comply with Freescale's End User License Agreement. An example follows:

  ```
  LICENSE = "Proprietary"
  LIC_FILES_CHKSUM = "file://EULA.txt;md5=93b784b1c11b3fffb1638498
  a8dde3f6"
  ```

- Provide multiple licensing options, such as an open source license and a commercial license. In this case, the `LICENSE` variable is used to specify the open licenses, and the `LICENSE_FLAGS` variable is used for the commercial licenses. A typical example is the `gst-plugins-ugly` package in Poky:

  ```
  LICENSE = "GPLv2+ & LGPLv2.1+ & LGPLv2+"
  LICENSE_FLAGS = "commercial"
  LIC_FILES_CHKSUM =
    "file://COPYING;md5=a6f89e2100d9b6cdffcea4f398e37343 \
    file://gst/synaesthesia/synaescope.h;beginline=1;endline=20
    ;md5=99f301df7b80490c6ff8305fcc712838 \
    file://tests/check/elements/xingmux.c;beginline=1;endline=2
    1;md5=4c771b8af188724855cb99cadd390068 \
    file://gst/mpegstream/gstmpegparse.h;beginline=1;endline=18
    ;md5=ff65467b0c53cdfa98d0684c1bc240a9"
  ```

When the `LICENSE_FLAGS` variable is set on a recipe, the package will not be built unless the license appears on the `LICENSE_FLAGS_WHITELIST` variable too, typically defined in your `conf/local.conf` file. For the earlier example, we would add:

```
LICENSE_FLAGS_WHITELIST = "commercial"
```

The `LICENSE` and `LICENSE_FLAGS_WHITELIST` variables can match exactly for a very narrow match or broadly, as in the preceding example, which matches all licenses that begin with the word `commercial`. For narrow matches, the package name must be appended to the license name; for instance, if we only wanted to whitelist the `gst-plugins-ugly` package from the earlier example but nothing else, we could use the following:

```
LICENSE_FLAGS_WHITELIST = "commercial_gst-plugins-ugly"
```

See also

> ▸ You should refer to the specific licenses for a complete understanding of the requirements imposed by them. You can find a complete list of open source licenses and their documentation at `http://spdx.org/licenses/`.

4
Application Development

In this chapter, we will cover the following recipes:

- ► Introducing toolchains
- ► Preparing and using an SDK
- ► Using the Application Development Toolkit
- ► Using the Eclipse IDE
- ► Developing GTK+ applications
- ► Using the Qt Creator IDE
- ► Developing Qt applications
- ► Describing workflows for application development
- ► Working with GNU make
- ► Working with the GNU build system
- ► Working with the CMake build system
- ► Working with the SCons builder
- ► Developing with libraries
- ► Working with the Linux framebuffer
- ► Using the X Windows system
- ► Using Wayland
- ► Adding Python applications
- ► Integrating the Oracle Java Runtime Environment
- ► Integrating the Open Java Development Kit
- ► Integrating Java applications

Introduction

Dedicated applications are what define an embedded product, and Yocto offers helpful application development tools as well as the functionality to integrate with popular **Integrated Development Environments** (**IDE**) like Eclipse and Qt Creator. It also provides a wide range of utility classes to help in the integration of finished applications into the build system and the target images.

This chapter will introduce the IDEs and show us how they are used to build and debug C and C++ applications on real hardware, and will explore application development, including graphical frameworks and Yocto integration, not only for C and C++ but also Python and Java applications.

Introducing toolchains

A toolchain is a set of tools, binaries, and libraries used to build applications to run on a computer platform. In Yocto, the toolchains are based on GNU components.

Getting ready

A GNU toolchain contains the following components:

- **Assembler (GNU as)**: This is part of the binutils package
- **Linker (GNU ld)**: This is also part of the binutils package
- **Compiler (GNU gcc)**: This has support for C, C++, Java, Ada, Fortran, and Objective C
- **Debugger (GNU gdb)**: This is the GNU debugger
- **Binary file tools (objdump, nm, objcopy, readelf, strip, and so on)**: These are part of the binutils package.

These components are enough to build bare metal applications, bootloaders like U-Boot, or operating systems like the Linux kernel, as they don't need a C library and they implement the C library functions they need. However, for Linux user space applications, a POSIX-compliant C library is needed.

The GNU C library, `glibc`, is the default C library used in the Yocto project. Yocto is introducing support for musl, a smaller C library, but as we have mentioned before, there is still work to be done until it is ready to be used with the hardware platforms supported by the FSL community layer.

But on embedded systems, it is not just a toolchain we need, but a cross-compilation toolchain. This is because we build in a host computer but run the resulting binaries on the target, which is usually a different architecture. In reality, there are several types of toolchains, based on the architecture of the machine building the toolchain (build machine), running the toolchain (host machine), and running the binaries built by the toolchain (target machine). The most common combinations are:

- **Native**: An example of this is an x86 machine running a toolchain that has also been built on an x86 machine producing binaries to run on an x86 machine. This is common in desktop computers.

- **Cross-compilation**: This is the most common on embedded systems; for example, an x86 machine running a toolchain that has also been built on an x86 machine but producing binaries to run on a different architecture, like ARM.

- **Cross-native**: This is typically the toolchain running on targets. An example of this is where a toolchain has been built on an x86 machine but runs on ARM and produces binaries for ARM.

- **Canadian**: Rarely seen, this is where the build, host, and target machines are all different.

The process of building a cross-compilation toolchain is complex and fault prone, so automated tools for toolchain building have emerged, like **buildroot** and **crosstool-NG**. The Yocto build system also compiles its own toolchain on every build, and as we will see, you can use this toolchain for application development too.

But the cross-compilation toolchain and C library are not the only things we need in order to build applications; we also need a `sysroot`; that is, a root filesystem on the host with the libraries and header files that can be found on the target root filesystem.

The combination of the cross-compilation toolchain, the `sysroot`, and sometimes other development tools such as an IDE is referred to as an SDK, or Software Development Kit.

How to do it...

There are several ways to obtain an SDK with the Yocto project:

- Using the **Application Development Toolkit** (**ADT**).

  If you are using a hardware platform supported by Poky (that is, a virtualized QEMU machine or one of the reference boards), the recommendation is to use ADT, which will install all the required SDK components for you.

▶ Downloading a precompiled toolchain.

The easiest way to obtain a cross-compilation toolchain for a supported platform is to download a precompiled one; for example from the Yocto project downloads site, `http://downloads.yoctoproject.org/releases/yocto/yocto-1.7.1/toolchain/`. The Yocto project provides prebuilt toolchains for both 32- and 64-bit i686 host machines, and prebuilt ARM toolchains both for **armv5** and **armv7** architectures. These contain `sysroot` that match the `core-image-sato` target image. However, the prebuilt `sysroot` is soft floating point, so it can't be used with the target images built by the FSL community layer for i.MX6-based platforms, which are hard floating point. To install the prebuilt armv7 toolchain for an x86_64 host, run the following:

```
$ wget http://downloads.yoctoproject.org/releases/yocto/yocto-
  1.7.1/toolchain/x86_64/poky-glibc-x86_64-core-image-sato-
  armv7a-vfp-neon-toolchain-1.7.1.sh

$ chmod a+x poky-glibc-x86_64-core-image-sato-armv7a-vfp-neon-
  toolchain-1.7.1.sh

$ ./poky-glibc-x86_64-core-image-sato-armv7a-vfp-neon-
  toolchain-1.7.1.sh
```

▶ Building your own toolchain installer.

On most embedded Linux projects, your machine will be supported by an external layer, and you will have a customized root filesystem that your `sysroot` will need to match. So building your own toolchain installer is recommended when you have a customized root filesystem. For example, the ideal toolchain to work with the Wandboard would be **Cortex-A9**-specific and targeted to produce hard floating point binaries.

▶ Using the Yocto project build system.

Finally, if you already have a Yocto build system installation on your host, you can also use it for application development. Usually, application developers do not need the complexity of a Yocto build system installation, so a toolchain installer for the target system will be enough.

Preparing and using an SDK

The Yocto build system can be used to generate a cross-compilation toolchain and matching `sysroot` for a target system.

Getting ready

We will use the previously used `wandboard-quad` build directory and source the `setup-environment` script as follows:

```
$ cd /opt/yocto/fsl-community-bsp/
$ source setup-environment wandboard-quad
```

How to do it...

There are several ways to build an SDK with the Yocto build system:

- ▸ The `meta-toolchain` target.

    This method will build a toolchain that matches your target platform, and a basic `sysroot` that will not match your target root filesystem. However, this toolchain can be used to build bare metal software like the U-Boot bootloader or the Linux kernel, which do not need a `sysroot`. The Yocto project offers downloadable `sysroot` for the supported hardware platforms. You can also build this toolchain yourself with:

    ```
    $ bitbake meta-toolchain
    ```

    Once built, it can be installed with:

    ```
    $ cd tmp/deploy/sdk
    $ ./poky-glibc-x86_64-meta-toolchain-cortexa9hf-vfp-neon-
      toolchain-1.7.1.sh
    ```

- ▸ The `populate_sdk` task.

    This is the recommended way to build a toolchain matching your target platform with a `sysroot` matching your target root filesystem. You build it with:

    ```
    $ bitbake core-image-sato -c populate_sdk
    ```

    You should replace `core-image-sato` for the target root filesystem image you want the `sysroot` to match. The resulting toolchain can be installed with:

    ```
    $ cd tmp/deploy/sdk
    $ ./poky-glibc-x86_64-core-image-sato-cortexa9hf-vfp-neon-
      toolchain-1.7.1.sh
    ```

    Also, if you want your toolchain to be able to build static applications, you need to add static libraries to it. You can do this by adding specific static libraries to your target image, which could also be used for native compilation. For example, to add the static `glibc` libraries, add the following to your `conf/local.conf` file:

    ```
    IMAGE_INSTALL_append = " glibc-staticdev"
    ```

And then build the toolchain to match your root filesystem as explained previously.

You usually won't want the static libraries added to your image, but do you want to be able to cross-compile static applications, so you can also add all the static libraries to the toolchain by adding:

```
SDKIMAGE_FEATURES_append = " staticdev-pkgs"
```

▶ The `meta-toolchain-qt` target.

This method will extend `meta-toolchain` to build Qt applications. We will see how to build Qt applications later on. To build this toolchain, execute the following command:

```
$ bitbake meta-toolchain-qt
```

Once built, it can be installed with:

```
$ cd tmp/deploy/sdk
$ ./poky-glibc-x86_64-meta-toolchain-qt-cortexa9hf-vfp-neon-
  toolchain-qt-1.7.1.sh
```

The resulting toolchain installers will be located under `tmp/deploy/sdk` for all the cases mentioned here.

▶ The `meta-ide-support` target.

This method does not generate a toolchain installer, but it prepares the current build project to use its own toolchain. It will generate an `environment-setup` script inside the tmp directory.

```
$ bitbake meta-ide-support
```

To use the bundled toolchain, you can now source that script as follows:

```
$ source tmp/environment-setup-cortexa9hf-vfp-neon-poky-linux-
  gnueabi
```

Using the Application Development Toolkit

The ADT is an SDK installation script that installs the following for Poky-supported hardware platforms:

▶ A prebuilt cross-compilation toolchain, as explained previously

▶ A `sysroot` that matches the `core-image-sato` target image

▶ The QEMU emulator

▶ Other development user space tools used for system profiling (these will be discussed in the following chapters)

Getting ready

To install the ADT, you can choose either of the following options:

- Download a precompiled tarball from the Yocto project downloads site with the following command:

  ```
  $ wget http://downloads.yoctoproject.org/releases/yocto/yocto-
    1.7.1/adt-installer/adt_installer.tar.bz2
  ```

- Build one using your Yocto `build` directory.

The ADT installer is an automated script to install precompiled Yocto SDK components, so it will be the same whether you download the prebuilt version or you build one yourself.

You can then configure it before running it to customize the installation.

Note that it only makes sense to use the ADT for the Poky-supported platforms. For instance, it is not that useful for external hardware like `wandboard-quad` unless you provide your own components.

How to do it...

To build the ADT from your Yocto `build` directory, open a new shell and execute the following:

```
$ cd /opt/yocto/poky
$ source oe-init-build-env qemuarm
$ bitbake adt-installer
```

The ADT tarball will be located in the `tmp/deploy/sdk` directory.

How it works...

To install it, follow these steps:

1. Extract the tarball on a location of your choice:

   ```
   $ cd /opt/yocto
   $ cp
     /opt/yocto/poky/qemuarm/tmp/deploy/sdk/adt_installer.tar.bz2
     /opt/yocto
   $ tar xvf adt_installer.tar.bz2
   $ cd /opt/yocto/adt-installer
   ```

2. Configure the installation by editing the `adt_installer.conf` file. Some of the options are:

- ❏ YOCTOADT_REPO: This is a repository with the packages and root filesystem to be used. By default, it uses the one on the Yocto project web site, `http://adtrepo.yoctoproject.org/1.7.1/`, but you could set one up yourself with your customized packages and root filesystem.

- ❏ YOCTOADT_TARGETS: This defines the machine targets the SDK is for. By default, this is ARM and x86.

- ❏ YOCTOADT_QEMU: This option controls whether to install the QEMU emulator. The default is to install it.

- ❏ YOCTOADT_NFS_UTIL: This option controls whether to install user mode NFS. It is recommended if you are going to use the Eclipse IDE with QEMU-based machines. The default is to install it.

And then for the specific target architectures (only shown for ARM):

- ❏ YOCTOADT_ROOTFS_arm: This defines the specific root filesystem images to download from the ADT repository. By default it installs the `minimal` and `sato-sdk` images.

- ❏ YOCTOADT_TARGET_SYSROOT_IMAGE_arm: This is the root filesystem used to create the `sysroot`. This must also be included in the YOCTOADT_ROOTFS_arm selection that was explained earlier. By default this is the `sato-sdk` image.

- ❏ YOCTOADT_TARGET_MACHINE_arm: This is the machine that the images are downloaded for. By default this is `qemuarm`.

- ❏ YOCTOADT_TARGET_SYSROOT_LOC_arm: This is the path on the host to install the target's `sysroot`. By default this is `$HOME/test-yocto/`.

3. Run the ADT installer as follows:

```
$ ./adt_installer
```

It will ask for an installation location (by default `/opt/poky/1.7.1`) and whether you want to run it in interactive or silent mode.

Using the Eclipse IDE

Eclipse is an open source IDE that is written mostly in Java and released under the **Eclipse Public License** (**EPL**). It can be extended using plugins, and the Yocto project releases a Yocto plugin that allows us to use Eclipse for application development.

Getting ready

Yocto 1.7 provides Eclipse Yocto plugins for two different Eclipse versions, Juno and Kepler. They can be downloaded at `http://downloads.yoctoproject.org/releases/yocto/yocto-1.7.1/eclipse-plugin/`. We will use Kepler 4.3, as it is the newest. We will start with the Eclipse Kepler standard edition and install all the required plugins we need.

It is recommended to run Eclipse under Oracle Java 1.7, although other Java providers are supported. You can install Oracle Java 1.7 from Oracle's web site, `https://www.java.com/en/`, or using a Ubuntu Java Installer PPA, `https://launchpad.net/~webupd8team/+archive/ubuntu/java`. The latter will integrate Java with your package management system, so it's preferred. To install it, follow these steps:

```
$ sudo add-apt-repository ppa:webupd8team/java
$ sudo apt-get update
$ sudo apt-get install oracle-java7-set-default
```

To download and install Eclipse Kepler standard edition for an x86_64 host, follow these steps:

1. Fetch the tarball from the Eclipse download site, `http://eclipse.org/downloads/packages/release/Kepler/SR2`. For example:

   ```
   $ wget http://download.eclipse.org/technology/epp/downloads/
   release/kepler/SR2/eclipse-standard-kepler-SR2-linux-gtk-x86_64.
   tar.gz
   ```

2. Unpack it on a location of your choice as follows:

   ```
   $ tar xvf eclipse-standard-kepler-SR2-linux-gtk-x86_64.tar.gz
   ```

3. Start the Eclipse IDE with the following:

   ```
   $ nohup eclipse/eclipse &
   ```

4. Select **Install New Software** from the **Help** pull-down menu. Then select the **Kepler - http://download.eclipse.org/releases/kepler** source.

5. Install the following Eclipse components:

   ❏ Linux tools:

   LTTng - Linux Tracing Toolkit

   ❏ Mobile and device development:

   C/C++ Remote Launch

   Remote System Explorer End-user Runtime

   Remote System Explorer User Actions

Target Management Terminal

TCF Remote System Explorer add-in

TCF Target Explorer

    ❏   Programming languages:

C/C++ Autotools Support

C/C++ Development Tools

6. Install the Eclipse Yocto plugin by adding this repository source: `http://downloads.yoctoproject.org/releases/eclipse-plugin/1.7.1/kepler`, as shown in the following screenshot:

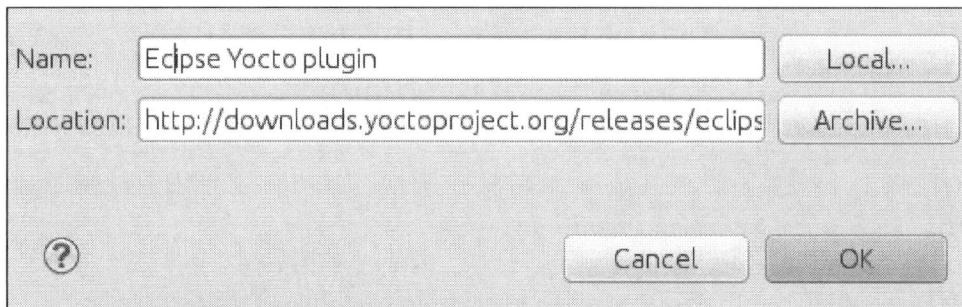

Name:	`Eclipse Yocto plugin` Local...
Location:	`http://downloads.yoctoproject.org/releases/eclips` Archive...
⑦	Cancel OK

7. Choose **Yocto Project ADT plug-in** and ignore the unsigned content warning. We won't be covering other plugin extensions.

How to do it...

To configure Eclipse to use a Yocto toolchain, go to **Window | Preferences | Yocto Project ADT**.

The ADT configuration offers two cross-compiler options:

1. **Standalone pre-built toolchain**: Choose this when you have installed a toolchain either from a toolchain installer or the ADT installer.

2. **Build system derived toolchain**: Choose this when using a Yocto `build` directory prepared with `meta-ide-support` as explained previously.

It also offers two target options:

1. **The QEMU emulator**: Choose this if you are using Poky with a virtualized machine and you have used the ADT installer to install a `qemuarm` Linux kernel and root filesystem.

2. **External hardware**: Choose this if you are using real hardware like the `wandboard-quad` hardware. This option is the most useful for embedded development.

An example configuration when using the ADT installer with its default configuration would be to choose the standalone prebuilt toolchain option along with the QEMU emulator as follows:

- Cross-compiler options:

    - Standalone pre-built toolchain:

Toolchain root location: `/opt/poky/1.7.1`

Sysroot location: `${HOME}/test-yocto/qemuarm`

Target architecture: `armv5te-poky-linux-gnueabi`

    - Target options:

QEMU kernel: `/tmp/adt-installer/download_image/zImage-qemuarm.bin`

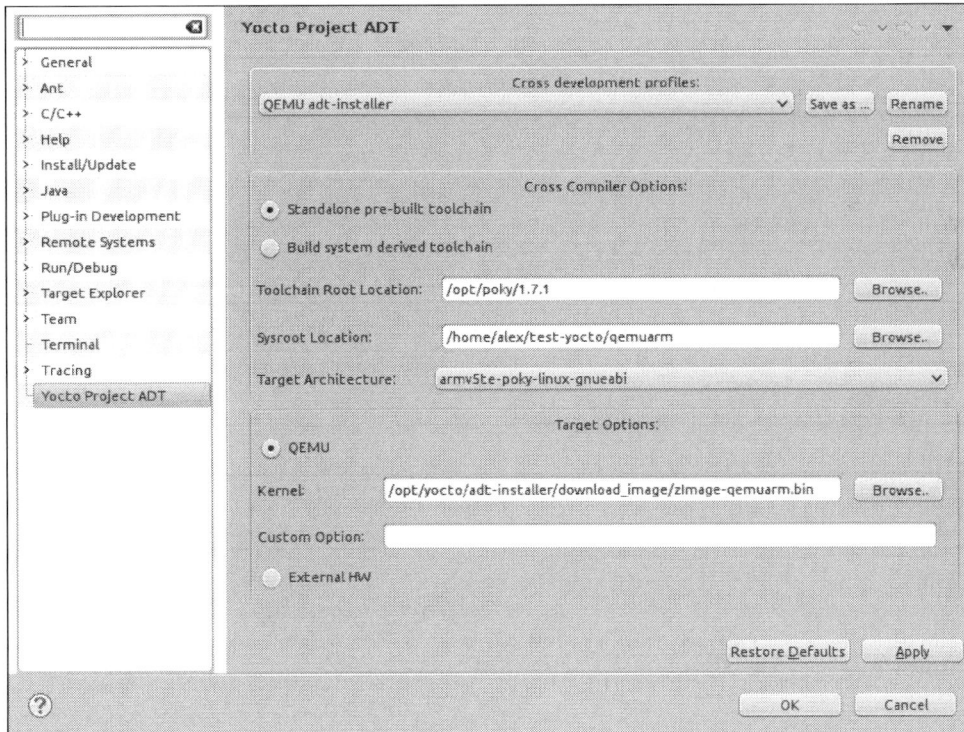

And for a build system derived toolchain using the `wandboard-quad` reference board, this is what you will need:

- ▶ Cross-compiler options:
    - ❑ Build system derived toolchain:

Toolchain root location: `/opt/yocto/fsl-community-bsp/wandboard-quad`

Sysroot location: `/opt/yocto/fsl-community-bsp/wandboard-quad/tmp/sysroots/wandboard-quad`

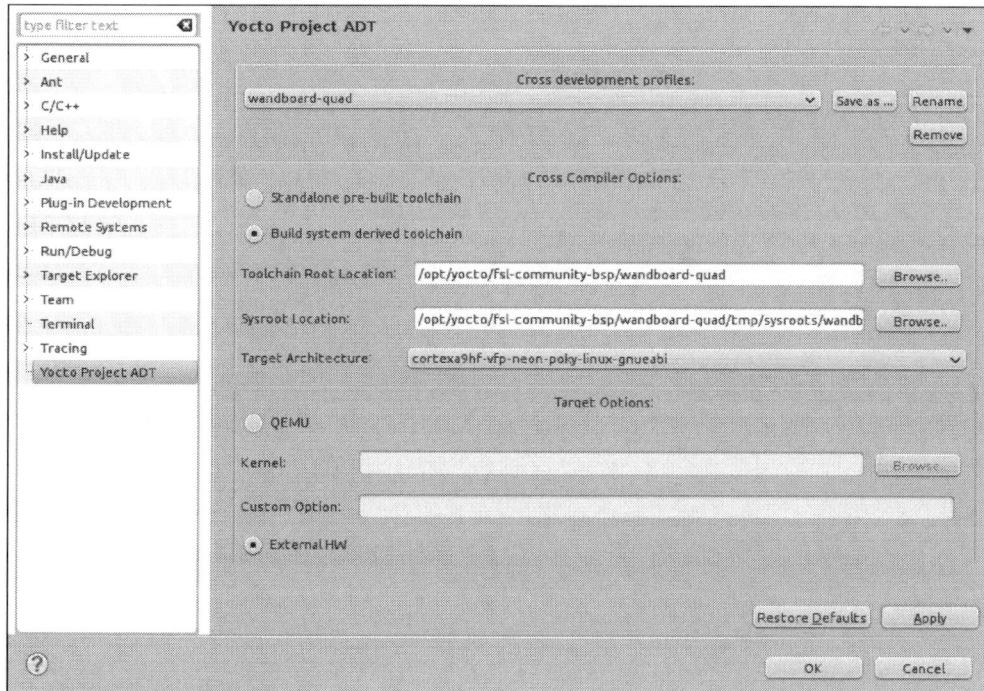

There's more...

In order to perform debugging on a remote target, it needs to be running the `tcf-agent` daemon. It is included by default on the SDK images, but you can also include it in any other image by adding the following to your `conf/local.conf` file:

```
EXTRA_IMAGE_FEATURES += "eclipse-debug"
```

▶ For more information, refer to the *Yocto Project Application Developer's Guide* at `http://www.yoctoproject.org/docs/1.7.1/adt-manual/adt-manual.html`

Developing GTK+ applications

This recipe will show how to build, run, and debug a graphical GTK+ application using the Eclipse IDE.

Getting ready

1. Add the `eclipse-debug` feature to your project's `conf/local.conf` file as follows:

   ```
   EXTRA_IMAGE_FEATURES += "eclipse-debug"
   ```

2. Build a `core-image-sato` target image as follows:

   ```
   $ cd /opt/yocto/fsl-community-bsp/
   $ source setup-environment wandboard-quad
   $ bitbake core-image-sato
   ```

3. Build a `core-image-sato` toolchain as follows:

   ```
   $ bitbake -c populate_sdk core-image-sato
   ```

4. Install the toolchain as follows:

   ```
   $ cd tmp/deploy/sdk
   $ ./poky-glibc-x86_64-core-image-sato-cortexa9hf-vfp-neon-toolchain-1.7.1.sh
   ```

Before launching the Eclipse IDE, we can check whether we are able to build and launch a GTK application manually. We will build the following GTK+ hello world application:

The following is a code for `gtk_hello_world.c`:

```
#include <gtk/gtk.h>

int main(int argc, char *argv[])
{
  GtkWidget *window;
  gtk_init (&argc, &argv);
  window = gtk_window_new (GTK_WINDOW_TOPLEVEL);
  gtk_widget_show (window);
```

```
    gtk_main ();
    return 0;
}
```

To build it, we use the `core-image-sato` toolchain installed as described previously:

```
$ source /opt/poky/1.7.1/environment-setup-cortexa9hf-vfp-neon-poky-
  linux-gnueabi
$ ${CC} gtk_hello_world.c -o helloworld `pkg-config --cflags --libs
  gtk+-2.0`
```

This command uses the `pkg-config` helper tool to read the `.pc` files that are installed with the GTK libraries in the `sysroot` to determine which compiler switches (`--cflags` for `include` directories and `--libs` for the libraries to link with) are needed to compile programs that use GTK.

We can manually copy the resulting binary to our Wandboard while booting `core-image-sato` over NFS and run it from the target's console with:

```
# DISPLAY=:0 helloworld
```

This will open a GTK+ window over the SATO desktop.

How to do it...

We can now configure the Eclipse ADT plugin using the standalone toolchain as described before, or we could decide to use the build system derived toolchain instead.

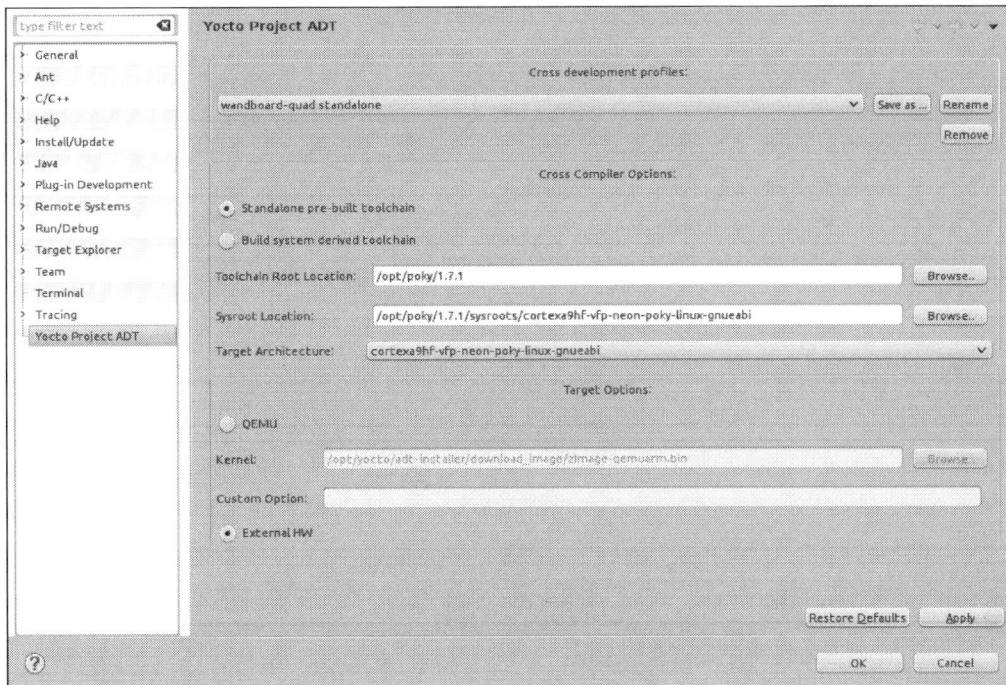

Follow the next steps to build and run an example hello world application:

1. Create a new hello world GTK autotools project. Accept all the defaults in the project creation wizard. Browse to **File | New | Project | C/C++ | C Project | Yocto Project ADT Autotools Project | Hello World GTK C Autotools Project**.

> When choosing a name for your project, avoid using special characters like dashes, as they could cause problems with the build tools.

2. Build the project by going to **Project | Build Project**.

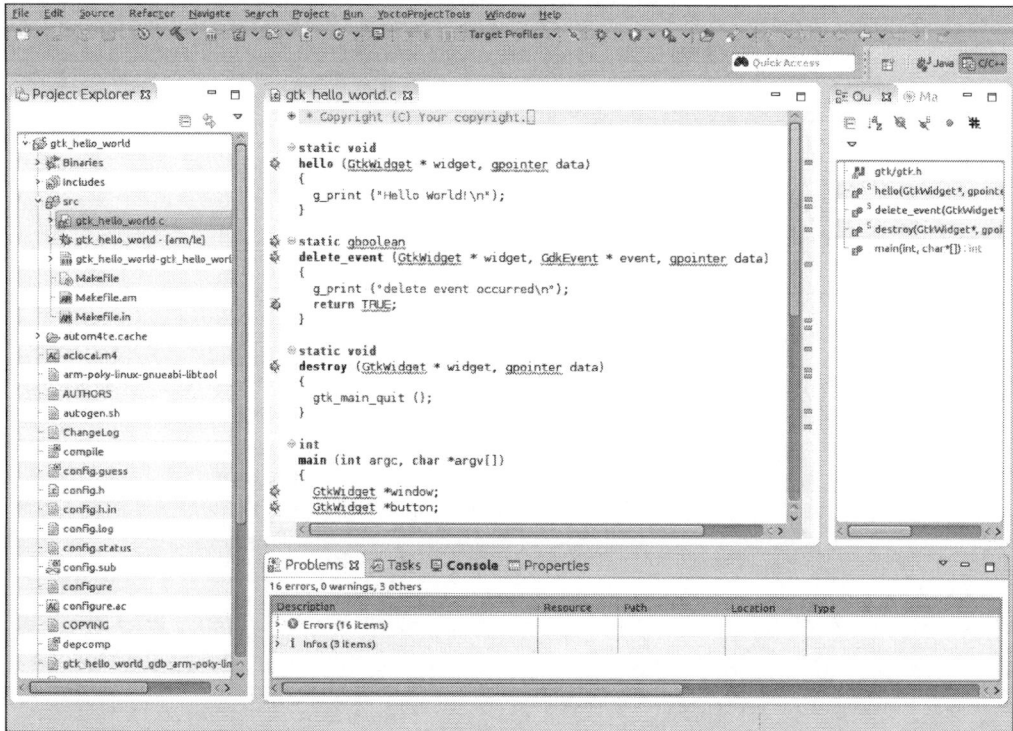

3. Even though the project builds successfully, you may see errors both marked in the source and in the **Problems** tab. This is because the Eclipse's code analysis feature cannot resolve all the project's symbols. To resolve it, add the needed `include` header files to your project's properties by going to **Project | Properties | C/C++ General | Paths and Symbols | Includes**.

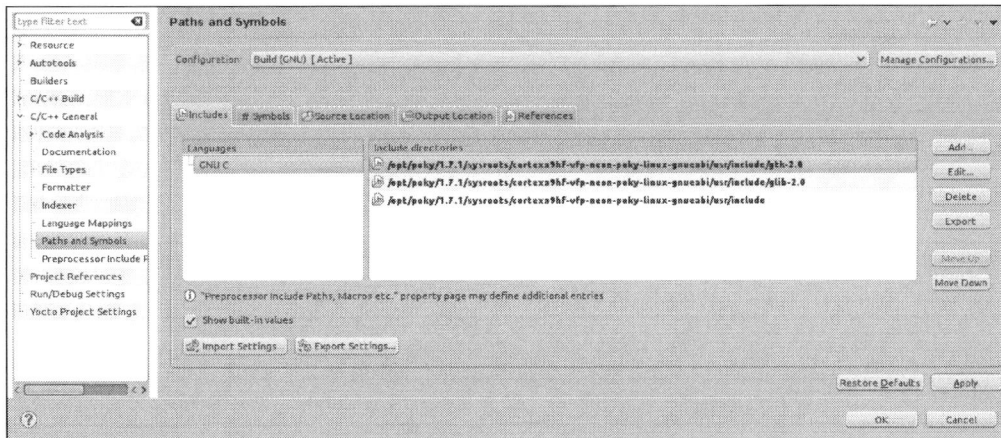

4. Under **Run** | **Run Configurations**, you should have **C/C++ Remote Application** with a TCF target called `<project_name>_gdb_arm-poky-linux-gnueabi`. If you don't, create one.

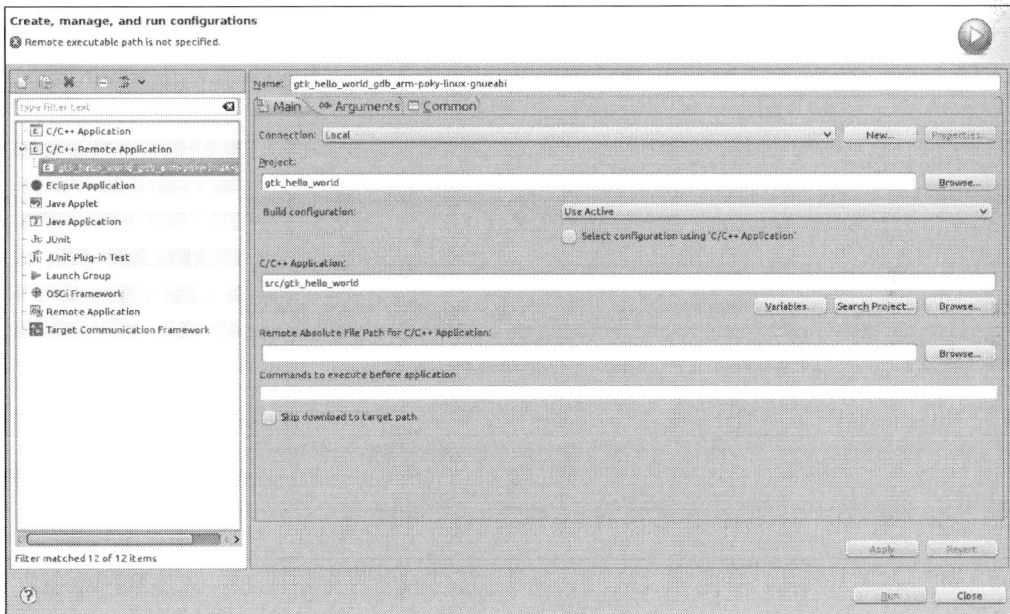

5. Create a new TCF connection to the target's IP address using the **New...** button in the **Main** tab.

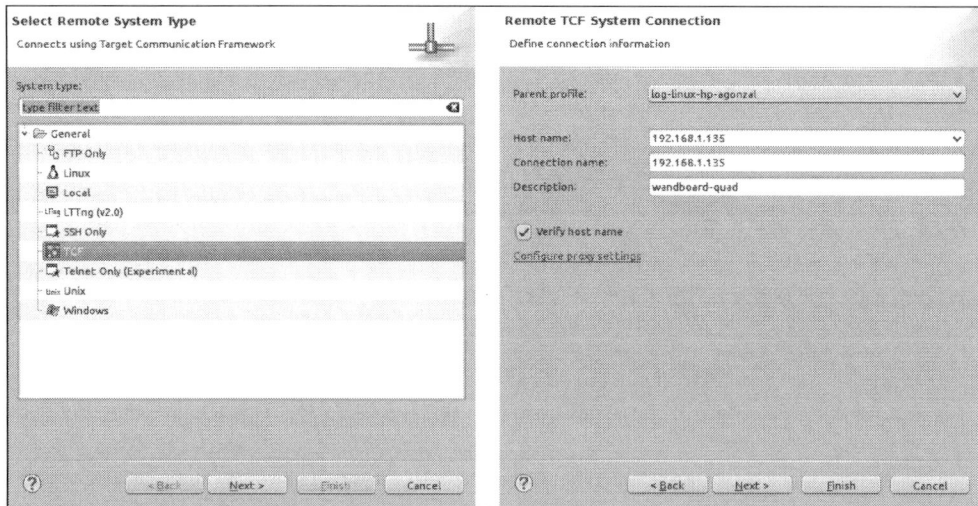

6. Fill in the **Remote Absolute File Path for C/C++ Application** field with the path to the binary and include the binary name; for example, /gtk_hello_world.

7. In the **Commands to execute before application** field, enter export DISPLAY=:0.

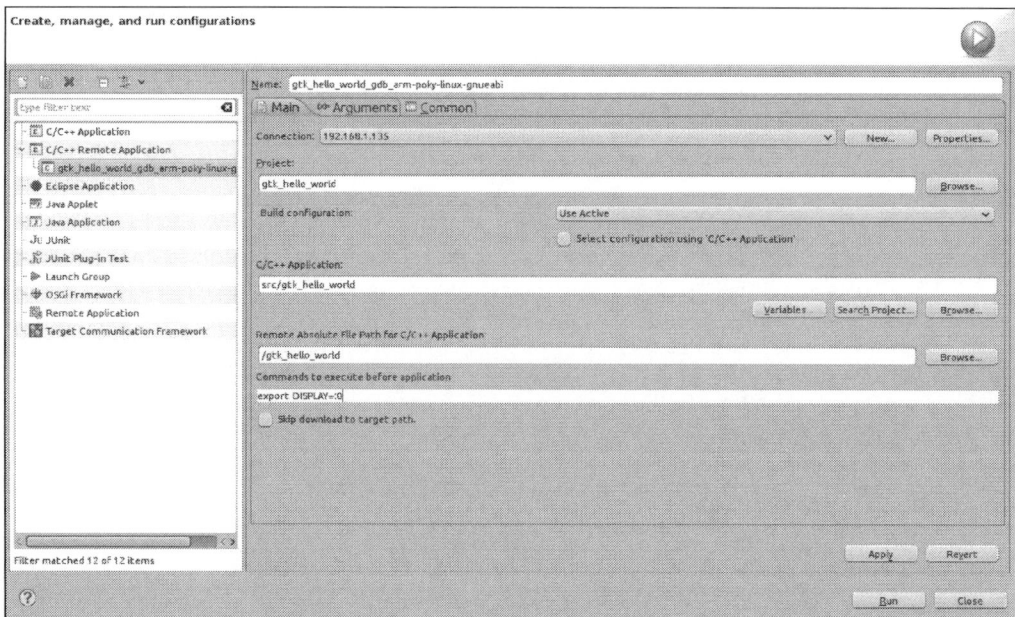

8. Run the application and log in as `root` with an empty password. You should see the GTK application on your SATO desktop, and the following output in the Console tab:

> If you have problems connecting to the target, verify that it is running `tcf-agent` by typing in the following on the target's console:
>
> ```
> # ps w | grep tcf
> 735 root       11428 S    /usr/sbin/tcf-agent -d -L-
> -10
> ```
>
> If you have login problems, you can use Eclipse's **Remote System Explorer (RSE)** perspective to clear passwords and debug the connection to the target. Once the connection can be established and you are able to browse the target's filesystem through RSE, you can come back to the run configuration.

There's more...

To debug the application, follow these steps:

1. Go to **Run | Debug Configuration**.

2. Under the **Debugger** tab, verify the GDB debugger path is the correct toolchain debugger location.

    ```
    /opt/poky/1.7.1/sysroots/x86_64-pokysdk-linux/usr/bin/arm-
        poky-linux-gnueabi/arm-poky-linux-gnueabi-gdb
    ```

    If it isn't, point it to the correct location.

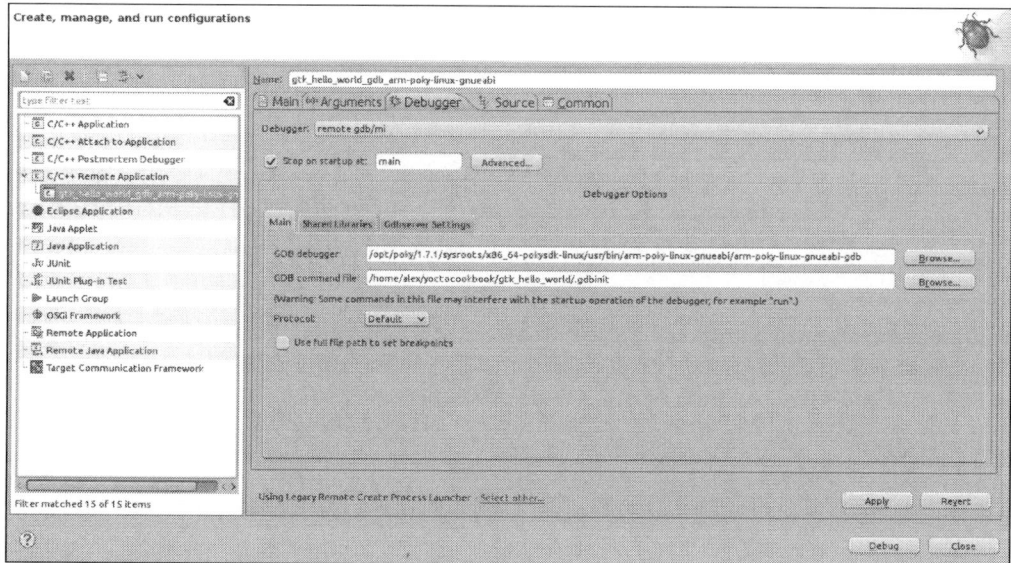

3. Double-click on the `main` function in the source file to add a breakpoint. A blue dot will appear on the side bar.

4. Click on the **Debug** button. The debug perspective appears with the application executing on the remote Wandboard hardware.

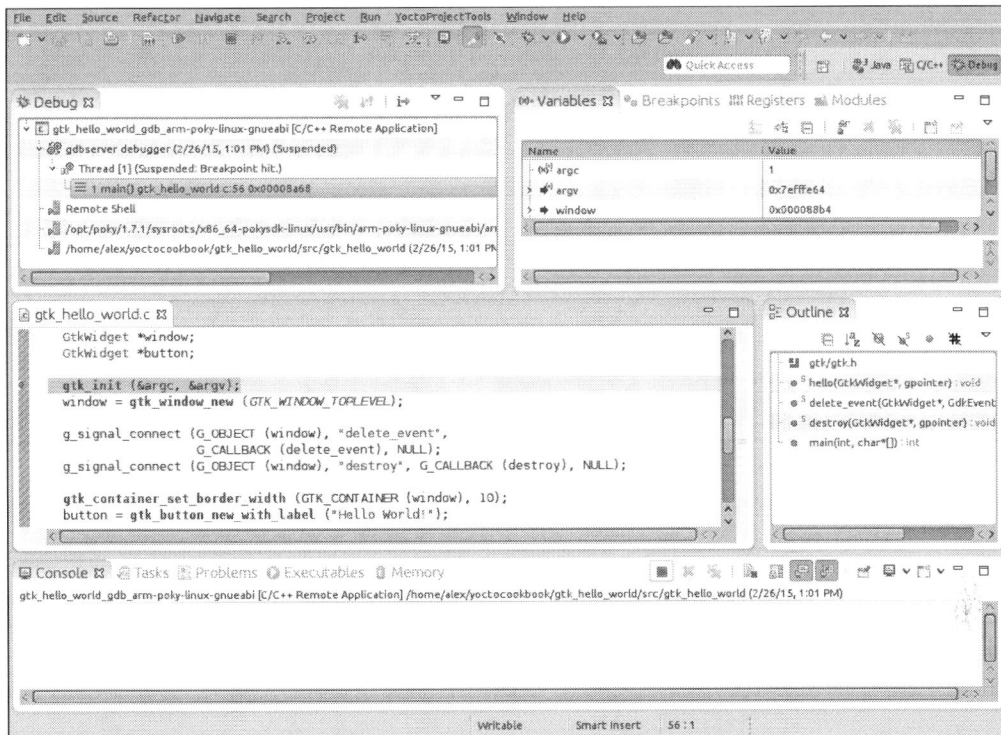

> If you get **Text file busy** error, remember to close the application we ran on the previous point.

Using the Qt Creator IDE

Qt Creator is a multiplatform IDE part of the Qt Application Development Framework SDK. It is the IDE of choice for Qt application development and is available with multiple licenses, including GPLv3, LGPLv2, and commercial licenses as well.

Getting ready

1. Download and install the Qt Creator 3.3.0 for your host from the Qt project downloads website. For downloading and installing an x86_64 Linux host, you can use the following commands:

```
$ wget
  http://download.qt.io/official_releases/qtcreator/3.3/3.3.0/qt
  -creator-opensource-linux-x86_64-3.3.0.run
```

```
$ chmod u+x qt-creator-opensource-linux-x86_64-3.3.0.run

$ ./qt-creator-opensource-linux-x86_64-3.3.0.run
```

2. Build a toolchain that is ready to develop Qt applications with the following:

```
$ cd /opt/yocto/fsl-community-bsp/

$ source setup-environment wandboard-quad

$ bitbake meta-toolchain-qt
```

3. Install it as follows:

```
$ cd tmp/deploy/sdk

$ ./poky-glibc-x86_64-meta-toolchain-qt-cortexa9hf-vfp-neon-
  toolchain-qt-1.7.1.sh
```

How to do it...

Before launching Qt Creator, we need to set up the development environment. To make this happen automatically when we launch Qt Creator, we can patch its initialization script by adding the following line right at the beginning of the bin/qtcreator.sh file:

```
source /opt/poky/1.7.1/environment-setup-cortexa9hf-vfp-neon-poky-
  linux-gnueabi
#! /bin/sh
```

> Note that the environment initialization script is placed before the hash bang.

Now we can run Qt Creator as follows:

```
$ ./bin/qtcreator.sh &
```

And configure it by going to **Tools | Options** and using the following steps:

1. First we configure a new device for our Wandboard. Under **Devices | Add**, we select **Generic Linux Device**.

Set the root password in the target by using the `passwd` command from the target's root console and type it in the password field.

2. Under **Build & Run**, we configure a new compiler pointing to the Yocto `meta-toolchain-qt` compiler path we just installed. Here's the path as shown in the following screenshot:

```
/opt/poky/1.7.1/sysroots/x86_64-pokysdk-linux/usr/bin/arm-
    poky-linux-gnueabi/arm-poky-linux-gnueabi-g++
```

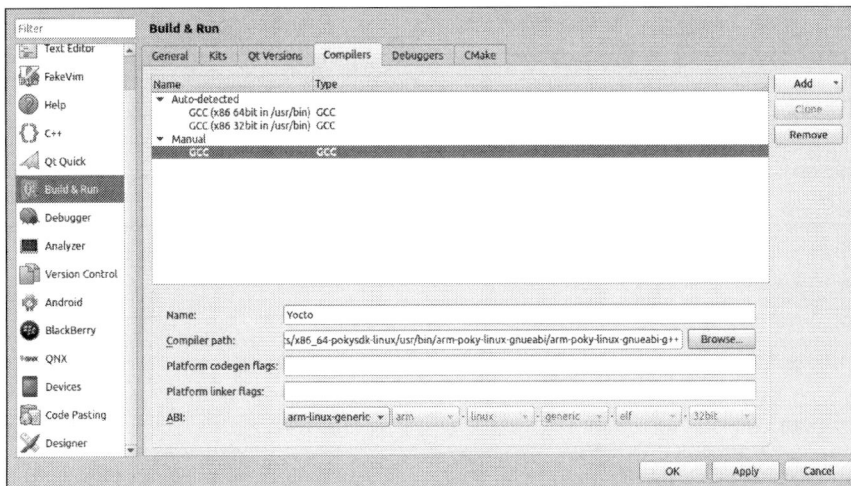

3. Similarly for a cross-debugger, the following is the path which is also mentioned in the following screenshot:

```
/opt/poky/1.7.1/sysroots/x86_64-pokysdk-linux/usr/bin/arm-
    poky-linux-gnueabi/arm-poky-linux-gnueabi-gdb
```

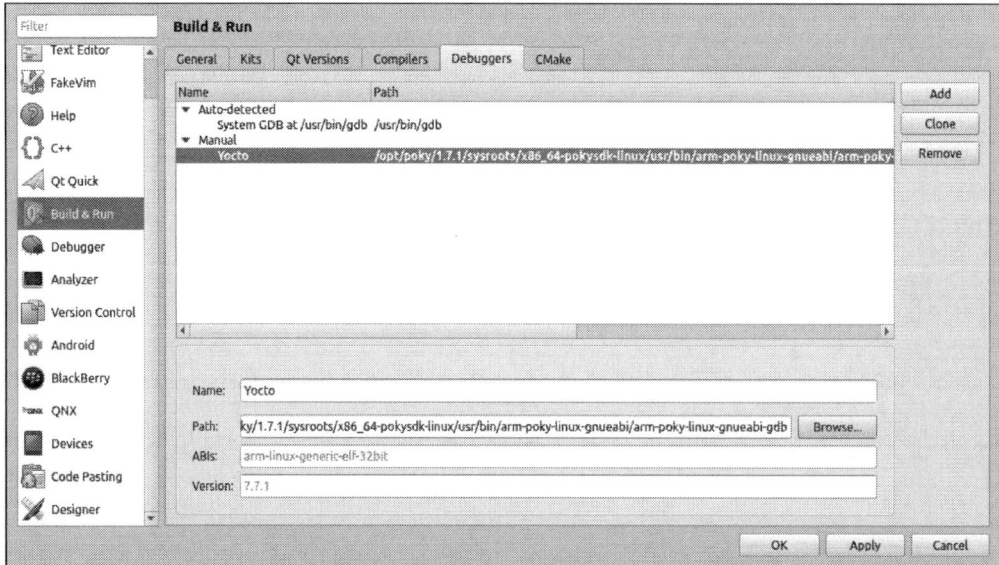

4. And then we configure Qt by selecting the `qmake` builder from the toolchain. Here's the path which is also mentioned in the following screenshot:

```
/opt/poky/1.7.1/sysroots/x86_64-pokysdk-linux/usr/bin/qmake
```

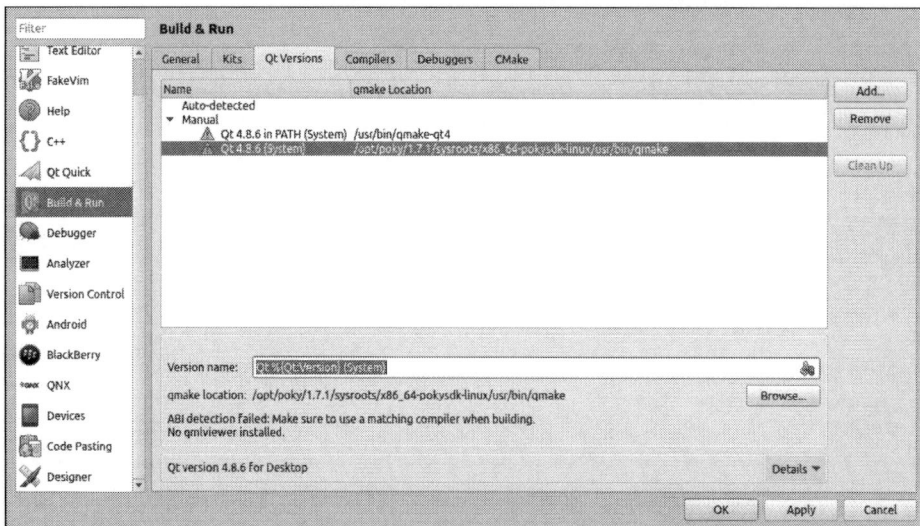

5. Finally we configure a new kit as follows:

   1. Select **Generic Linux Device** and configure its `sysroot` to:

      `/opt/poky/1.7.1/sysroots/cortexa9hf-vfp-neon-poky-linux-`
      `   gnueabi/`

   2. Select the compiler, debugger, and Qt version we just defined.

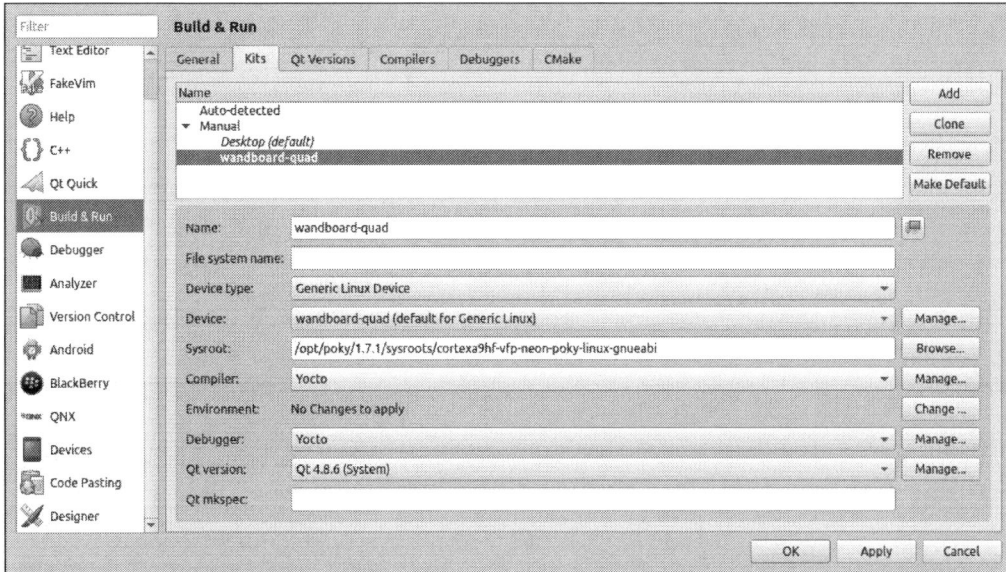

> In Ubuntu, Qt Creator stores its configuration on the user's home directory under `.config/QtProject/`.

Developing Qt applications

This recipe will show how to build, run, and debug a graphical Qt application using Qt Creator.

Getting ready

Before launching Qt Creator, we check whether we are able to build and launch a Qt application manually. We will build a Qt hello world application.

Here is the code for `qt_hello_world.cpp`:

```cpp
#include <QApplication>
#include <QPushButton>

int main(int argc, char *argv[])
{
    QApplication app(argc, argv);

    QPushButton hello("Hello world!");

    hello.show();
    return app.exec();
}
```

To build it, we use the `meta-toolchain-qt` installed as described previously:

```
$ source /opt/poky/1.7.1/environment-setup-cortexa9hf-vfp-neon-poky-
  linux-gnueabi
$ qmake -project
$ qmake
$ make
```

This uses `qmake` to create a project file and a `Makefile` file with all the relevant code files in the folder.

To run it, we first need to build a filesystem with Qt support. We first prepare the environment as follows:

```
$ cd /opt/yocto/fsl-community-bsp/
$ source setup-environment wandboard-quad
```

And configure our project with the `qt4-pkgs` extra feature by adding the following to `conf/local.conf`:

```
EXTRA_IMAGE_FEATURES += "qt4-pkgs"
```

And for Qt applications, we also need the **International Component for Unicode (ICU)** library, as the Qt libraries are compiled with support for it.

```
IMAGE_INSTALL_append = " icu"
```

And build it with:

```
$ bitbake core-image-sato
```

Once finished, we can program the microSD card image and boot the Wandboard. Copy the `qt_hello_world` binary to the target and run:

```
# DISPLAY=:0 qt_hello_world
```

You should see the Qt hello world window on the X11 desktop.

How to do it...

Follow these steps to build and run an example hello world application:

1. Create a new empty project by going to **File | New File or Project | Other project | Empty qmake project**.

2. Select only the **wandboard-quad** kit we just created.

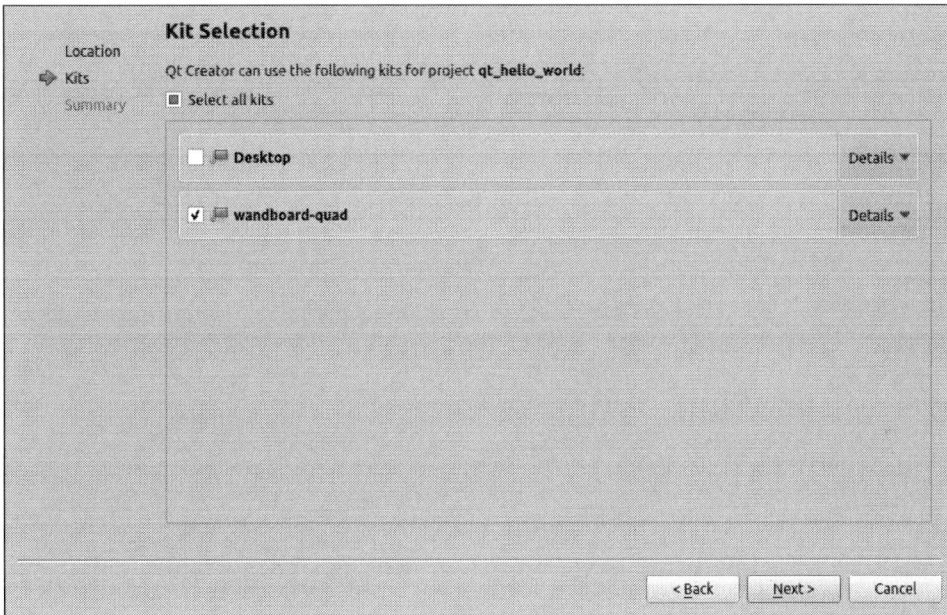

3. Add a new C++ file, `qt_hello_world.cpp`, by going to **File | New File or Project | C++ | C++ Source File**.

4. Paste the contents of the `qt_hello_world.cpp` file into Qt Creator, as shown in the following screenshot:

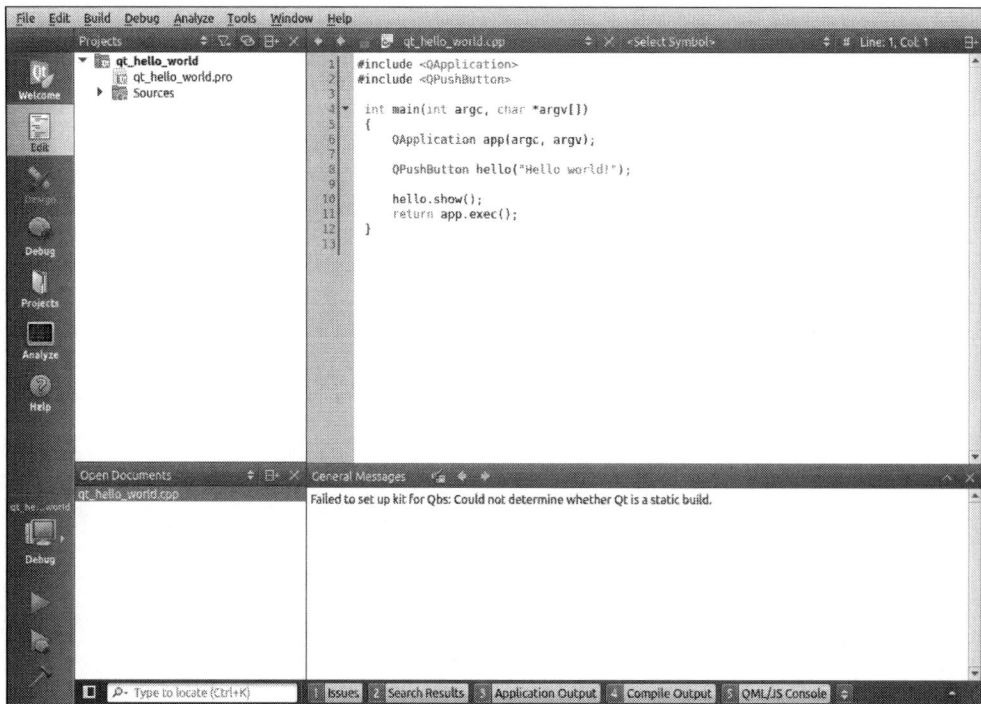

5. Configure your project with the target installation details by adding the following to your `hw.pro` file:

```
SOURCES += \
    qt_hello_world.cpp

TARGET =  qt_hello_world
    target.files =  qt_hello_world
    target.path = /

INSTALLS += target
```

Replace `qt_hello_world` with the name of your project.

6. Build the project. If you have build errors, verify that the Yocto build environment has been correctly set up.

> You can try to manually run the toolchain `environment-setup` script before launching Qt Creator.

7. Go to **Projects | Run** and check your project settings.

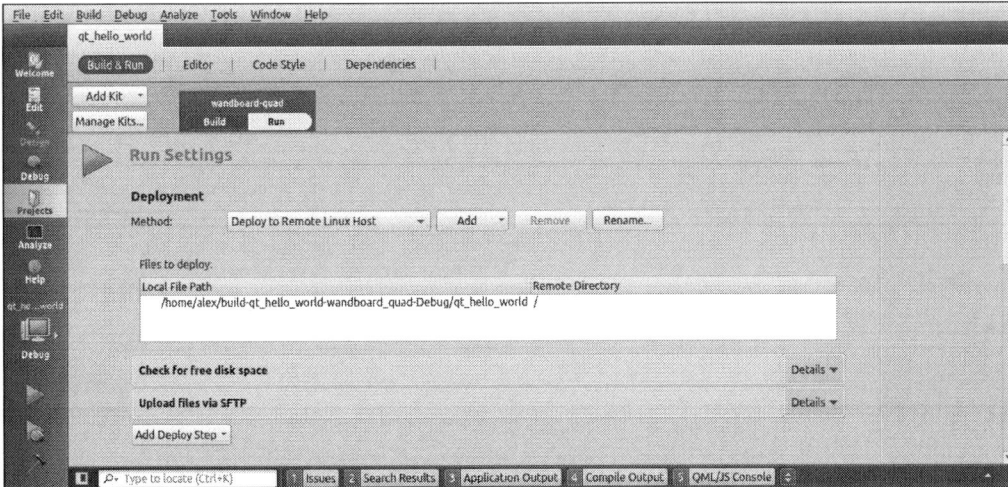

8. As can be seen in this screenshot, Qt Creator will use the SFTP protocol to transfer the files to the target. By default, the dropbear SSH server running on `core-image-sato` does not have SFTP support. We need to add it to our image to allow Qt Creator to work by adding the `openssh-sftp-server` package to the project's `conf/local.conf` file.

```
IMAGE_INSTALL_append =  " openssh-sftp-server"
```

However, there are other tools we will need, like the **gdbserver** if we want to debug our application, so it's easier to add the `eclipse-debug` feature, which will add all of the needed applications to the target image.

```
EXTRA_IMAGE_FEATURES += "eclipse-debug"
```

9. You can now run the project.

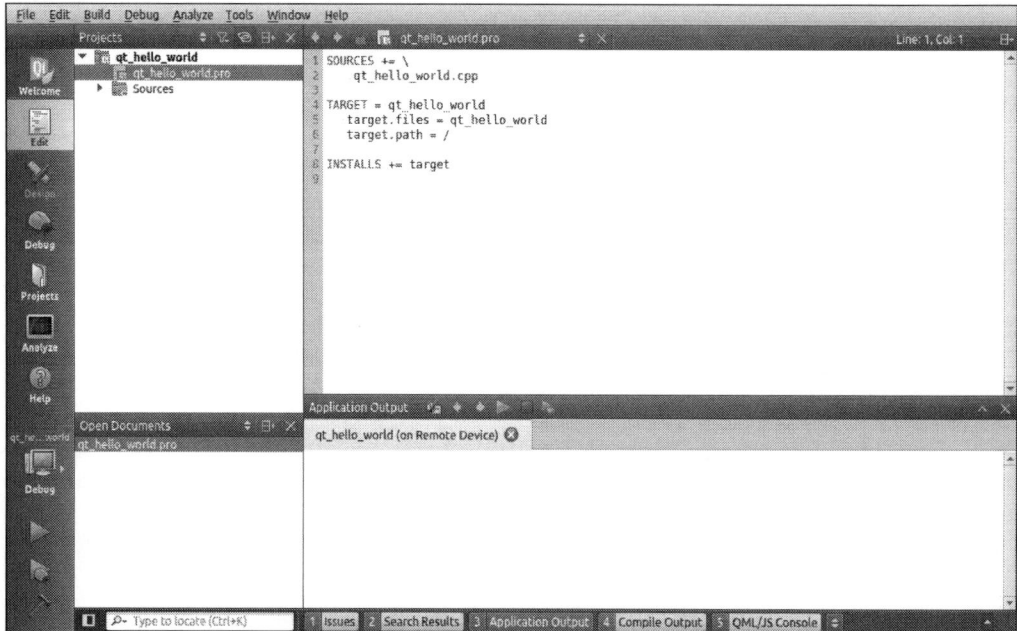

> If the application fails to be deployed with a login error, verify that you have set a root password in the target as explained in the recipe previously, or that you are using SSH key authentication.

You should now see the example Qt hello world application running on your SATO desktop.

There's more...

To debug the application, toggle a breakpoint on the source and click on the **Debug** button.

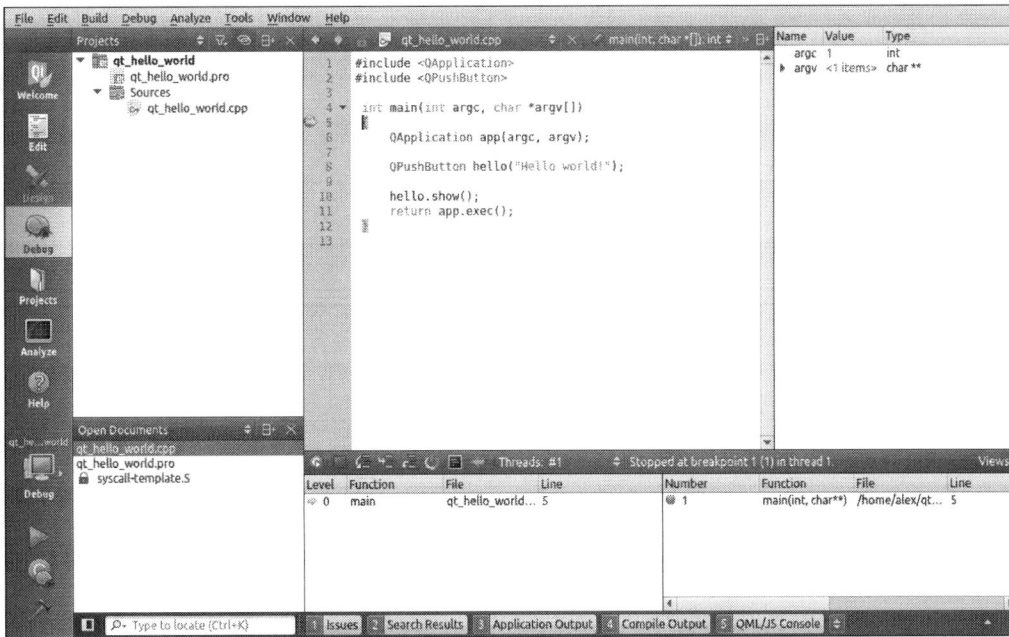

Describing workflows for application development

The workflows for application development are similar to the ones we already saw for U-Boot and the Linux kernel back in *Chapter 2, The BSP Layer*.

How to do it...

We will see how the following development workflows are applied to application development:

▸ External development

▸ Working directory development

▸ External source development

How it works...

External development

This is what we have been using on the recipes we saw before when building from the command line using a standalone toolchain, and also when using both the Eclipse and Qt Creator IDEs. This workflow produces binaries that have to be individually copied to the hardware to run and debug. It can be used in conjunction with the other workflows.

Working directory development

When the application is being built by the Yocto build system, we use this workflow to debug sporadic problems. However, it is not the recommended workflow for long developments. Note, though, that it is usually the first step when debugging third-party packages.

We will use the `helloworld_1.0.bb` custom recipe we saw back in the *Adding new packages* recipe in *Chapter 3, The Software Layer,* `meta-custom/recipes-example/helloworld/helloworld_1.0.bb`, as an example.

```
DESCRIPTION = "Simple helloworld application"
SECTION = "examples"
LICENSE = "MIT"
LIC_FILES_CHKSUM =
    "file://${COMMON_LICENSE_DIR}/MIT;md5=0835ade698e0bcf8506ecda2f7b4
    f302"

SRC_URI = "file://helloworld.c"

S = "${WORKDIR}"

do_compile() {
            ${CC} helloworld.c -o helloworld
}

do_install() {
            install -d ${D}${bindir}
            install -m 0755 helloworld ${D}${bindir}
}
```

Here, the `helloworld.c` source file is the following:

```
#include <stdio.h>

int main(void)
{
    return printf("Hello World");
}
```

The workflow steps are:

1. Start the package compilation from scratch.

   ```
   $ cd /opt/yocto/fsl-community-bsp/
   $ source setup-environment wandboard-quad
   $ bitbake -c cleanall helloworld
   ```

   This will erase the package's build folder, shared state cache, and downloaded package source.

2. Start a development shell:

   ```
   $ bitbake -c devshell helloworld
   ```

   This will fetch, unpack, and patch the `helloworld` sources and spawn a new shell with the environment ready for compilation. The new shell will change to the package's `build` directory.

3. Depending on the `SRC_URI` variable, the package's `build` directory can be revision controlled already. If not, as is the case in this example, we will create a local Git repository as follows:

   ```
   $ git init
   $ git add helloworld.c
   $ git commit -s -m "Original revision"
   ```

4. Perform the modifications we need; for example, change `helloworld.c` to print `Howdy world` as follows:

   ```
   #include <stdio.h>

   int main(void)
   {
       return printf("Howdy World");
   }
   ```

5. Exit `devshell` and build the package without erasing our modifications.

   ```
   $ bitbake -C compile helloworld
   ```

   > 💡 Note the capital C (which invokes the compile task) and also all the tasks that follow it.

6. Test your changes on the hardware by copying the generated package and installing it. Because you have only modified one package, the rest of the dependencies should be already installed in the running root filesystem. Run the following:

   ```
   $ bitbake -e helloworld | grep ^WORKDIR=
   WORKDIR="/opt/yocto/fsl-community-bsp/wandboard-
       quad/tmp/work/cortexa9hf-vfp-neon-poky-linux-
       gnueabi/helloworld/1.0-r0"
   $ scp ${WORKDIR_PATH}/deploy-rpms/deploy-
       rpms/cortexa9hf_vfp_neon/helloworld-1.0-
       r0.cortexa9hf_vfp_neon.rpm root@<target_ip_address>:/
   $ rpm -i /helloworld-1.0-r0.cortexa9hf_vfp_neon.rpm
   ```

   This assumes the target's root filesystem has been built with the `package-management` feature and the `helloworld` package is added to the `RM_WORK_EXCLUDE` variable when using the `rm_work` class.

7. Go back to `devshell` and commit your change to the local Git repository as follows:

   ```
   $ bitbake -c devshell helloworld
   $ git add  helloworld.c
   $ git commit -s -m "Change greeting message"
   ```

8. Generate a patch into the recipe's patch directory:

   ```
   $ git format-patch -1 -o /opt/yocto/fsl-community-
       bsp/sources/meta-custom/recipes-
       example/helloworld/helloworld-1.0
   ```

9. Finally, add the patch to the recipe's `SRC_URI` variable, as shown here:

   ```
   SRC_URI  =  "file://helloworld.c \
               file://0001-Change-greeting-message.patch"
   ```

External source development

This workflow is recommended for development work once the application has been integrated into the Yocto build system. It can be used in conjunction with external development using an IDE, for example.

In the example recipe we saw earlier, the source file was placed on the `meta-custom` layer along with the metadata.

It is more common to have the recipe fetch directly from a revision control system like Git, so we will change the `meta-custom/recipes-example/helloworld/helloworld_1.0.bb` file to source from a Git directory as follows:

```
DESCRIPTION = "Simple helloworld application"
SECTION = "examples"
LICENSE = "MIT"
LIC_FILES_CHKSUM =
    "file://${COMMON_LICENSE_DIR}/MIT;md5=0835ade698e0bcf8506ecda2f7b4
    f302"

SRC_URI = "git://github.com/yoctocookbook/helloworld"

S = "${WORKDIR}/git"

do_compile() {
            ${CC} helloworld.c -o helloworld
}

do_install() {
            install -d ${D}${bindir}
            install -m 0755 helloworld ${D}${bindir}
}
```

We can then clone it into a local directory as follows:

```
$ cd /opt/yocto/
$ git clone git://github.com/yoctocookbook/helloworld
```

An alternative to using a remote revision controlled repository it to use a local one. To do so, follow these steps:

1. Create a local Git repository that will hold the source:

   ```
   $ mkdir -p /opt/yocto/helloworld
   $ cd /opt/yocto/helloworld
   $ git init
   ```

2. Copy our `helloworld.c` file over here, and add it to the repository:

   ```
   $ git add helloworld.c
   ```

3. Finally, commit it with a signature and a message:

   ```
   $ git commit -s -m "Original revision"
   ```

In any case, we have the version-controlled source in a local directory. We will then configure our `conf/local.conf` file to work from it as follows:

```
INHERIT += "externalsrc"
EXTERNALSRC_pn-helloworld = "/opt/yocto/helloworld"
EXTERNALSRC_BUILD_pn-helloworld = "/opt/yocto/helloworld"
```

And build it with:

```
$ cd /opt/yocto/fsl-community-bsp/

$ source setup-environment wandboard-quad

$ bitbake helloworld
```

We can then work directly in the local folder without the risk of accidentally having BitBake erase our code. Once development is complete, the modifications to `conf/local.conf` are removed and the recipe will fetch the source from its original `SRC_URI` location.

Working with GNU make

GNU make is a make implementation for Linux systems. It is used by a wide variety of open source projects, including the Linux kernel. The build is managed by a `Makefile`, which tells make how to build the source code.

How to do it...

Yocto recipes inherit `base.bbclass` and hence their default behavior is to look for a `Makefile`, `makefile`, or `GNU Makefile` and use GNU make to build the package.

If your package already contains a `Makefile`, then all you need to worry about are the arguments that need to be passed to make. Make arguments can be passed using the `EXTRA_OEMAKE` variable, and a `do_install` override that calls the `oe_runmake` install needs to be provided, otherwise an empty install is run.

For example, the `logrotate` recipe is based on a `Makefile` and looks as follows:

```
SUMMARY = "Rotates, compresses, removes and mails system log
    files"
SECTION = "console/utils"
HOMEPAGE = "https://fedorahosted.org/logrotate/"
```

```
LICENSE = "GPLv2"

DEPENDS="coreutils popt"

LIC_FILES_CHKSUM =
    "file://COPYING;md5=18810669f13b87348459e611d31ab760"

SRC_URI =
    "https://fedorahosted.org/releases/l/o/logrotate/logrotate-
    ${PV}.tar.gz \"
SRC_URI[md5sum] = "99e08503ef24c3e2e3ff74cc5f3be213"
SRC_URI[sha256sum] =
    "f6ba691f40e30e640efa2752c1f9499a3f9738257660994de70a45fe00d12b64"

EXTRA_OEMAKE = ""

do_install(){
    oe_runmake install DESTDIR=${D} PREFIX=${D} MANDIR=${mandir}
    mkdir -p ${D}${sysconfdir}/logrotate.d
    mkdir -p ${D}${sysconfdir}/cron.daily
    mkdir -p ${D}${localstatedir}/lib
    install -p -m 644 examples/logrotate-default
${D}${sysconfdir}/logrotate.conf
    install -p -m 755 examples/logrotate.cron
${D}${sysconfdir}/cron.daily/logrotate
    touch ${D}${localstatedir}/lib/logrotate.status
}
```

See also

▸ For more information about GNU make, visit `https://www.gnu.org/software/make/manual/`

Working with the GNU build system

A `Makefile` is a good solution when you are always going to build and run your software on the same system, and things like `glibc` and `gcc` versions and the available library versions are known. However, most software need to be built and run in a variety of systems.

Getting ready

The GNU build system, or `autotools`, is a set of tools whose aim is to create a `Makefile` for your software in a variety of systems. It's made up of three main tools:

> ▶ `autoconf`: This parses the contents of a `configure.ac` file that describes the source code to be built and creates a `configure` script. This script will then be used to generate the final `Makefile`.

> ▶ `automake`: This parses the contents of a `Makefile.am` file and converts it into a `Makefile.in` file. This is then used by the `configure` script generated earlier to obtain a `config.status` script that gets automatically executed to obtain the final `Makefile`.

> ▶ `libtools`: This manages the creation of both static and dynamic libraries.

How to do it...

The Yocto build system contains classes with the required knowledge to build `autotools` packages. All your recipe needs to do is to inherit the `autotools` class and configure the arguments to be passed to the `configure` script in the `EXTRA_OECONF` variable. Usually, the `autotools` system understands how to install the software, so you do not need a `do_install` override.

There is a wide variety of open source projects that use `autotools` as the build system.

An example, `meta-custom/recipes-example/hello/hello_2.9.bb`, that does not need any extra configure options, follows:

```
DESCRIPTION = "GNU helloworld autotools recipe"
SECTION = "examples"

LICENSE = "GPLv3"
LIC_FILES_CHKSUM = "file://${COREBASE}/meta/files/common-
    licenses/GPL-3.0;md5=c79ff39f19dfec6d293b95dea7b07891"

SRC_URI = "${GNU_MIRROR}/hello/hello-${PV}.tar.gz"
SRC_URI[md5sum] = "67607d2616a0faaf5bc94c59dca7c3cb"
SRC_URI[sha256sum] =
"ecbb7a2214196c57ff9340aa71458e1559abd38f6d8d169666846935df191ea7"

inherit autotools gettext
```

See also

▶ For more information about the GNU build system, visit `http://www.gnu.org/software/automake/manual/html_node/GNU-Build-System.html`

Working with the CMake build system

The GNU make system is a great tool when you build exclusively for Linux systems. However, some packages are multiplatform and need a way to manage `Makefile` files on different operating systems. **CMake** is a cross-platform build system that can work not only with GNU make, but also Microsoft Visual Studio and Apple's Xcode.

Getting ready

The CMake tool parses the `CMakeLists.txt` files in every directory to control the build process. An example `CMakeLists.txt` file to compile the hello world example follows:

```
cmake_minimum_required(VERSION 2.8.10)
project(helloworld)
add_executable(helloworld helloworld.c)
install(TARGETS helloworld RUNTIME DESTINATION bin)
```

How to do it...

The Yocto build system also contains classes with the required knowledge to build CMake packages. All your recipe needs to do is to inherit the `cmake` class and configure the arguments to be passed to the `configure` script in the `EXTRA_OECMAKE` variable. Usually, the CMake system understands how to install the software, so you do not need a `do_install` override.

A recipe to build the `helloworld.C` example application, `meta-custom/recipes-example/helloworld-cmake/helloworld-cmake_1.0.bb`, follows:

```
DESCRIPTION = "Simple helloworld cmake application"
SECTION = "examples"
LICENSE = "MIT"
LIC_FILES_CHKSUM = "file://${COMMON_LICENSE_DIR}/MIT;md5=0835ade698e0b
cf8506ecda2f7b4
  f302"

SRC_URI = "file://CMakeLists.txt \
           file://helloworld.c"
```

```
S = "${WORKDIR}"

inherit cmake

EXTRA_OECMAKE = ""
```

See also

> ▸ For more information about CMake, visit `http://www.cmake.org/documentation/`

Working with the SCons builder

SCons is also a multiplatform build system written in Python, with its configuration files also written in the same language. It also includes support for Microsoft Visual Studio among other features.

Getting ready

SCons parses the `SConstruct` files, and by default it does not propagate the environment into the build system. This is to avoid build issues caused by environment differences. This is a complication for Yocto, as it configures the environment with the cross-compilation toolchain settings.

SCons does not define a standard way to support cross-compilation, so every project will implement it differently. For a simple example as the hello world program, we can just initialize the `CC` and `PATH` variables from the external environment as follows:

```
import os
env = Environment(CC = os.environ['CC'],
                  ENV = {'PATH': os.environ['PATH']})
env.Program("helloworld", "helloworld.c")
```

How to do it...

The Yocto build system also contains classes with the required knowledge to build SCons packages. All your recipe needs to do is to inherit the `SCons` class and configure the arguments to be passed to the configure script in the `EXTRA_OESCONS` variable. Although some packages using `SCons` might deal with installation through an install alias as required by the `SCons` class, your recipe will mostly need to provide a `do_install` task override.

An example recipe to build the `helloworld.c` example application, `meta-custom/recipes-example/helloworld-scons/helloworld-scons_1.0.bb`, follows:

```
DESCRIPTION = "Simple helloworld scons application"
SECTION = "examples"
LICENSE = "MIT"
LIC_FILES_CHKSUM = "file://${COMMON_LICENSE_DIR}/MIT;md5=0835ade698e0b
cf8506ecda2f7b4
  f302"

SRC_URI = "file://SConstruct \
           file://helloworld.c"

S = "${WORKDIR}"

inherit scons

EXTRA_OESCONS = ""

do_install() {
    install -d ${D}/${bindir}
    install -m 0755 helloworld ${D}${bindir}
}
```

See also

▸   For more information about SCons, visit `http://www.scons.org/doc/HTML/scons-user/`

Developing with libraries

Most applications make use of shared libraries, which saves system memory and disk space, as they are shared between different applications. Modularizing code into libraries also allows for easier versioning and code management.

This recipe will explain how to work with both static and shared libraries in Linux and Yocto.

Getting ready

By convention, library files start with the `lib` prefix.

There are basically two library types:

- **Static libraries** (.a): When the object code is linked and becomes part of the application
- **Dynamic libraries** (.so): Linked at compile time but not included in the application, so they need to be available at runtime. Multiple applications can share a dynamic library so they need less disk space.

Libraries are placed in the following standard root filesystem locations:

- /lib: Libraries required for startup
- /usr/lib: Most system libraries
- /usr/local/lib: Non-system libraries

Dynamic libraries follow certain naming conventions on running systems so that multiple versions can co-exist, so a library can be referenced by different names. Some of them are explained as follows:

- The linker name with the .so suffix; for example, libexample.so.
- The fully qualified name or soname, a symbolic link to the library name. For example, libexample.so.x, where x is the version number. Increasing the version number means the library is not compatible with previous versions.
- The real name. For example, libexample.so.x.y[.z], where x is the major version number, y is the minor version number, and the optional z is a release number. Increasing minor or release numbers retains compatibility.

In GNU glibc, starting an ELF binary calls a program loader, /lib/ld-linux-X. Here, X is the version number, which finds all the needed shared libraries. This process uses a couple of interesting files:

- /etc/ld.so.conf: This stores the directories searched by the loader
- /etc/ld.so.preload: This is used to override libraries

The ldconfig tool reads the ld.so.conf file and creates a cache file (/etc/ld.so.cache) to increase access speed.

The following environment variables can also be helpful:

- LD_LIBRARY_PATH: This is a colon-separated directory list to search libraries in. It is used when debugging or using non-standard library locations.
- LD_PRELOAD: This is used to override shared libraries.

Building a static library

We will build a static library, `libhelloworld`, from two source files, `hello.c` and `world.c`, and use it to build a hello world application. The source files for the library are presented here.

The following is the code for the `hello.c` file:

```
char * hello (void)
{
  return "Hello";
}
```

This is the code for `world.c` file:

```
char * world (void)
{
  return "World";
}
```

To build the library, follow these steps:

1. Configure the build environment:

   ```
   $ source /opt/poky/1.7.1/environment-setup-cortexa9hf-vfp-
     neon-poky-linux-gnueabi
   ```

2. Compile and link the library:

   ```
   ${CC} -c hello.c world.c
   ${AR} -cvq libhelloworld.a hello.o world.o
   ```

3. Verify the contents of the library:

   ```
   ${AR} -t libhelloworld.a
   ```

The application source code is presented next.

- For the `helloworld.c` file the following is the code:

  ```
  #include <stdio.h>
  int main (void)
  {
    return printf("%s %s\n",hello(),world());
  }
  ```

- To build it we run:

  ```
  ${CC} -o helloworld helloworld.c libhelloworld.a
  ```

▶ We can check which libraries it links with using `readelf`:

```
$ readelf -d helloworld
Dynamic section at offset 0x534 contains 24 entries:
   Tag        Type                      Name/Value
 0x00000001 (NEEDED)                    Shared library:
   [libc.so.6]
```

Building a shared dynamic library

To build a dynamic library from the same sources, we would run:

```
${CC} -fPIC -g -c hello.c world.c
${CC} -shared -Wl,-soname,libhelloworld.so.1 -o libhelloworld.so.1.0
  hello.o world.o
```

We can then use it to build our `helloworld` C application, as follows:

```
${CC} helloworld.c libhelloworld.so.1.0 -o helloworld
```

And again, we can check the dynamic libraries using `readelf`, as follows:

```
$ readelf -d helloworld
Dynamic section at offset 0x6ec contains 25 entries:
  Tag        Type                      Name/Value
 0x00000001 (NEEDED)                    Shared library:
   [libhelloworld.so.1]
 0x00000001 (NEEDED)                    Shared library: [libc.so.6]
```

How to do it...

An example recipe for the static library example we just saw follows, `meta-custom/recipes-example/libhelloworld-static/libhelloworldstatic_1.0.bb`:

```
DESCRIPTION = "Simple helloworld example static library"
SECTION = "libs"
LICENSE = "MIT"
LIC_FILES_CHKSUM = "file://${COMMON_LICENSE_DIR}/MIT;md5=0835ade698e0b
cf8506ecda2f7b4
  f302"

SRC_URI = "file://hello.c \
          file://world.c \
          file://helloworld.pc"
```

```
S = "${WORKDIR}"

do_compile() {
        ${CC} -c hello.c world.c
        ${AR} -cvq libhelloworld.a hello.o world.o
}

do_install() {
        install -d ${D}${libdir}
        install -m 0755 libhelloworld.a ${D}${libdir}
}
```

By default, the configuration in meta/conf/bitbake.conf places all static libraries in a -staticdev package. It is also placed in the sysroot so that it can be used.

For a dynamic library, we would use the following recipe, meta-custom/recipes-example/libhelloworld-dyn/libhelloworlddyn_1.0.bb:

```
meta-custom/recipes-example/libhelloworld-dyn/libhelloworlddyn_1.0.bb
DESCRIPTION = "Simple helloworld example dynamic library"
SECTION = "libs"
LICENSE = "MIT"
LIC_FILES_CHKSUM = "file://${COMMON_LICENSE_DIR}/MIT;md5=0835ade698e0b
cf8506ecda2f7b4
  f302"

SRC_URI = "file://hello.c \
           file://world.c \
           file://helloworld.pc"

S = "${WORKDIR}"

do_compile() {
        ${CC} -fPIC -g -c hello.c world.c
        ${CC} -shared -Wl,-soname,libhelloworld.so.1 -o
  libhelloworld.so.1.0 hello.o world.o
}

do_install() {
        install -d ${D}${libdir}
        install -m 0755 libhelloworld.so.1.0 ${D}${libdir}
        ln -s libhelloworld.so.1.0
  ${D}/${libdir}/libhelloworld.so.1
        ln -s libhelloworld.so.1 ${D}/${libdir}/libhelloworld.so
}
```

Usually we would list the library dependencies (if any) in the RDEPENDS variable, but this is not always needed as the build system performs some automatic dependency checking by inspecting both the library file and the pkg-config file and adding the dependencies it finds to RDEPENDS automatically.

Multiple versions of the same library can co-exist on the running system. For that, you need to provide different recipes with the same package name but different package revision. For example, we would have libhelloworld-1.0.bb and libhelloworld-1.1.bb.

And to build an application using the static library, we would create a recipe in meta-custom/recipes-example/helloworld-static/helloworldstatic_1.0.bb, as follows:

```
DESCRIPTION = "Simple helloworld example"
SECTION = "examples"
LICENSE = "MIT"
LIC_FILES_CHKSUM = "file://${COMMON_LICENSE_DIR}/MIT;md5=0835ade698e0b
cf8506ecda2f7b4
  f302"

DEPENDS = "libhelloworld-static"

SRC_URI = "file://helloworld.c"

S = "${WORKDIR}"

do_compile() {
        ${CC} -o helloworld helloworld.c
  ${STAGING_LIBDIR}/libhelloworld.a
}

do_install() {
        install -d ${D}${bindir}
        install -m 0755 helloworld ${D}${bindir}
}
```

To build using the dynamic library, we would just need to change the recipe in meta-custom/recipes-example/helloworld-shared/helloworldshared_1.0.bb to meta-custom/recipes-example/helloworld-shared/helloworldshared_1.0.bb:

```
meta-custom/recipes-example/helloworld-shared/helloworldshared_1.0.bb
DESCRIPTION = "Simple helloworld example"
SECTION = "examples"
LICENSE = "MIT"
```

```
LIC_FILES_CHKSUM =
    "file://${COMMON_LICENSE_DIR}/MIT;md5=0835ade698e0bcf8506ecda2f7b4
    f302"

DEPENDS = "libhelloworld-dyn"

SRC_URI = "file://helloworld.c"

S = "${WORKDIR}"

do_compile() {
        ${CC} -o helloworld helloworld.c -lhelloworld
}

do_install() {
        install -d ${D}${bindir}
        install -m 0755 helloworld ${D}${bindir}
}
```

How it works...

Libraries should provide the information required to use them, such as `include` headers and `library` dependencies. The Yocto Project provides two ways for libraries to provide build settings:

  ▸ The `binconfig` class. This is a legacy class used for libraries that provide a `-config` script to provide build settings.

  ▸ The `pkgconfig` class. This is the recommended method for libraries to provide build settings.

A `pkg-config` build settings file has the `.pc` suffix, is distributed with the library, and is installed in a common location known to the `pkg-config` tool.

The `helloworld.pc` file for the dynamic library looks as follows:

```
prefix=/usr/local
exec_prefix=${prefix}
includedir=${prefix}/include
libdir=${exec_prefix}/lib

Name: helloworld
Description: The helloworld library
Version: 1.0.0
Cflags: -I${includedir}/helloworld
Libs: -L${libdir} -lhelloworld
```

However, for the static library, we would change the last line to:

```
Libs: -L${libdir} libhelloworld.a
```

A package wanting to use this `.pc` file would inherit the `pkgconfig` class.

There's more...

There's a provision for packages that build both a library and an executable but do not want both of them installed together. By inheriting the `lib_package` class, the package will create a separate `-bin` package with the executables.

See also

> ▸ More details regarding `pkg-config` can be found at `http://www.freedesktop.org/wiki/Software/pkg-config/`

Working with the Linux framebuffer

The Linux kernel provides an abstraction for the graphical hardware in the form of framebuffer devices. These allow applications to access the graphics hardware through a well-defined API. The framebuffer is also used to provide a graphical console to the Linux kernel, so that it can, for example, display colors and a logo.

In this recipe, we will explore how applications can use the Linux framebuffer to display graphics and video.

Getting ready

Some applications, especially in embedded devices, are able to access the framebuffer by mapping the memory and accessing it directly. For example, the `gstreamer` framework is able to work directly over the framebuffer, as is the Qt graphical framework.

Qt is a cross-platform application framework written in C++ and developed both by Digia, under the Qt company name, and the open source Qt project community.

For Qt applications, Poky provides a `qt4e-demo-image` and the FSL community BSP provides a `qte-in-use-image`, both of which include support for Qt4 Extended over the framebuffer. The provided framework also includes support for hardware acceleration – not only video but also 2D and 3D graphical acceleration provided through the OpenGL and OpenVG APIs.

How to do it...

To compile the Qt hello world application we saw in the _Developing Qt applications_ recipe earlier, we could use the following `meta-custom/recipes-qt/qt-helloworld/qt-helloworld_1.0.bb` Yocto recipe:

```
DESCRIPTION = "Simple QT helloworld example"
SECTION = "examples"
LICENSE = "MIT"
LIC_FILES_CHKSUM =
    "file://${COMMON_LICENSE_DIR}/MIT;md5=0835ade698e0bcf8506ecda2f7b4
    f302"

RDEPENDS_${PN} += "icu"

SRC_URI = "file://qt_hello_world.cpp \
            file://qt_hello_world.pro"

S = "${WORKDIR}"

inherit qt4e

do_install() {
        install -d ${D}${bindir}
        install -m 0755 qt_hello_world ${D}${bindir}
}
```

Here the `meta-custom/recipes-qt/qt-helloworld/qt-helloworld-1.0/qt_hello_world.cpp` source file is as follows:

```
#include <QApplication>
#include <QPushButton>

int main(int argc, char *argv[])
{
    QApplication app(argc, argv);

    QPushButton hello("Hello world!");

    hello.show();
    return app.exec();
}
```

And the `meta-custom/recipes-qt/qt-helloworld/qt-helloworld-1.0/qt_ hello_world.pro` project file is as follows:

```
SOURCES += \
    qt_hello_world.cpp
```

Then we add it to the image by using the following in your project's `conf/local.conf` file:

```
IMAGE_INSTALL_append = " qt-helloworld"
```

And we build the image with:

```
$ bitbake qt4e-demo-image
```

We can then program the SD card image, boot it, log in to the Wandboard, and launch the application by running:

```
# qt_hello_world -qws
```

The `-qws` command-line option is needed to run the server application.

How it works...

The framebuffer devices are located under `/dev`. The default framebuffer device is `/dev/fb0`, and if the graphics hardware provides more than one, they will be sequentially numbered.

By default, the Wandboard boots with two framebuffer devices, `fb0` and `fb1`. The first is the default video display, and the second one is an overlay plane that can be used to combine content on the display.

However, the i.MX6 SoC supports up to four displays, so it could have up to four framebuffer devices in addition to two overlay framebuffers.

You can change the default framebuffer used by applications with the `FRAMEBUFFER` environment variable. For example, if your hardware supports several framebuffers, you could use the second one by running:

```
# export FRAMEBUFFER=/dev/fb1
```

The framebuffer devices are memory mapped and you can perform file operations on them. For example, you can clear the contents of the screen by running:

```
# cat /dev/zero > /dev/fb0
```

Or copy it with:

```
# cat /dev/fb0 > fb.raw
```

You may even restore the contents with:

```
# cat fb.raw > /dev/fb0
```

User space programs can also interrogate the framebuffers or modify their configuration programmatically using `ioctls`, or from the console by using the `fbset` application, which is included in Yocto's core images as a BusyBox applet.

```
# fbset -fb /dev/fb0
mode "1920x1080-60"
        # D: 148.500 MHz, H: 67.500 kHz, V: 60.000 Hz
        geometry 1920 1080 1920 1080 24
        timings 6734 148 88 36 4 44 5
        accel false
        rgba 8/16,8/8,8/0,0/0
endmode
```

You can configure the framebuffer HDMI device with a specific resolution, bits per pixel, and refresh rate by passing the `video` command-line option from the U-Boot bootloader to the Linux kernel. The specific format depends on the device framebuffer driver, and for the Wandboard it is as follows:

```
video=mxcfbn:dev=hdmi,<xres>x<yres>M[@rate]
```

Where:

- `n` is the framebuffer number
- `xres` is the horizontal resolution
- `yres` is the vertical resolution
- `M` specifies that the timings are to be calculated using the VESA coordinated video timings instead of from a look-up table
- `rate` is the refresh rate

For example, for the `fb0` framebuffer, you could use:

```
video=mxcfb0:dev=hdmi,1920x1080M@60
```

> Note that after some time of inactivity, the virtual console will blank out. To unblank the display, use:
> ```
> # echo 0 > /sys/class/graphics/fb0/blank
> ```

There's more...

The FSL community BSP layer also provides a `fsl-image-multimedia` target image that includes the `gstreamer` framework, including plugins that make use of the hardware acceleration features within the i.MX6 SoC. A `fsl-image-multimedia-full` image is also provided, which extends the supported `gstreamer` plugins.

To build the `fsl-image-multimedia` image with framebuffer support, you need to remove the graphical distribution features by adding the following to your `conf/local.conf` file:

```
DISTRO_FEATURES_remove = "x11 directfb wayland"
```

And build the image with:

```
$ bitbake fsl-image-multimedia
```

The resulting `fsl-image-multimedia-wandboard-quad.sdcard` image at `tmp/deploy/images` can be programmed into a microSD card and booted.

The default Wandboard device tree defines an `mxcfb1` node as follows:

```
mxcfb1: fb@0 {
          compatible = "fsl,mxc_sdc_fb";
          disp_dev = "hdmi";
          interface_pix_fmt = "RGB24";
          mode_str ="1920x1080M@60";
          default_bpp = <24>;
          int_clk = <0>;
          late_init = <0>;
};
```

So, connecting a 1920x1080 HDMI monitor should show a virtual terminal with the Poky login prompt.

We can then use the `gstreamer` command-line tool, `gst-launch`, to construct `gstreamer` pipelines. For example, to view a hardware-accelerated video over the framebuffer, you can download the Big Bunny teaser full HD video file and play it over the framebuffer using the `gstreamer` framework's `gst-launch` command-line tool as follows:

```
# cd /home/root
# wget
  http://video.blendertestbuilds.de/download.blender.org/peach/trailer_
  1080p.mov
# gst-launch playbin2 uri=file:///home/root/trailer_1080p.mov
```

The video will use Freescale's `h.264` video decoder plugin, `vpudec`, which makes use of the hardware video processing unit inside the i.MX6 SoC to decode the `h.264` video.

You can see a list of the available i.MX6-specific plugins by running:

```
# gst-inspect | grep imx
h264.imx:  mfw_h264decoder: h264 video decoder
audiopeq.imx:  mfw_audio_pp: audio post equalizer
aiur.imx: webm: webm
aiur.imx:  aiurdemux: aiur universal demuxer
mpeg2dec.imx:  mfw_mpeg2decoder: mpeg2 video decoder
tvsrc.imx:  tvsrc: v4l2 based tv src
ipucsc.imx:  mfw_ipucsc: IPU-based video converter
mpeg4dec.imx:  mfw_mpeg4aspdecoder: mpeg4 video decoder
vpu.imx:  vpudec: VPU-based video decoder
vpu.imx:  vpuenc: VPU-based video encoder
mp3enc.imx:  mfw_mp3encoder: mp3 audio encoder
beep.imx: ac3: ac3
beep.imx: 3ca: ac3
beep.imx:  beepdec: beep audio decoder
beep.imx:  beepdec.vorbis: Vorbis decoder
beep.imx:  beepdec.mp3: MP3 decoder
beep.imx:  beepdec.aac: AAC LC decoder
isink.imx:  mfw_isink: IPU-based video sink
v4lsink.imx:  mfw_v4lsink: v4l2 video sink
v4lsrc.imx:  mfw_v4lsrc: v4l2 based camera src
amrdec.imx:  mfw_amrdecoder: amr audio decoder
```

See also

> ▸ The framebuffer API is documented in the Linux kernel documentation at `https://www.kernel.org/doc/Documentation/fb/api.txt`

> ▸ For more information regarding Qt for Embedded Linux, refer to `http://qt-project.org/doc/qt-4.8/qt-embedded-linux.html`

> ▸ Documentation for the gstreamer 0.10 framework can be found at `http://www.freedesktop.org/software/gstreamer-sdk/data/docs/2012.5/gstreamer-0.10/`

Using the X Windows system

The X Windows system provides the framework for a GUI environment – things like drawing and moving windows on the display and interacting with input devices like the mouse, the keyboard, and touchscreens. The protocol version has been X11 for over two decades, so it also known as X11.

Getting ready

The reference implementation for the X Windows system is the **X.Org** server, which is released under permissive licenses such as MIT. It uses a client/server model, with the server communicating with several client programs, serving user input, and accepting graphical output. The X11 protocol is network transparent so that the clients and the server may run on different machines, with different architectures and operating systems. However, mostly, they both run on the same machine and communicate using local sockets.

User interface specifications, such as buttons or menu styles, are not defined in X11, which leaves it to other window manager applications that are usually part of desktop environments, such as Gnome or KDE.

X11 has input and video drivers to handle the hardware. For example, it has a framebuffer driver, `fbdev`, that can output to a non-accelerated Linux framebuffer, and `evdev`, a generic Linux input device driver with support for mice, keyboards, tablets, and touchscreens.

The design of the X11 Windows systems makes it heavy for embedded devices, and although a powerful device like the quad-core i.MX6 has no trouble using it, many embedded devices choose other graphical alternatives. However, there are many graphical applications, mostly from the desktop environment, that run over the X11 Windows system.

The FSL community BSP layer provides a hardware-accelerated X video driver for the i.MX6 SoC, `xf86-video-imxfb-vivante`, which is included in the X11-based `core-image-sato` target image and other graphical images.

The X server is configured by an `/etc/X11/xorg.conf` file that configures the accelerated device as follows:

```
Section "Device"
    Identifier   "i.MX Accelerated Framebuffer Device"
    Driver       "vivante"
    Option       "fbdev"       "/dev/fb0"
    Option       "vivante_fbdev" "/dev/fb0"
    Option       "HWcursor"    "false"
EndSection
```

The graphical acceleration is provided by the Vivante GPUs included in the i.MX6 SoC.

Low-level X11 development is not recommended, and toolkits such as GTK+ and Qt are preferred. We will see how to integrate both types of graphical applications into our Yocto target image.

How to do it...

SATO is the default visual style for the Poky distribution based on **Gnome Mobile and Embedded** (**GMAE**). It is a desktop environment based on GTK+ that uses the matchbox-window-manager. It has the peculiarity of showing one single fullscreen window at a time.

To build the GTK hello world application, `meta-custom/recipes-graphics/gtk-helloworld/gtk-helloworld-1.0/gtk_hello_world.c`, that we introduced earlier, as follows:

```c
#include <gtk/gtk.h>

int main(int argc, char *argv[])
{
    GtkWidget *window;
    gtk_init (&argc, &argv);
    window = gtk_window_new (GTK_WINDOW_TOPLEVEL);
    gtk_widget_show (window);
    gtk_main ();
    return 0;
}
```

We can use the following `meta-custom/recipes-graphics/gtk-helloworld/gtk-helloworld_1.0.bb` recipe:

```
DESCRIPTION = "Simple GTK helloworld application"
SECTION = "examples"
LICENSE = "MIT"
LIC_FILES_CHKSUM = "file://${COMMON_LICENSE_DIR}/MIT;md5=0835ade698e0b
cf8506ecda2f7b4
  f302"

SRC_URI = "file://gtk_hello_world.c"

S = "${WORKDIR}"

DEPENDS = "gtk+"

inherit pkgconfig

do_compile() {
```

```
        ${CC} gtk_hello_world.c -o helloworld `pkg-config --cflags --
    libs gtk+-2.0`
}

do_install() {
    install -d ${D}${bindir}
    install -m 0755 helloworld ${D}${bindir}
}
```

We can then add the package to the `core-image-sato` image by using:

```
IMAGE_INSTALL_append = " gtk-helloworld"
```

And we can build it, program it, and run the application from the serial terminal with:

```
# export DISPLAY=:0
# helloworld
```

There's more...

Accelerated graphical output is also supported on the Qt framework, either directly on the framebuffer (like in the `qt4e-demo-image` target we saw before) or using the X11 server available in `core-image-sato`.

To build the Qt hello world source we introduced in the previous recipe but over X11, we can use the `meta-custom/recipes-qt/qtx11-helloworld/qtx11-helloworld_1.0.bb` Yocto recipe shown as follows::

```
DESCRIPTION = "Simple QT over X11 helloworld example"
SECTION = "examples"
LICENSE = "MIT"
LIC_FILES_CHKSUM = "file://${COMMON_LICENSE_DIR}/MIT;md5=0835ade698e0b
cf8506ecda2f7b4
    f302"

RDEPENDS_${PN} += "icu"

SRC_URI = "file://qt_hello_world.cpp \
           file://qt_hello_world.pro"

S = "${WORKDIR}"

inherit qt4x11

do_install() {
```

```
                install -d ${D}${bindir}
                install -m 0755 qt_hello_world ${D}${bindir}
        }
```

We then need to add the Qt4 framework to the target image as well as the application.

```
        EXTRA_IMAGE_FEATURES += "qt4-pkgs"
        IMAGE_INSTALL_append = " qtx11-helloworld"
```

We can then build `core-image-sato` using the following command:

$ bitbake core-image-sato

Program and boot our target. Then run the application with:

 # export DISPLAY=:0

 # qt_hello_world

See also

▸   More information on the X.Org server can be found at `http://www.x.org`

▸   The Qt application framework documentation can be found at `https://qt-project.org/`

▸   More information and documentation about GTK+ can be found at `http://www.gtk.org/`

Using Wayland

Wayland is a display server protocol that is intended to replace the X Window system, and it is licensed under the MIT license.

This recipe will provide an overview of Wayland, including some key differences with the X Window system, and will show how to make use of it in Yocto.

Getting ready

The Wayland protocol follows a client/server model in which clients are the graphical applications requesting the display of pixel buffers on the screen, and the server, or compositor, is the service provider that controls the display of these buffers.

The Wayland compositor can be a Linux display server, an X application, or a special Wayland client. Weston is the reference Wayland compositor in the Wayland project. It is written in C and works with the Linux kernel APIs. It relies on `evdev` for the handling of input events.

Wayland uses **Direct Rendering Manager (DRM)** in the Linux kernel and does not need something like an X server. The client renders the window contents to a buffer shared with the compositor by itself, using a rendering library, or an engine like Qt or GTK+.

Wayland lacks the network transparency features of X, but it is likely that similar functionality will be added in the future.

It also has better security features than X and is designed to provide confidentiality and integrity. Wayland does not allow applications to look at the input of other programs, capture other input events, or generate fake input events. It also makes a better job out of protecting the Window outputs. However, this also means that it currently offers no way to provide some of the features we are used to in desktop X systems like screen capturing, or features common in accessibility programs.

Being lighter than X.Org and more secure, Wayland is better suited to use with embedded systems. If needed, X.Org can run as a client of Wayland for backwards compatibility.

However, Wayland is not as established as X11, and the Wayland-based images in Poky do not receive as much community attention as the X11-based ones.

How to do it...

Poky offers a `core-image-weston` image that includes the Weston compositor.

Modifying our GTK hello world example from the *Using the X Windows system* recipe to use GTK3 and run it with Weston is straightforward.

```
DESCRIPTION = "Simple GTK3 helloworld application"
SECTION = "examples"
LICENSE = "MIT"
LIC_FILES_CHKSUM = "file://${COMMON_LICENSE_DIR}/MIT;md5=0835ade698e0b
cf8506ecda2f7b4
  f302"

SRC_URI = "file://gtk_hello_world.c"

S = "${WORKDIR}"

DEPENDS = "gtk+3"

inherit pkgconfig

do_compile() {
    ${CC} gtk_hello_world.c -o helloworld `pkg-config --cflags --
  libs gtk+-3.0`
}
```

```
do_install() {
    install -d ${D}${bindir}
    install -m 0755 helloworld ${D}${bindir}
}
```

To build it, configure your `conf/local.conf` file by removing the `x11` distribution feature as follows:

```
DISTRO_FEATURES_remove = "x11"
```

> You will need to build from scratch by removing both the `tmp` and `sstate-cache` directories when changing the `DISTRO_FEATURES` variable.

Add the application to the image with:

```
IMAGE_INSTALL_append = " gtk3-helloworld"
```

And build the image with:

```
$ cd /opt/yocto/fsl-community-bsp/
$ source setup-environment wandboard-quad
$ bitbake core-image-weston
```

Once the build finishes, you will find the microSD card image ready to be programmed under `tmp/deploy/images/wandboard-quad`.

You can then launch the application by running:

```
# export XDG_RUNTIME_DIR=/var/run/user/root
# helloworld
```

There's more...

The FSL community BSP release supports hardware-accelerated graphics in Wayland using the Vivante GPU included in the i.MX6 SoC.

This means that applications like `gstreamer` will be able to offer hardware-accelerated output when running with the Weston compositor.

Wayland support can also be found in graphical toolkits like Clutter and GTK3+.

See also

▶ You can find more information about Wayland on the project's web page at `http://wayland.freedesktop.org/`

Adding Python applications

In Yocto 1.7, Poky has support for building both Python 2 and Python 3 applications, and includes a small set of Python development tools in the `meta/recipes-devtools/python` directory.

A wider variety of Python applications are available in the `meta-python` layer included as part of `meta-openembedded`, which you can add to your `conf/bblayers.conf` file if you want to.

Getting ready

The standard tool for packaging Python modules is `distutils`, which is included for both Python 2 and Python 3. Poky includes the `distutils` class (`distutils3` in Python 3), which is used to build Python packages that use `distutils`. An example recipe in `meta-python` that uses the `distutils` class is `meta-python/recipes-devtools/python/python-pyusb_1.0.0a2.bb`.

```
SUMMARY = "PyUSB provides USB access on the Python language"
HOMEPAGE = "http://pyusb.sourceforge.net/"
SECTION = "devel/python"
LICENSE = "BSD"
LIC_FILES_CHKSUM =
   "file://LICENSE;md5=a53a9c39efcfb812e2464af14afab013"
DEPENDS = "libusb1"
PR = "r1"

SRC_URI = "\
    ${SOURCEFORGE_MIRROR}/pyusb/${SRCNAME}-${PV}.tar.gz \
"
SRC_URI[md5sum] = "9136b3dc019272c62a5b6d4eb624f89f"
SRC_URI[sha256sum] =
   "dacbf7d568c0bb09a974d56da66d165351f1ba3c4d5169ab5b734266623e1736"

SRCNAME = "pyusb"
S = "${WORKDIR}/${SRCNAME}-${PV}"

inherit distutils
```

However, `distutils` does not install package dependencies, allow package uninstallation, or allow us to install several versions of the same package, so it is only recommended for simple requirements. Hence, `setuptools` was developed to extend on `distutils`. It is not included in the standard Python libraries, but it is available in Poky. There is also a `setuptools` class in Poky (`setuptools3` for Python 3) that is used to build Python packages distributed with `setuptools`.

How to do it...

To build a Python hello world example application with `setuptools`, we would use a Yocto `meta-custom/recipes-python/python-helloworld/pythonhelloworld_1.0.bb` recipe as follows:

```
DESCRIPTION = "Simple Python setuptools hello world application"
SECTION = "examples"
LICENSE = "MIT"
LIC_FILES_CHKSUM =
    "file://${COMMON_LICENSE_DIR}/MIT;md5=0835ade698e0bcf8506ecda2f7b4
    f302"

SRC_URI = "file://setup.py \
      file://python-helloworld.py \
      file://helloworld/__init__.py \
            file://helloworld/main.py"

S = "${WORKDIR}"

inherit setuptools

do_install_append () {
    install -d ${D}${bindir}
    install -m 0755 python-helloworld.py ${D}${bindir}
}
```

To create an example hello world package, we create the directory structure shown in the following screenshot:

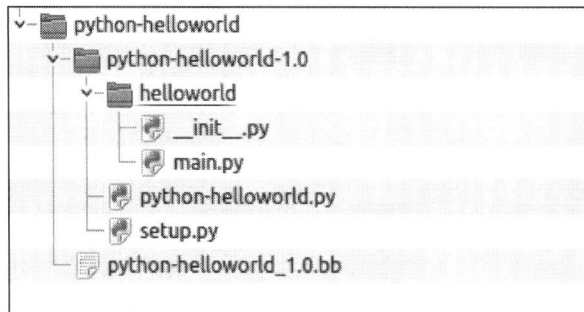

Here is the code for the same directory structure:

```
$ mkdir -p meta-custom/recipes-python/python-helloworld/python-
  helloworld-1.0/helloworld/
```

```
$ touch meta-custom/recipes-python/python-helloworld/python-
  helloworld-1.0/helloworld/__init__.py
```

And create the following meta-custom/recipes-python/python-helloworld/
python-helloworld-1.0/setup.py Python setup file:

```
import sys
from setuptools import setup

setup(
    name = "helloworld",
    version = "0.1",
    packages=["helloworld"],
    author="Alex Gonzalez",
    author_email = "alex@example.com",
    description = "Hello World packaging example",
    license = "MIT",
    keywords= "example",
    url = "",
)
```

As well as the meta-custom/recipes-python/python-helloworld/python-
helloworld-1.0/helloworld/main.py python file:

```
import sys

def main(argv=None):
    if argv is None:
```

```
        argv = sys.argv
    print "Hello world!"
    return 0
```

And a `meta-custom/recipes-python/python-helloworld/python-helloworld-1.0/python-helloworld.py` test script that makes use of the module:

```
#!/usr/bin/env python
import sys
import helloworld.main

if __name__ == '__main__':
        sys.exit(helloworld.main.main())
```

We can then add it to our image with:

```
IMAGE_INSTALL_append = " python-helloworld"
```

And build it using:

```
$ cd /opt/yocto/fsl-community-bsp/
$ source setup-environment wandboard-quad
$ bitbake core-image-minimal
```

Once programmed and booted, we can test the module by running the example script:

```
# /usr/bin/python-helloworld.py
Hello world!
```

There's more...

In `meta-python`, you can also find the `python-pip` recipe that will add the `pip` utility to your target image. It can be used to install packages from the **Python Package Index** (**PyPI**).

You can add it to your image with:

```
IMAGE_INSTALL_append  = " python-pip python-distribute"
```

You will need to add the `meta-openembedded/meta-python` layer to your `conf/bblayers.conf` file in order to build your image, and also the `python-distribute` dependency, which is needed by `python-pip`. Then you can build for the `core-image-minimal` image with:

```
$ cd /opt/yocto/fsl-community-bsp/
$ source setup-environment wandboard-quad
$ bitbake core-image-minimal
```

Once installed, you can use it from the target as follows:

```
# pip search <package_name>
# pip install <package_name>
```

Integrating the Oracle Java Runtime Environment

Oracle provides two specialized Java editions for embedded development:

> ▸ **Java SE embedded**: This is a large subset of the desktop version of the standard Java SE. It contains optimizations with respect to the standard edition, like size and memory usage, to adapt it to the needs of mid-sized embedded devices.

> ▸ **Java Micro Edition** (**ME**): This is targeted at headless low- and mid-range devices, and is a subset of Java SE complying with the **Connected Limited Device Configuration** (**CLDC**), and including some extra features and tools for the embedded market. Oracle offers a couple of reference implementations, but Java ME will have to be individually integrated from source into specific platforms.

We will focus on Java SE embedded, which can be downloaded in binary format from the Oracle download site.

Java SE embedded is commercially licensed and requires royalty payments for embedded deployments.

Getting ready

Yocto has a `meta-oracle-java` layer that is meant to help in the integration of the official Oracle **Java Runtime Environment** (**JRE**) Version 7. However, installation without user intervention is not possible, as the Oracle's web page requires login and the acceptance of its license.

In Java SE embedded Version 7, Oracle offered both soft and hard floating point versions of headless and headful JREs for ARMv6/v7, and a headless version JRE for soft floating point user spaces for ARMv5. Java SE embedded version 7 provides two different **Java Virtual Machines** (**JVMs**) for ARM Linux:

> ▸ A client JVM optimized for responsiveness

> ▸ A server JVM identical to the client JVM but optimized for long-running applications

At the time of writing, the `meta-oracle-java` layer only has a recipe for the headless hard floating-point version with the client JVM. We will add recipes for the latest Java 7 SE embedded, which is update 75, for both headless and headful hard floating point JREs, which are appropriate to run on an i.MX6-based board like `wandboard-quad`.

How to do it...

To install the Java SE embedded runtime environment, first we need to clone the `meta-oracle-java` layer into our sources directory and add it to our `conf/bblayers.conf` file as follows:

```
$ cd /opt/yocto/fsl-community-bsp/sources
$ git clone git://git.yoctoproject.org/meta-oracle-java
```

Then we need to explicitly accept the Oracle Java license by adding the following to our `conf/local.conf` file:

```
LICENSE_FLAGS_WHITELIST += "oracle_java"
```

We want to build the newest update available, so we add the following `meta-custom/recipes-devtools/oracle-java/oracle-jse-ejre-arm-vfphflt-client-headless_1.7.0.bb` recipe to our `meta-custom` layer:

```
SUMMARY = "Oracle Java SE runtime environment binaries"

JDK_JRE = "ejre"
require recipes-devtools/oracle-java/oracle-jse.inc

PV_UPDATE = "75"
BUILD_NUMBER = "13"

LIC_FILES_CHKSUM = "\
        file://${WORKDIR}/${JDK_JRE}${PV}_${PV_UPDATE}/
COPYRIGHT;md5=0b204
  bd2921accd6ef4a02f9c0001823 \
        file://${WORKDIR}/${JDK_JRE}${PV}_${PV_UPDATE}/
THIRDPARTYLICENSERE
  ADME.txt;md5=f3a388961d24b8b72d412a079a878cdb \
        "

SRC_URI =
  "http://download.oracle.com/otn/java/ejre/7u${PV_UPDATE}-
  b${BUILD_NUMBER}/ejre-7u${PV_UPDATE}-fcs-b${BUILD_NUMBER}-linux-
  arm-vfp-hflt-client_headless-18_dec_2014.tar.gz"
```

```
SRC_URI[md5sum] = "759ca6735d77778a573465b1e84b16ec"
SRC_URI[sha256sum] =
"ebb6499c62fc12e1471cff7431fec5407ace59477abd0f48347bf6e89c6bff3b"

RPROVIDES_${PN} += "java2-runtime"
```

Try to build the recipe with the following:

$ bitbake oracle-jse-ejre-arm-vfp-hflt-client-headless

You will see that we get a checksum mismatch. This is caused by the license acceptance step in Oracle's website. To get around this, we will need to manually download the file into the downloads directory as specified in our project's DL_DIR configuration variable.

Then we can add the JRE to our target image:

```
IMAGE_INSTALL_append = " oracle-jse-ejre-arm-vfp-hflt-client-
    headless"
```

And build it with:

$ cd /opt/yocto/fsl-community-bsp/

$ source setup-environment wandboard-quad

$ bitbake core-image-minimal

We can now log in to the target and run it with:

 # /usr/bin/java -version

java version "1.7.0_75"

Java(TM) SE Embedded Runtime Environment (build 1.7.0_75-b13, headless)

Java HotSpot(TM) Embedded Client VM (build 24.75-b04, mixed mode)

We can also build the headful version using the following meta-custom/recipes-devtools/oracle-java/oracle-jse-ejre-arm-vfphflt-client-headful_1.7.0.bb recipe:

```
SUMMARY = "Oracle Java SE runtime environment binaries"

JDK_JRE = "ejre"
require recipes-devtools/oracle-java/oracle-jse.inc

PV_UPDATE = "75"
BUILD_NUMBER = "13"

LIC_FILES_CHKSUM = "\
```

```
        file://${WORKDIR}/${JDK_JRE}${PV}_${PV_UPDATE}/
COPYRIGHT;md5=0b204
  bd2921accd6ef4a02f9c0001823 \
        file://${WORKDIR}/${JDK_JRE}${PV}_${PV_UPDATE}/
THIRDPARTYLICENSERE
  ADME.txt;md5=f3a388961d24b8b72d412a079a878cdb \
        "


SRC_URI =
    "http://download.oracle.com/otn/java/ejre/7u${PV_UPDATE}-
    b${BUILD_NUMBER}/ejre-7u${PV_UPDATE}-fcs-b${BUILD_NUMBER}-linux-
    arm-vfp-hflt-client_headful-18_dec_2014.tar.gz"


SRC_URI[md5sum] = "84dba4ffb47285b18e6382de2991edfc"
SRC_URI[sha256sum] =
    "5738ffb8ce2582b6d7b39a3cbe16137d205961224899f8380eebe3922bae5c61"


RPROVIDES_${PN} += "java2-runtime"
```

And add it to the target image with:

```
IMAGE_INSTALL_append =  " oracle-jse-ejre-arm-vfp-hflt-client-
    headful"
```

And build `core-image-sato` with:

```
$ cd cd /opt/yocto/fsl-community-bsp/
$ source setup-environment wandboard-quad
$ bitbake core-image-sato
```

In this case, the reported Java version is:

```
# /usr/bin/java -version
java version "1.7.0_75"
Java(TM) SE Embedded Runtime Environment (build 1.7.0_75-b13)
Java HotSpot(TM) Embedded Client VM (build 24.75-b04, mixed mode)
```

There's more...

The latest release at the time of this writing is Java SE embedded Version 8 update 33 (8u33).

Oracle offers the download of the JDK only, and a host tool, **jrecreate**, needs to be used to configure and create an appropriate JRE from the JDK. The tool allows us to choose between different JVMs (minimal, client, and server) as well as soft or hard floating point ABIs, extensions like JavaFX, locales, and several other tweakings to the JVM.

Oracle Java SE embedded Version 8 provides support for headful X11 development using Swing, AWT, and JavaFX only for ARMv7 hard floating point user spaces, and includes support for JavaFX (the graphical framework aimed to replace Swing and AWT) on the Freescale i.MX6 processor.

There is no Yocto recipe to integrate Java Version 8 at the time of this writing.

Integrating the Open Java Development Kit

The open source alternative to the Oracle Java SE embedded is the **Open Java Development Kit** (**OpenJDK**), an open source implementation of Java SE licensed under the GPLv2, with the classpath exception, which means that applications are allowed to link without being bound by the GPL license.

This recipe will show how to build OpenJDK with Yocto and integrate the JRE into our target images.

Getting ready

The main components of OpenJDK are:

- ▶ The HotSpot Java Virtual Machine
- ▶ The **Java Class Library** (**JCL**)
- ▶ The Java compiler, **javac**

Initially, OpenJDK needed to be built using a proprietary JDK. However, the **IcedTea** project allowed us to build OpenJDK using the GNU classpath, the GNU compiler for Java (GCJ), and bootstrap a JDK to build OpenJDK. It also complements OpenJDK with some missing components available on Java SE like a web browser plugin and web start implementations.

Yocto can build meta-java using the `meta-java` layer, which includes recipes for cross-compiling OpenJDK using IcedTea.

You can download OpenJDK from its Git repository at `http://git.yoctoproject.org/cgit/cgit.cgi/meta-java/`.

Development discussions can be followed and contributed to by visiting the development mailing list at `http://lists.openembedded.org/mailman/listinfo/openembedded-devel`.

The `meta-java` layer also includes recipes for a wide variety of Java libraries and VMs, and tools for application development like **ant** and **fastjar**.

How to do it...

To build OpenJDK 7, you need to clone the `meta-java` layer as follows:

```
$ cd /opt/yocto/fsl-community-bsp/sources/
$ git clone http://git.yoctoproject.org/cgit/cgit.cgi/meta-java/
```

At the time of this writing, there is no 1.7 Dizzy branch yet, so we will work directly from the master branch.

Add the layer to your `conf/bblayers.conf` file:

```
  + ${BSPDIR}/sources/meta-java \
    "
```

And configure the project by adding the following to your `conf/local.conf` file:

```
PREFERRED_PROVIDER_virtual/java-initial = "cacao-initial"
PREFERRED_PROVIDER_virtual/java-native = "jamvm-native"
PREFERRED_PROVIDER_virtual/javac-native = "ecj-bootstrap-native"
PREFERRED_VERSION_openjdk-7-jre = "25b30-2.3.12"
PREFERRED_VERSION_icedtea7-native = "2.1.3"
```

You can then add the OpenJDK package to your image with:

```
IMAGE_INSTALL_append = " openjdk-7-jre"
```

And build the image of your choice:

```
$ cd /opt/yocto/fsl-community-bsp/
$ source setup-environment wandboard-quad
$ bitbake core-image-sato
```

When you run the target image, you will get the following Java version:

```
# java -version
java version "1.7.0_25"
OpenJDK Runtime Environment (IcedTea 2.3.12) (25b30-2.3.12)
OpenJDK Zero VM (build 23.7-b01, mixed mode)
```

How it works...

To test the JVM, we can byte-compile a Java class on our host and copy it to the target to execute it. For instance, we can use the following simple `HelloWorld.java` example:

```
class HelloWorld {
  public static void main(String[] args) {
    System.out.println("Hello World!");
  }
}
```

To byte-compile it in the host, we need to have a Java SDK installed. To install a Java SDK in Ubuntu, just run:

```
$ sudo apt-get install openjdk-7-jdk
```

To byte-compile the example, we execute:

```
$ javac HelloWorld.java
```

To run it, we copy the `HelloWorld.class` to the target, and from the same folder we run:

```
# java HelloWorld
```

There's more...

When using OpenJDK on a production system, it is recommended to always use the latest available release, which contains bug and security fixes. At the time of this writing, the latest OpenJDK 7 release is update 71 (jdk7u71b14), buildable with IcedTea 2.5.3, so the `meta-java` recipes should be updated.

See also

   ▶ Up-to-date information regarding openJDK can be obtained at `http://openjdk.java.net/`

Integrating Java applications

The `meta-java` layer also offers helper classes to ease the integration of Java libraries and applications into Yocto. In this recipe, we will see an example of building a Java library using the provided classes.

Getting ready

The `meta-java` layer provides two main classes to help with the integration of Java applications and libraries:

▸ **The Java bbclass**: This provides the default target directories and some auxiliary functions, namely:

  ❏ `oe_jarinstall`: This installs and symlinks a JAR file

  ❏ `oe_makeclasspath`: This generates a classpath string from JAR filenames

  ❏ `oe_java_simple_wrapper`: This wraps your Java application in a shell script

▸ **The java-library bbclass**: This inherits the Java bbclass and extends it to create and install JAR files.

How to do it...

We will use the following `meta-custom/recipes-java/java-helloworld/java-helloworld-1.0/HelloWorldSwing.java` graphical Swing hello world as an example:

```
import javax.swing.JFrame;
import javax.swing.JLabel;

public class HelloWorldSwing {
    private static void createAndShowGUI() {
        JFrame frame = new JFrame("Hello World!");
        frame.setDefaultCloseOperation(JFrame.EXIT_ON_CLOSE);

        JLabel label = new JLabel("Hello World!");
        frame.getContentPane().add(label);

        frame.pack();
        frame.setVisible(true);
    }
    public static void main(String[] args) {
        javax.swing.SwingUtilities.invokeLater(new Runnable() {
            public void run() {
                createAndShowGUI();
            }
        });
    }
}
```

To integrate this `HelloWorldSwing` application, we can use a Yocto `meta-custom/` `recipes-java/java-helloworld/java-helloworld_1.0.bb` recipe as follows:

```
DESCRIPTION = "Simple Java Swing hello world application"
SECTION = "examples"
LICENSE = "MIT"
LIC_FILES_CHKSUM = "file://${COMMON_LICENSE_DIR}/MIT;md5=0835ade698e0b
cf8506ecda2f7b4
  f302"

RDEPENDS_${PN} = "java2-runtime"

SRC_URI = "file://HelloWorldSwing.java"

S = "${WORKDIR}"

inherit java-library

do_compile() {
        mkdir -p build
        javac -d build `find . -name "*.java"`
        fastjar cf ${JARFILENAME} -C build .
}

BBCLASSEXTEND = "native"
```

The recipe is also buildable for the host native architecture. We can do this either by providing a separate `java-helloworld-native` recipe that inherits the `native` class or by using the `BBCLASSEXTEND` variable as we did earlier. In both cases, we could then use the `_class-native` and `_class-target` overrides to differentiate between native and target functionality.

Even though Java is byte-compiled and the compiled class will be the same for both, it still makes sense to add the native support explicitly.

How it works...

The `java-library` class will create a library package with the name `lib<package>-java`.

To add it to a target image, we would use:

```
IMAGE_INSTALL_append = " libjava-helloworld-java"
```

We can then decide whether we want to run the application with the Oracle JRE or OpenJDK. For OpenJDK, we will add the following packages to our image:

```
IMAGE_INSTALL_append = " openjdk-7-jre openjdk-7-common"
```

And for the Oracle JRE, we will use the following:

```
IMAGE_INSTALL_append = " oracle-jse-ejre-arm-vfp-hflt-client-
    headful"
```

The available JREs do not currently run over the framebuffer or Wayland, so we will use an X11-based graphical image like `core-image-sato`:

```
$ cd /opt/yocto/fsl-community-bsp/
$ source setup-environment wandboard-quad
$ bitbake core-image-sato
```

We can then boot it, log in to the target, and execute the example with OpenJDK by running:

```
# export DISPLAY=:0
# java -cp /usr/share/java/java-helloworld.jar HelloWorldSwing
```

There's more...

At the time of this writing, OpenJDK as built from the `meta-java` layer master branch is not able to run X11 applications and will fail with this exception:

```
Exception in thread "main" java.awt.AWTError: Toolkit not found:
    sun.awt.X11.XToolkit
        at java.awt.Toolkit$2.run(Toolkit.java:875)
        at java.security.AccessController.doPrivileged(Native
    Method)
        at java.awt.Toolkit.getDefaultToolkit(Toolkit.java:860)
        at java.awt.Toolkit.getEventQueue(Toolkit.java:1730)
        at java.awt.EventQueue.invokeLater(EventQueue.java:1217)
        at javax.swing.SwingUtilities.invokeLater(SwingUtilities.
java:1287)
        at HelloWorldSwing.main(HelloWorldSwing.java:17)
```

However, the precompiled Oracle JRE runs the application without issues with:

```
# export DISPLAY=:0
# /usr/bin/java -cp /usr/share/java/java-helloworld.jar
  HelloWorldSwing
```

> If you see build errors when building packages with the Oracle JRE, try using a different package format, for example, IPK, by adding the following to your `conf/local.conf` configuration file:
>
> `PACKAGE_CLASSES = "package_ipk"`
>
> This is due to dependency problems in the `meta-oracle-java` layer with the RPM package manager, as explained in the layer's README file.

5
Debugging, Tracing, and Profiling

In this chapter, we will cover the following recipes:

- ▶ Analyzing core dumps
- ▶ Native GDB debugging
- ▶ Cross GDB debugging
- ▶ Using strace for application debugging
- ▶ Using the kernel's performance counters
- ▶ Using static kernel tracing
- ▶ Using dynamic kernel tracing
- ▶ Using dynamic kernel events
- ▶ Exploring Yocto's tracing and profiling tools
- ▶ Tracing and profiling with perf
- ▶ Using SystemTap
- ▶ Using OProfile
- ▶ Using LTTng
- ▶ Using blktrace

Introduction

Debugging an embedded Linux product is a common task not only during development, but also in deployed production systems.

Application debugging in embedded Linux is different from debugging in a traditional embedded device in that we don't have a flat memory model with an operating system and applications sharing the same address space. Instead, we have a virtual memory model with the Linux operating system, sharing the address space and assigning virtual memory areas to running processes.

With this model, the mechanisms used for kernel and user space debugging differ. For example, the traditional model of using a JTAG-based hardware debugger is useful for kernel debugging, but unless it knows about the user space processes memory mapping, it will not be able to debug user space applications.

Application debugging is approached with the use of a user space debugger service. We have seen an example of this methodology in action with the TCF agent used in the Eclipse GDB. The other commonly used agent is the **gdbserver**, which we will use in this chapter.

Finally we will explore the area of tracing and profiling. Tracing is a low-level logging of frequent system events, and the statistical analysis of these captured traces is called profiling.

We will use some of the tools embedded Linux and Yocto offer to trace and profile our systems so that they run to their maximum potential.

Analyzing core dumps

Even after extensive quality assurance testing, embedded systems in-field also fail and need to be debugged. Moreover, often the failure is not something that can be easily reproduced in a laboratory environment, so we are left with production, often hardened system, to debug.

Assuming we have designed our system with the aforementioned scenario in mind, our first debugging choice is usually to extract as much information about the failing system—for example, by obtaining and analyzing a core dump of the misbehaving processes.

Getting ready

In the process of debugging embedded Linux systems, we can use the same toolbox as standard Linux systems. One of the tools enables applications to generate into the disk a memory core dump upon crashing. This assumes that we have enough disk space to store the application's entire memory map, and that writing to disk is quick enough that it will not drag the system to a halt.

Once the memory core dump is generated, we use the host's GDB to analyze the core dump. GDB needs to have debug information available. Debug information can be in the executable itself—for example, when we install the -dbg version of a package, or we configure our project to not strip binaries—or can be kept in a separate file. To install debug information separately from the executable, we use the dbg-pkgs feature. By default, this installs the debug information of a package in a .debug directory in the same location as the executable itself. To add debug information for all packages in a target image, we add the following to our conf/local.conf configuration file:

```
EXTRA_IMAGE_FEATURES += "dbg-pkgs"
```

We can then build an appropriate toolchain generated to match our filesystem, as we saw in the *Preparing and using an SDK* recipe in *Chapter 4, Application Development*. The core dump contains build IDs for the executables and libraries in use at the time of the crash, so it's important to match the toolchain and the target image.

How to do it...

We can display the limits of the system-wide resources with the ulimit tool. We are interested in the core file size, which by default is set to zero to avoid the creation of application core dumps. In our failing system, preferably in a test environment, make your application dump a memory core upon crashing with:

```
$ ulimit -c unlimited
```

You can then verify the change with:

```
$ ulimit -a
-f: file size (blocks)            unlimited
-t: cpu time (seconds)            unlimited
-d: data seg size (kb)            unlimited
-s: stack size (kb)               8192
-c: core file size (blocks)       unlimited
-m: resident set size (kb)        unlimited
-l: locked memory (kb)            64
-p: processes                     5489
-n: file descriptors              1024
-v: address space (kb)            unlimited
-w: locks                         unlimited
-e: scheduling priority           0
-r: real-time priority            0
```

For this example, we will be using the `wvdial` application in a real segmentation fault scenario. The purpose is not to debug the application itself but to showcase the methodology used for core dump analysis; so, details regarding the application-specific configuration and system setup are not provided. However, being a real crash, the example is more illustrative.

To run `wvdial` on the target, use the following code:

```
# wvdial
--> WvDial: Internet dialer version 1.61
--> Initializing modem.
--> Sending: ATZ
ATZ
OK
--> Sending: ATQ0 V1 E1 S0=0 &C1 &D2 +FCLASS=0
ATQ0 V1 E1 S0=0 &C1 &D2 +FCLASS=0
OK
--> Sending: AT+CGDCONT=1,"IP","internet"
AT+CGDCONT=1,"IP","internet"
OK
--> Modem initialized.
--> Idle Seconds = 3000, disabling automatic reconnect.
Segmentation fault (core dumped)
```

The application will create a core file in the same folder, which you can then copy to your host system to analyze.

> You can also simulate a core dump by sending a `SIGQUIT` signal to a running process. For example, you could force the sleep command to core dump with a `SIGQUIT` signal as follows:
>
> ```
> $ ulimit -c unlimited
> $ sleep 30 &
> $ kill -QUIT <sleep-pid>
> ```

How it works...

Once in possession of the core dump, use the cross GDB in the host to load it and get some useful information, such as the backtrace, using the following steps:

1. First set up the environment in the host:

   ```
   $ cd /opt/poky/1.7.1/
   $ source environment-setup-cortexa9hf-vfp-neon-poky-linux-
     gnueabi
   ```

2. You can then start the cross GDB debugger, passing it a debug version of the application. Debug versions are stored in the `sysroot` file in the same location as the unstripped binary, but under a `.debug` directory.

The whole GDB banner is showed below but will be omitted in future examples.

```
$ arm-poky-linux-gnueabi-gdb /opt/yocto/fsl-community-
    bsp/wandboard-quad/tmp/work/cortexa9hf-vfp-neon-poky-linux-
    gnueabi/wvdial/1.61-r0/packages-split/wvdial-
    dbg/usr/bin/.debug/wvdial core
GNU gdb (GDB) 7.7.1
Copyright (C) 2014 Free Software Foundation, Inc.
License GPLv3+: GNU GPL version 3 or later <http://gnu.org/
    licenses/gpl.html>
This is free software: you are free to change and redistribute
    it.
There is NO WARRANTY, to the extent permitted by law.  Type
    "show copying"
and "show warranty" for details.
This GDB was configured as "--host=x86_64-pokysdk-linux --
    target=arm-poky-linux-gnueabi".
Type "show configuration" for configuration details.
For bug reporting instructions, please see:
<http://www.gnu.org/software/gdb/bugs/>.
Find the GDB manual and other documentation resources online
    at:
<http://www.gnu.org/software/gdb/documentation/>.
For help, type "help".
Type "apropos word" to search for commands related to
    "word"...
Reading symbols from /opt/yocto/fsl-community-bsp/wandboard-
    quad/tmp/work/cortexa9hf-vfp-neon-poky-linux-
    gnueabi/wvdial/1.61-r0/packages-split/wvdial-
    dbg/usr/bin/.debug/wvdial...done.
[New LWP 1050]


warning: Could not load shared library symbols for 14
    libraries, e.g. /usr/lib/libwvstreams.so.4.6.
Use the "info sharedlibrary" command to see the complete
    listing.
Do you need "set solib-search-path" or "set sysroot"?
Core was generated by `wvdial'.
```

```
Program terminated with signal SIGSEGV, Segmentation fault.
#0  0x76d524c4 in ?? ()
```

3. Now point GDB to the location of the toolchain's `sysroot`:

```
(gdb) set sysroot /opt/poky/1.7.1/sysroots/cortexa9hf-vfp-
   neon-poky-linux-gnueabi/
Reading symbols from /opt/poky/1.7.1/sysroots/cortexa9hf-vfp-
   neon-poky-linux-gnueabi/usr/lib/libwvstreams.so.4.6...Reading
symbols from
   /opt/poky/1.7.1/sysroots/cortexa9hf-vfp-neon-poky-linux-
   gnueabi/usr/lib/.debug/libwvstreams.so.4.6...done.
done.
Loaded symbols for /opt/poky/1.7.1/sysroots/cortexa9hf-vfp-
   neon-poky-linux-gnueabi/usr/lib/libwvstreams.so.4.6
Reading symbols from /opt/poky/1.7.1/sysroots/cortexa9hf-vfp-
   neon-poky-linux-gnueabi/usr/lib/libwvutils.so.4.6...Reading
   symbols from /opt/poky/1.7.1/sysroots/cortexa9hf-vfp-neon-
   poky-linux-gnueabi/usr/lib/.debug/libwvutils.so.4.6...done.
done.
[...]
Loaded symbols for /opt/poky/1.7.1/sysroots/cortexa9hf-vfp-
   neon-poky-linux-gnueabi/lib/libdl.so.2
```

4. You can now inquire GDB for the application's backtrace as follows:

```
(gdb) bt
#0  0x76d524c4 in WvTaskMan::_stackmaster () at
   utils/wvtask.cc:416
#1  0x00000000 in ?? ()
```

See also

▸ The usage documentation for GDB found at `http://www.gnu.org/software/gdb/documentation/`

Native GDB debugging

On devices as powerful as the Wandboard, native debugging is also an option to debug sporadic failures. This recipe will explore the native debugging method.

Getting ready

For native development and debugging, Yocto offers the `-dev` and `-sdk` target images. To add developing tools to the `-dev` images, we can use the `tools-sdk` feature. We also want to install debug information and debug tools, and we do this by adding the `dbg-pkgs` and `tools-debug` features to our image. For example, for `core-image-minimal-dev`, we would add the following to our `conf/local.conf` file:

```
EXTRA_IMAGE_FEATURES += "tools-sdk dbg-pkgs tools-debug"
```

To prepare a development-ready version of the `core-image-minimal-dev` target image, we would execute the following commands:

```
$ cd /opt/yocto/fsl-community-bsp/
$ source setup-environment wandboard-quad
$ bitbake core-image-minimal-dev
```

We will then program the development image to our target.

How to do it...

Once the target has booted, you can start the `wvdial` application through the native GDB using the following steps:

1. In the target command prompt, start the GDB debugger with the application as argument:

   ```
   $ gdb wvdial
   ```

2. Now instruct GDB to run the application:

   ```
   (gdb) run
   Starting program: /usr/bin/wvdial
   Cannot access memory at address 0x0
   Cannot access memory at address 0x0

   Program received signal SIGILL, Illegal instruction.
   0x7698afe8 in ?? () from /lib/libcrypto.so.1.0.0
   (gdb) sharedlibrary libcrypto
   Symbols already loaded for /lib/libcrypto.so.1.0.0
   ```

3. Then request to print a backtrace:

```
(gdb) bt
#0  0x7698afe8 in ?? () from /lib/libcrypto.so.1.0.0
#1  0x769878e8 in OPENSSL_cpuid_setup () from /lib/libcrypto.
so.1.0.0
#2  0x76fe715c in ?? () from /lib/ld-linux-armhf.so.3
Cannot access memory at address 0x48535540
```

This is not the same backtrace you got when analyzing the core dump. What is going on here? The clue is on libcrypto, part of the OpenSSL library. OpenSSL probes the capabilities of the system by trying each capability and trapping the illegal instruction errors. So the SIGILL signal you are seeing during startup is normal and you should instruct GDB to continue.

4. Instruct GDB to continue:

```
(gdb) c
Continuing.
--> WvDial: Internet dialer version 1.61
--> Initializing modem.
--> Sending: ATZ
ATZ
OK
--> Sending: ATQ0 V1 E1 S0=0 &C1 &D2 +FCLASS=0
ATQ0 V1 E1 S0=0 &C1 &D2 +FCLASS=0
OK
--> Sending: AT+CGDCONT=1,"IP","internet"
AT+CGDCONT=1,"IP","internet"
OK
--> Modem initialized.
--> Idle Seconds = 3000, disabling automatic reconnect.

Program received signal SIGSEGV, Segmentation fault.
0x76db74c4 in WvTaskMan::_stackmaster () () from /usr/lib/
libwvbase.so.4.6
```

This result is now compatible with the core dump you saw in the previous recipe.

There's more...

When debugging applications, it is sometimes useful to reduce the level of optimization used by the compiler. This will reduce the application's performance but will facilitate debugging by improving the accuracy of the debug information. You can configure the build system to reduce optimization and add debug information by adding the following line of code to your `conf/local.conf` file:

```
DEBUG_BUILD = "1"
```

By using this configuration, the optimization is reduced from `FULL_OPTIMIZATION (-O2)` to `DEBUG_OPTIMIZATION (-O -fno-omit-frame-pointer)`. But sometimes this is not enough, and you may like to build with no optimization. You can achieve this by overriding the `DEBUG_OPTIMIZATION` variable either globally or for a specific recipe.

See also

► The example on using a debug-optimized build in the upcoming recipe on *Cross GDB debugging*

Cross GDB debugging

When we run a cross compiled GDB in the host, which connects to a native gdbserver running on the target, it is referred to as cross debugging. This is the same scenario we saw in the *Using the Eclipse IDE* recipe earlier, except that Eclipse uses the **Target Communications Framework** (**TCF**). Cross debugging has the advantage of not needing debug information on target images, as they are already available in the host.

This recipe will show how to use a cross GDB and gdbserver.

Getting ready

To include gdbserver in your target image, you can use an `-sdk` image, or you can add the `tools-debug` feature to your image by adding the following to your `conf/local.conf` configuration file:

```
EXTRA_IMAGE_FEATURES += "tools-debug"
```

So that GDB can access debug information of the shared libraries and executables, add the following to the `conf/local.conf` file:

```
EXTRA_IMAGE_FEATURES += "dbg-pkgs"
```

The images running on the target and the toolchain's `sysroot` need to match. For example, if you are using `core-image-minimal` images, the toolchain needs to have been generated in the same project with:

```
$ bitbake -c populate_sdk core-image-minimal
```

This will generate a `sysroot` containing debug information for binaries and libraries.

How to do it...

Once the toolchain is installed, you can run the application to be debugged on the target using gdbserver—in this case, `wvdial`—in the following steps:

1. Launch gdbserver with the application to run as argument:

   ```
   # gdbserver localhost:1234 /usr/bin/wvdial
   Process wvdial created; pid = 879
   Listening on port 1234
   ```

   The gdbserver is launched listening on localhost on a random 1234 port and is waiting for a connection from the remote GDB.

2. In the host, you can now set up the environment using the recently installed toolchain:

   ```
   $ cd /opt/poky/1.7.1/
   $ source environment-setup-cortexa9hf-vfp-neon-poky-linux-gnueabi
   ```

   You can then launch the cross GDB, passing to it the absolute path to the debug version of the application to debug, which is located in a `.debug` directory on the sysroot:

   ```
   $ arm-poky-linux-gnueabi-gdb
   /opt/poky/1.7.1/sysroots/cortexa9hf-vfp-neon-poky-linux-gnueabi/usr/bin/.debug/wvdial
   Reading symbols from /opt/poky/1.7.1/sysroots/cortexa9hf-vfp-neon-poky-linux-gnueabi/usr/bin/.debug/wvdial...done.
   (gdb)
   ```

3. Next configure GDB to consider all files as trusted so that it auto loads whatever it needs:

   ```
   (gdb) set auto-load safe-path /
   ```

4. Also as you know, `wvdial` will generate a `SIGILL` signal that will interrupt our debugging session, instruct GDB not to stop when that signal is seen:

```
(gdb) handle SIGILL nostop
```

5. You can then connect to the remote target on the `1234` port with:

```
(gdb) target remote <target_ip>:1234
Remote debugging using 192.168.128.6:1234
Cannot access memory at address 0x0
0x76fd7b00 in ?? ()
```

6. The first thing to do is to set `sysroot` so that GDB is able to find dynamically loaded libraries:

```
(gdb) set sysroot /opt/poky/1.7.1/sysroots/cortexa9hf-vfp-
    neon-poky-linux-gnueabi
Reading symbols from /opt/poky/1.7.1/sysroots/cortexa9hf-
    vfp-neon-poky-linux-gnueabi/lib/ld-linux-
    armhf.so.3...done.
Loaded symbols for /opt/poky/1.7.1/sysroots/cortexa9hf-vfp-
    neon-poky-linux-gnueabi/lib/ld-linux-armhf.so.3
```

7. Type `c` to continue with the program's execution. You will see `wvdial` continuing on the target:

```
--> WvDial: Internet dialer version 1.61

--> Initializing modem.

--> Sending: ATZ

ATZ

OK

--> Sending: ATQ0 V1 E1 S0=0 &C1 &D2 +FCLASS=0

ATQ0 V1 E1 S0=0 &C1 &D2 +FCLASS=0

OK

--> Sending: AT+CGDCONT=1,"IP","internet"

AT+CGDCONT=1,"IP","internet"

OK

--> Modem initialized.

--> Idle Seconds = 3000, disabling automatic reconnect.
```

8. You will then see GDB intercepting a `SIGILL` and `SEGSEGV` signal on the host:

```
Program received signal SIGILL, Illegal instruction.

Program received signal SIGSEGV, Segmentation fault.
0x76dc14c4 in WvTaskMan::_stackmaster () at
  utils/wvtask.cc:416
416      utils/wvtask.cc: No such file or directory.
```

9. You can now ask to see a backtrace:

```
(gdb) bt
#0  0x76dc14c4 in WvTaskMan::_stackmaster () at
  utils/wvtask.cc:416
#1  0x00000000 in ?? ()
```

Although limited, this backtrace could still be useful to debug the application.

How it works...

We see a limited backtrace because the compiled binaries are not suitable for debugging, as they omit stack frames. To keep information on stack frames, add the following to the `conf/local.conf` configuration file:

```
DEBUG_BUILD = "1"
```

This changes the compilation flags to debug optimization as follows:

```
DEBUG_OPTIMIZATION = "-O -fno-omit-frame-pointer ${DEBUG_FLAGS} -
  pipe"
```

The `-fno-omit-frame-pointer` flag will tell `gcc` to keep stack frames. The compiler will also reduce the optimization level to provide a better debugging experience.

A debug build will also make it possible to trace variables and set breakpoints and watchpoints, as well as other common debugging features.

After building and installing the target images and toolchain again, you can now follow the same process as in the preceding recipe:

1. Use the following code for connecting to the remote target:

```
(gdb) target remote <target_ip>:1234
Remote debugging using 192.168.128.6:1234
warning: Unable to find dynamic linker breakpoint function.
GDB will be unable to debug shared library initializers
and track explicitly loaded dynamic code.
Cannot access memory at address 0x0
0x76fdd800 in ?? ()
```

Set the `sysroot` as follows:

```
(gdb) set sysroot /opt/poky/1.7.1/sysroots/cortexa9hf-vfp-
    neon-poky-linux-gnueabi
Reading symbols from /opt/poky/1.7.1/sysroots/cortexa9hf-
    vfp-neon-poky-linux-gnueabi/lib/ld-linux-
    armhf.so.3...done.
Loaded symbols for /opt/poky/1.7.1/sysroots/cortexa9hf-vfp-
    neon-poky-linux-gnueabi/lib/ld-linux-armhf.so.3
```

2. Once you are done with the setup, instruct the program to continue as follows:

```
(gdb) c
Continuing.

Program received signal SIGILL, Illegal instruction.

Program received signal SIGABRT, Aborted.
0x76b28bb4 in __GI_raise (sig=sig@entry=6) at
    ../sysdeps/unix/sysv/linux/raise.c:55
55          ../sysdeps/unix/sysv/linux/raise.c: No such file or
    directory.
(gdb) bt
#0  0x76b28bb4 in __GI_raise (sig=sig@entry=6) at
    ../sysdeps/unix/sysv/linux/raise.c:55
#1  0x76b2cabc in __GI_abort () at abort.c:89
#2  0x76decfa8 in __assert_fail (__assertion=0x76df4600
    "magic_number == -0x123678",
        __file=0x1 <error: Cannot access memory at address
    0x1>, __line=427,
        __function=0x76df4584
    <WvTaskMan::_stackmaster()::__PRETTY_FUNCTION__> "static
    void WvTaskMan::_stackmaster()")
        at utils/wvcrashbase.cc:98
#3  0x76dc58c8 in WvTaskMan::_stackmaster () at
    utils/wvtask.cc:427
Cannot access memory at address 0x123678
#4  0x00033690 in ?? ()
Cannot access memory at address 0x123678
Backtrace stopped: previous frame identical to this frame
    (corrupt stack?)
```

You can now see a complete backtrace.

Using strace for application debugging

Debugging does not always involve working with source code. Sometimes it is a change in an external factor that is causing the problem.

Strace is a tool that is useful for scenarios where we are looking for problems outside of the binary itself; for example configuration files, input data, and kernel interfaces. This recipe will explain how to use it.

Getting ready

To include strace in your system, add the following to your `conf/local.conf` file:

```
IMAGE_INSTALL_append = " strace"
```

Strace is also part of the `tools-debug` image feature, so you can also add it with:

```
EXTRA_IMAGE_FEATURES += "tools-debug"
```

Strace is also included in the `-sdk` images.

Before starting, we will also include `pgrep`, a process utility that will make our debugging easier by looking up process IDs by name. To do so, add the following to your `conf/local.conf` configuration file:

```
IMAGE_INSTALL_append = " procps"
```

How to do it...

When printing a system call, strace prints the values passed to the kernel or returned from the kernel. The verbose option prints more details for some system calls.

For example, filtering just the `sendto()` system calls from a single ping looks as follows:

```
# strace -f -t -e sendto /bin/bash -c "ping -c 1 127.0.0.1"
5240  17:18:04 sendto(0,
  "\10\0;\220x\24\0\0\225m\256\355\0\0\0\0\0\0\0\0\0\0\0\0\0\0\0\0\0\
  0\0"..., 64, 0, {sa_family=AF_INET, sin_port=htons(0),
  sin_addr=inet_addr("127.0.0.1")}, 28) = 64
```

How it works...

Strace allows the monitoring of system calls of running processes into the Linux kernel. It uses the `ptrace()` system call to do so. This means that other programs that use `ptrace()`, such as `gdb`, will not run simultaneously.

Strace is a disruptive monitoring tool, and the process being monitored will slow down and create many more context switches. A generic way of running strace on a given program is:

```
strace -f -e <filter> -t -s<num> -o <log file>.strace <program>
```

The arguments are explained below:

- ▶ `f`: Tells strace to trace all child processes.
- ▶ `e`: Filters the output to a selection of comma separated system calls.
- ▶ `t`: Prints absolute timestamps. Use `r` for timestamps relative to the last syscall, and `T` to add the time spent in the syscall.
- ▶ `s`: Increases the maximum length of strings from the default of `32`.
- ▶ `o`: Redirects the output to a file that can then be analyzed offline.

It can also attach to running processes using the following command:

```
$ strace -p $( pgrep <program> )
```

Or several instances of a process using the following command:

```
$ strace $( pgrep <program> | sed 's/^/-p' )
```

To detach, just press _Ctrl + C_.

See also

- ▶ The corresponding man pages for more information about strace at `http://man7.org/linux/man-pages/man1/strace.1.html`

Using the kernel's performance counters

Hardware performance counters are perfect for code optimization, especially in embedded systems with a single workload. They are actively used by a wide range of tracing and profiling tools. This recipe will introduce the Linux performance counters subsystem and show how to use it.

Getting ready

The **Linux Kernel Performance Counters Subsystem** (**LPC**), commonly known as `linux_perf`, is an abstraction interface to different CPU-specific performance measurements. The `perf_events` subsystem not only exposes hardware performance counters from the CPU, but also kernel software events using the same API. It also allows the mapping of events to processes, although this has a performance overhead. Further, it provides generalized events which are common across architectures.

Events can be categorized into three main groups:

- **Software events**: Based on kernel counters, these events are used for things such as context switches and minor faults tracking.

- **Hardware events**: These come from the processor's CPU **Performance Monitoring Unit** (**PMU**) and are used to track architecture-specific items, such as the number of cycles, cache misses, and so on. They vary with each processor type.

- **Hardware cache events**: These are common hardware events that will only be available if they actually map to a CPU hardware event.

To know whether `perf_event` support is available for your platform, you can check for the existence of the `/proc/sys/kernel/perf_event_paranoid` file. This file is also used to restrict access to the performance counters, which by default are set to allow both user and kernel measurement. It can have the following values:

- `2`: Only allows user-space measurements

- `1`: Allows both kernel and user measurements (default)

- `0`: Allows access to CPU-specific data but not raw tracepoint samples

- `-1`: No restrictions

The i.MX6 SoC has a Cortex-A9 CPU which includes a PMU, providing six counters to gather statistics on the operation of the processor and memory, each one of them able to monitor any of 58 available events.

You can find a description of the available events in the *Cortex-A9 Technical Reference Manual*.

The i.MX6 performance counters do not allow exclusive access to just user or just kernel measurements. Also, i.MX6 SoC designers have unfortunately joined the PMU interrupts from all CPU cores, when ideally they should only be handled by the same CPU that raises them. You can start the i.MX6 with just one core, using the `maxcpus=1` kernel command-line argument, so that you can still use the `perf_events` interface.

To configure the Linux kernel to boot with one core, stop at the U-Boot prompt and change the `mmcargs` environment variable as follows:

```
> setenv mmcargs 'setenv bootargs console=${console},${baudrate}
root=${mmcroot} ${extra_bootargs}; run videoargs'
> setenv extra_bootargs maxcpus=1
```

The `mmcargs` environmental variable is only used when booting from an MMC device like the microSD card. If the target is booting from another source, such as a network, the corresponding environmental variable will have to be changed. You can dump the whole U-Boot environment with the `printenv` U-Boot command, and change the required variable with `setenv`.

How to do it...

The interface introduces a `sys_perf_event_open()` syscall, with the counters being started and stopped using `ioctls`, and read either with `read()` calls or `mmapping` samples into circular buffers. The `perf_event_open()` syscall is defined as follows:

```
#include <linux/perf_event.h>
#include <linux/hw_breakpoint.h>

int perf_event_open(struct perf_event_attr *attr,
                    pid_t pid, int cpu, int group_fd,
                    unsigned long flags);
```

There is no C library wrapper for it, so it needs to be called using `syscall()`.

How it works...

Following is an example, `perf_example.c`, program modified from the `perf_event_open` man page to measure instruction count for a `printf` call:

```
#include <stdlib.h>
#include <stdio.h>
#include <unistd.h>
#include <string.h>
#include <sys/ioctl.h>
#include <linux/perf_event.h>
#include <asm/unistd.h>

static long
perf_event_open(struct perf_event_attr *hw_event, pid_t pid,
                int cpu, int group_fd, unsigned long flags)
{
    int ret;

    ret = syscall(__NR_perf_event_open, hw_event, pid, cpu,
                  group_fd, flags);
```

```
        return ret;
    }

    int
    main(int argc, char **argv)
    {
        struct perf_event_attr pe;
        long long count;
        int fd;

        memset(&pe, 0, sizeof(struct perf_event_attr));
        pe.type = PERF_TYPE_HARDWARE;
        pe.size = sizeof(struct perf_event_attr);
        pe.config = PERF_COUNT_HW_INSTRUCTIONS;
        pe.disabled = 1;

        fd = perf_event_open(&pe, 0, -1, -1, 0);
        if (fd == -1) {
            fprintf(stderr, "Error opening leader %llx\n", pe.config);
            exit(EXIT_FAILURE);
        }

        ioctl(fd, PERF_EVENT_IOC_RESET, 0);
        ioctl(fd, PERF_EVENT_IOC_ENABLE, 0);

        printf("Measuring instruction count for this printf\n");

        ioctl(fd, PERF_EVENT_IOC_DISABLE, 0);
        read(fd, &count, sizeof(long long));

        printf("Used %lld instructions\n", count);

        close(fd);

        return 0;
    }
```

For compiling this program externally, we can use the following commands:

```
$ source /opt/poky/1.7.1/environment-setup-cortexa9hf-vfp-neon-poky-
  linux-gnueabi
$ ${CC} perf_example.c -o perf_example
```

After copying the binary to your target, you can then execute it with the help of the following code:

```
# ./perf_example
Measuring instruction count for this printf
Used 0 instructions
```

Obviously, using zero instructions for the `printf()` call can't be correct. Looking into possible causes, we find a documented erratum (ERR006259) on i.MX6 processors that states that in order for the PMU to be used, the SoC needs to receive at least 4 JTAG clock cycles after power on reset.

Rerun the example with the JTAG connected:

```
# ./perf_example
Measuring instruction count for this printf
Used 3977 instructions
```

There's more...

Even though you can access the `perf_events` interface directly as in the preceding example, the recommended way to use it is through a user space application, such as perf, which we will see in the *Tracing and profiling with perf* recipe in this chapter.

See also

▶ The Technical Reference Manual at `http://infocenter.arm.com/help/index.jsp?topic=/com.arm.doc.ddi0388f/BEHGGDJC.html` for more information about the Cortex-A9 PMU

Using static kernel tracing

The Linux kernel is continuously being instrumented with static probe points called **tracepoints**, which when disabled have a very small overhead. They allow us to record more information than the function tracer we saw in *Chapter 2, The BSP Layer*. Tracepoints are used by multiple tracing and profiling tools in Yocto.

This recipe will explain how to use and define static tracepoints independently of user space tools.

Getting ready

Static tracepoints can be instrumented using custom kernel modules, and also through the event tracing infrastructure. Enabling any of the tracing features in the kernel will create a `/sys/kernel/debug/tracing/` directory; for example, the function tracing feature as explained in the *Using the kernel function tracing system* in *Chapter 2, The BSP Layer*.

So before continuing with this recipe, you need to configure the function tracing feature in the Linux kernel as explained before.

How to do it...

The static tracing functionality is exposed via the `debugfs` filesystem. The functionality offered by the interface includes:

▸ **Listing events**:

You can see a list of available tracepoints exposed via `sysfs` and ordered in subsystem directories with:

```
# ls /sys/kernel/debug/tracing/events/
```

asoc	ftrace	migrate	rcu	spi
block	gpio	module	regmap	sunrpc
cfg80211	header_event	napi	regulator	task
compaction	header_page	net	rpm	timer
drm	irq	oom	sched	udp
enable	jbd	power	scsi	vmscan
ext3	jbd2	printk	signal	workqueue
ext4	kmem	random	skb	writeback
filemap	mac80211	raw_syscalls	sock	

Or in the `available_events` file with the `<subsystem>:<event>` format using the following commands:

```
#  grep 'net'  /sys/kernel/debug/tracing/available_events
net:netif_rx
net:netif_receive_skb
net:net_dev_queue
net:net_dev_xmit
```

► **Describing events**:

Each event has a specific printing format that describes the information included in the log event, as follows:

```
#cat /sys/kernel/debug/tracing/events/net/netif_receive_skb/format
name: netif_receive_skb
ID: 378
format:
  field:unsigned short common_type;  offset:0;  size:2;
  signed:0;

  field:unsigned char common_flags;  offset:2;  size:1;
  signed:0;

  field:unsigned char common_preempt_count;  offset:3;
  size:1;  signed:0;

  field:int common_pid;  offset:4;  size:4;  signed:1;


  field:void * skbaddr;  offset:8;  size:4;  signed:0;

  field:unsigned int len;  offset:12;  size:4;  signed:0;

  field:__data_loc char[] name;  offset:16;  size:4;  signed:0;


print fmt: "dev=%s skbaddr=%p len=%u", __get_str(name), REC-
  >skbaddr, REC->len
```

► **Enabling and disabling events**:

You can enable or disable events in the following ways:

  ❑ By echoing 0 or 1 to the event `enable` file:

```
# echo 1 >
  /sys/kernel/debug/tracing/events/net/netif_receive_skb/
enable
```

  ❑ By subsystem directory, which will enable or disable all the tracepoints in the directory/subsystem:

```
# echo 1 > /sys/kernel/debug/tracing/events/net/enable
```

  ❑ By echoing the unique tracepoint name into the `set_event` file:

```
# echo netif_receive_skb >>
  /sys/kernel/debug/tracing/set_event
```

Note the append operation `>>` is used not to clear events.

❏ Events can be disabled by appending an exclamation mark to their names:

```
# echo '!netif_receive_skb' >>
  /sys/kernel/debug/tracing/set_event
```

❏ Events can also be enabled/disabled by subsystem:

```
# echo 'net:*' > /sys/kernel/debug/tracing/set_event
```

❏ To disable all events:

```
# echo > /sys/kernel/debug/tracing/set_event
```

You can also enable tracepoints from boot by passing a `trace_event=<comma separated event list>` kernel command line-argument.

▶ **Adding events to the tracing buffer**:

To see the tracepoints appear on the tracing buffer, turn tracing on:

```
# echo 1 > /sys/kernel/debug/tracing/tracing_on
```

Tracepoint events are integrated into the `ftrace` subsystem so that if you enable a tracepoint, when a tracer is running, it will show up in the trace. Take a look at the following commands:

```
# cd /sys/kernel/debug/tracing
# echo 1 > events/net/netif_receive_skb/enable
# echo netif_receive_skb > set_ftrace_filter
# echo function > current_tracer
# cat trace
        <idle>-0       [000] ..s2  1858.542206:
  netif_receive_skb <-napi_gro_receive
        <idle>-0       [000] ..s2  1858.542214:
  netif_receive_skb: dev=eth0 skbaddr=dcb5bd80 len=168
```

How it works...

A tracepoint is inserted using the `TRACE_EVENT` macro. It inserts a callback in the kernel source that gets called with the tracepoint parameters as arguments. Tracepoints added with the `TRACE_EVENT` macro allow `ftrace` or any other tracer to use them. The callback inserts the trace at the calling tracer's ring buffer.

To insert a new tracepoint into the Linux kernel, define a new header file with a special format. By default, tracepoint kernel files are located in `include/trace/events`, but the kernel has functionality so that the header files can be located in a different path. This is useful when defining a tracepoint in a kernel module.

To use the tracepoint, the header file must be included in any file that inserts the tracepoint, and a single C file must define CREATE_TRACE_POINT. For example, to extend the hello world Linux kernel module we saw in a previous chapter with a tracepoint, add the following code to meta-bsp-custom/recipes-kernel/hello-world-tracepoint/files/hello_world.c:

```c
#include <linux/module.h>
#include "linux/timer.h"
#define CREATE_TRACE_POINTS
#include "trace.h"

static struct timer_list hello_timer;

void hello_timer_callback(unsigned long data)
{
        char a[] = "Hello";
        char b[] = "World";
        printk("%s %s\n",a,b);
    /* Insert the static tracepoint */
        trace_log_dbg(a, b);
    /* Trigger the timer again in 8 seconds */
        mod_timer(&hello_timer, jiffies + msecs_to_jiffies(8000));
}

static int hello_world_init(void)
{
    /* Setup a timer to fire in 2 seconds */
        setup_timer(&hello_timer, hello_timer_callback, 0);
        mod_timer(&hello_timer, jiffies + msecs_to_jiffies(2000));
        return 0;
}

static void hello_world_exit(void)
{
    /* Delete the timer */
        del_timer(&hello_timer);
}

module_init(hello_world_init);
module_exit(hello_world_exit);

MODULE_LICENSE("GPL v2");
```

The tracepoint header file in `meta-bsp-custom/recipes-kernel/hello-world-tracepoint/files/trace.h` would be:

```
#undef TRACE_SYSTEM
#define TRACE_SYSTEM log_dbg

#if !defined(_HELLOWORLD_TRACE) || defined(TRACE_HEADER_MULTI_READ)
#define _HELLOWORLD_TRACE

#include <linux/tracepoint.h>

TRACE_EVENT(log_dbg,
            TP_PROTO(char *a, char *b),
            TP_ARGS(a, b),
            TP_STRUCT__entry(
                    __string(a, a)
                    __string(b, b)),
            TP_fast_assign(
                    __assign_str(a, a);
                    __assign_str(b, b);),
            TP_printk("log_dbg: a %s b %s",
                    __get_str(a), __get_str(b))
        );
#endif

/* This part must be outside protection */
#undef TRACE_INCLUDE_PATH
#undef TRACE_INCLUDE_FILE
#define TRACE_INCLUDE_PATH .
#define TRACE_INCLUDE_FILE trace
#include <trace/define_trace.h>
```

And the module's `Makefile` file in `meta-bsp-custom/recipes-kernel/hello-world-tracepoint/files/Makefile` would look as follows:

```
obj-m    := hello_world.o
CFLAGS_hello_world.o    += -I$(src)

SRC := $(shell pwd)

all:
        $(MAKE) -C "$(KERNEL_SRC)" M="$(SRC)"

modules_install:
```

```
$(MAKE) -C "$(KERNEL_SRC)" M="$(SRC)" modules_install

clean:
    rm -f *.o *~ core .depend .*.cmd *.ko *.mod.c
    rm -f Module.markers Module.symvers modules.order
    rm -rf .tmp_versions Modules.symvers
```

Note the highlighted line that includes the current folder in the search path for `include` files.

We can now build the module externally, as we saw in the *Building external kernel modules* recipe in *Chapter 2, The BSP Layer*. The corresponding Yocto recipe is included in the source that accompanies the book. Here is the code for the same:

$ cd /opt/yocto/fsl-community-bsp/sources/meta-bsp-custom/recipes-kernel/hello-world-tracepoint/files/

$ source /opt/poky/1.7.1/environment-setup-cortexa9hf-vfp-neon-poky-linux-gnueabi

$ KERNEL_SRC=/opt/yocto/linux-wandboard make

After copying the resulting `hello_world.ko` module to the Wandboard's root filesystem, you can load it with:

 # insmod hello_world.ko

Hello World

You can now see a new `log_dbg` directory inside `/sys/kernel/debug/tracing/events`, which contains a `log_dbg` event tracepoint with the following format:

 # cat /sys/kernel/debug/tracing/events/log_dbg/log_dbg/format

name: log_dbg

ID: 622

format:

```
    field:unsigned short common_type;       offset:0;
size:2; signed:0;
    field:unsigned char common_flags;       offset:2;
size:1; signed:0;
    field:unsigned char common_preempt_count;       offset:3;
size:1; signed:0;
    field:int common_pid;   offset:4;       size:4; signed:1;

    field:__data_loc char[] a;      offset:8;       size:4;
signed:0;
```

```
        field:__data_loc char[] b;        offset:12;        size:4;
    signed:0;
```

```
print fmt: "log_dbg: a %s b %s", __get_str(a), __get_str(b)
```

You can then enable the function tracer on the `hello_timer_callback` function:

```
# cd /sys/kernel/debug/tracing
# echo 1 > events/log_dbg/log_dbg/enable
# echo 1 > /sys/kernel/debug/tracing/tracing_on
# cat trace
        <idle>-0       [000] ..s2    57.425040: log_dbg: log_dbg: a
    Hello b World
```

There's more...

Static tracepoints can also be filtered. When an event matches a filter set, it is kept, otherwise it is discarded. Events without filters are always kept.

For example, to set a matching filter for the `log_dbg` event inserted in the preceding code, you could match either the a or b variables:

```
# echo "a == \"Hello\"" >
    /sys/kernel/debug/tracing/events/log_dbg/log_dbg/filter
```

See also

- ▶ The Linux kernel documentation at `https://git.kernel.org/cgit/linux/kernel/git/torvalds/linux.git/plain/Documentation/trace/events.txt` for more information regarding static tracepoints events

- ▶ The *Using the TRACE_EVENT() macro* article series by Steven Rostedt at `http://lwn.net/Articles/379903/`

Using dynamic kernel tracing

`kprobes` is a kernel debugging facility that allows us to dynamically break into almost any kernel function (except `kprobe` itself) to collect debugging and profiling information non-disruptively. Some architectures keep an array of blacklisted functions, which cannot be probed using `kprobe`, but on ARM the list is empty.

Because `kprobes` can be used to change a function's data and registers, it should only be used in development environments.

There are three types of probes:

- ▸ kprobes: This is the kernel probe which can be inserted into any location with more than one kprobe added at a single location, if needed.

- ▸ jprobe: This is the jumper probe inserted at the entry point of a kernel function to provide access to its arguments. Only one jprobe may be added at a given location.

- ▸ kretprobe: This is the return probe which triggers on a function return. Also, only one kretprobe may be added to the same location.

They are packaged into a kernel module, with the init function registering the probes and the exit function unregistering them.

This recipe will explain how to use all types of dynamic probes.

Getting ready

To configure the Linux kernel with kprobes support, you need to:

- ▸ Define the CONFIG_KPROBES configuration variable

- ▸ Define CONFIG_MODULES and CONFIG_MODULE_UNLOAD so that modules can be used to register probes

- ▸ Define CONFIG_KALLSYMS and CONFIG_KALLSYMS_ALL (recommended) so that kernel symbols can be looked up

- ▸ Optionally, define the CONFIG_DEBUG_INFO configuration variable so that probes can be inserted in the middle of functions as offsets from the entry point. To find the insertion point, you can use objdump, as seen in the following excerpt for the do_sys_open function:

```
arm-poky-linux-gnueabi-objdump -d -l vmlinux | grep
   do_sys_open
8010bfa8 <do_sys_open>:
do_sys_open():
8010c034:       0a000036       beq       8010c114
   <do_sys_open+0x16c>
8010c044:       1a000031       bne       8010c110
   <do_sys_open+0x168>
```

The kprobes API is defined in the kprobes.h file and includes registration/unregistration and enabling/disabling functions for the three types of probes as follows:

```
#include <linux/kprobes.h>
int register_kprobe(struct kprobe *kp);
int register_jprobe(struct jprobe *jp)
```

```
int register_kretprobe(struct kretprobe *rp);

void unregister_kprobe(struct kprobe *kp);
void unregister_jprobe(struct jprobe *jp);
void unregister_kretprobe(struct kretprobe *rp);
```

By default, a kprobe probe is enabled when registering, except when the KPROBE_FLAG_DISABLED flag is passed. The following function definitions enable or disable the probe:

```
int disable_kprobe(struct kprobe *kp);
int disable_kretprobe(struct kretprobe *rp);
int disable_jprobe(struct jprobe *jp);

int enable_kprobe(struct kprobe *kp);
int enable_kretprobe(struct kretprobe *rp);
int enable_jprobe(struct jprobe *jp);
```

The registered kprobe probes can be listed through debugfs:

```
$ cat /sys/kernel/debug/kprobes/list
```

They can globally be enabled or disabled with:

```
$ echo 0/1 > /sys/kernel/debug/kprobes/enabled
```

How to do it...

On registration, the kprobe probe places a breakpoint (or jump, if optimized) instruction at the start of the probed instruction. When the breakpoint is hit, a trap occurs, the registers are saved, and control passes to kprobes, which calls the pre-handler. It then single steps the breakpoint and calls the post-handler. If a fault occurs, the fault handler is called. Handlers can be NULL if desired.

A kprobe probe can be inserted either in a function symbol or into an address, using the offset field, but not in both.

> On occasions, kprobe will still be too intrusive to debug certain problems, as it slows the functions and may affect scheduling and be problematic when called from interrupt context.

For example, to place a `kprobe` probe in the open syscall, we would use the `meta-bsp-custom/recipes-kernel/open-kprobe/files/kprobe_open.c` custom module:

```c
#include <linux/kernel.h>
#include <linux/module.h>
#include <linux/kprobes.h>

static struct kprobe kp = {
  .symbol_name  = "do_sys_open",
};

static int handler_pre(struct kprobe *p, struct pt_regs *regs)
{
  pr_info("pre_handler: p->addr = 0x%p, lr = 0x%lx,"
    " sp = 0x%lx\n",
  p->addr, regs->ARM_lr, regs->ARM_sp);

  /* A dump_stack() here will give a stack backtrace */
  return 0;
}

static void handler_post(struct kprobe *p, struct pt_regs *regs,
      unsigned long flags)
{
  pr_info("post_handler: p->addr = 0x%p, status = 0x%lx\n",
    p->addr, regs->ARM_cpsr);
}

static int handler_fault(struct kprobe *p, struct pt_regs *regs,
  int trapnr)
{
  pr_info("fault_handler: p->addr = 0x%p, trap #%dn",
    p->addr, trapnr);
  /* Return 0 because we don't handle the fault. */
  return 0;
}

static int kprobe_init(void)
{
  int ret;
  kp.pre_handler = handler_pre;
  kp.post_handler = handler_post;
```

```
    kp.fault_handler = handler_fault;

    ret = register_kprobe(&kp);
    if (ret < 0) {
      pr_err("register_kprobe failed, returned %d\n", ret);
      return ret;
    }
    pr_info("Planted kprobe at %p\n", kp.addr);
    return 0;
}

static void kprobe_exit(void)
{
  unregister_kprobe(&kp);
  pr_info("kprobe at %p unregistered\n", kp.addr);
}

module_init(kprobe_init)
module_exit(kprobe_exit)
MODULE_LICENSE("GPL");
```

We compile it with a Yocto recipe, as explained in the *Building external kernel modules* recipe in *Chapter 2, The BSP Layer*. Here is the code for the `meta-bsp-custom/recipes-kernel/open-kprobe/open-kprobe.bb` Yocto recipe file:

```
SUMMARY = "kprobe on do_sys_open kernel module."
LICENSE = "GPLv2"
LIC_FILES_CHKSUM = "file://${COMMON_LICENSE_DIR}/GPL-
    2.0;md5=801f80980d171dd6425610833a22dbe6"

inherit module

PV = "0.1"

SRC_URI = " \
    file://kprobe_open.c \
    file://Makefile \
"

S = "${WORKDIR}"
```

With the `Makefile` file in `meta-bsp-custom/recipes-kernel/open-kprobe/files/`
`Makefile` being:

```
obj-m   := kprobe_open.o

SRC := $(shell pwd)

all:
  $(MAKE) -C "$(KERNEL_SRC)" M="$(SRC)"

modules_install:
  $(MAKE) -C "$(KERNEL_SRC)" M="$(SRC)" modules_install

clean:
  rm -f *.o *~ core .depend .*.cmd *.ko *.mod.c
  rm -f Module.markers Module.symvers modules.order
  rm -rf .tmp_versions Modules.symvers
```

Copy it to a target running the same kernel it has been linked against, and load it with
the following:

```
$ insmod kprobe_open.ko
Planted kprobe at 8010da84
```

We can now see the handlers printing in the console when a file is opened:

```
pre_handler: p->addr = 0x8010da84, lr = 0x8010dc34, sp = 0xdca75f98
post_handler: p->addr = 0x8010da84, status = 0x80070013
```

There's more...

A `jprobe` probe is implemented with a `kprobe`. It sets a breakpoint at the given symbol or
address (but it must be the first instruction of a function), and makes a copy of a portion of
the stack. When hit, it then jumps to the handler with the same registers and stack as the
probed function. The handler must have the same argument list and return type as the probed
function, and call `jprobe_return()` before returning to pass the control back to `kprobes`.
Then the original stack and CPU state are restored and the probed function is called.

Following is an example of a `jprobe` in the open syscall in the `meta-bsp-custom/`
`recipes-kernel/open-jprobe/files/jprobe_open.c` file:

```
#include <linux/kernel.h>
#include <linux/module.h>
#include <linux/kprobes.h>
```

```c
static long jdo_sys_open(int dfd, const char __user *filename, int
  flags, umode_t mode)
{
  pr_info("jprobe: dfd = 0x%x, filename = 0xs "
    "flags = 0x%x mode umode %x\n", dfd, filename, flags, mode);

  /* Always end with a call to jprobe_return(). */
  jprobe_return();
  return 0;
}

static struct jprobe my_jprobe = {
  .entry         = jdo_sys_open,
  .kp = {
    .symbol_name  = "do_sys_open",
  },
};

static int jprobe_init(void)
{
  int ret;

  ret = register_jprobe(&my_jprobe);
  if (ret < 0) {
    pr_err("register_jprobe failed, returned %d\n", ret);
    return -1;
  }
  pr_info("Planted jprobe at %p, handler addr %p\n",
        my_jprobe.kp.addr, my_jprobe.entry);
  return 0;
}

static void jprobe_exit(void)
{
  unregister_jprobe(&my_jprobe);
  pr_info("jprobe at %p unregistered\n", my_jprobe.kp.addr);
}

module_init(jprobe_init)
module_exit(jprobe_exit)
MODULE_LICENSE("GPL");
```

A `kretprobe` probe sets a `kprobe` at the given symbol or function address which when hit, replaces the return address with a trampoline, usually a nop instruction, where `kprobe` is registered. When the probed function returns, the `kprobe` probe on the trampoline is hit, calling the return handler and setting back the original return address before resuming execution.

Following is an example of a `kretprobe` probe in the open syscall in the `meta-bsp-custom/recipes-kernel/open-kretprobe/files/kretprobe_open.c` file:

```c
#include <linux/kernel.h>
#include <linux/module.h>
#include <linux/kprobes.h>
#include <linux/ktime.h>
#include <linux/limits.h>
#include <linux/sched.h>

/* per-instance private data */
struct my_data {
  ktime_t entry_stamp;
};

static int entry_handler(struct kretprobe_instance *ri, struct
  pt_regs *regs)
{
  struct my_data *data;

  if (!current->mm)
    return 1;  /* Skip kernel threads */

  data = (struct my_data *)ri->data;
  data->entry_stamp = ktime_get();
  return 0;
}

static int ret_handler(struct kretprobe_instance *ri, struct
  pt_regs *regs)
{
  int retval = regs_return_value(regs);
  struct my_data *data = (struct my_data *)ri->data;
  s64 delta;
  ktime_t now;

  now = ktime_get();
  delta = ktime_to_ns(ktime_sub(now, data->entry_stamp));
  pr_info("returned %d and took %lld ns to execute\n",
```

```
          retval, (long long)delta);
   return 0;
}

static struct kretprobe my_kretprobe = {
   .handler       = ret_handler,
   .entry_handler     = entry_handler,
   .data_size     = sizeof(struct my_data),
   .maxactive     = 20,
};

static int kretprobe_init(void)
{
   int ret;

   my_kretprobe.kp.symbol_name = "do_sys_open";
   ret = register_kretprobe(&my_kretprobe);
   if (ret < 0) {
     pr_err("register_kretprobe failed, returned %d\n",
         ret);
     return -1;
}
   pr_info("Planted return probe at %s: %p\n",
   my_kretprobe.kp.symbol_name,          my_kretprobe.kp.addr);
   return 0;
}

static void kretprobe_exit(void)
{
   unregister_kretprobe(&my_kretprobe);
   pr_info("kretprobe at %p unregistered\n",
       my_kretprobe.kp.addr);

   /* nmissed > 0 suggests that maxactive was set too low. */
   pr_info("Missed probing %d instances of %s\n",
     my_kretprobe.nmissed, my_kretprobe.kp.symbol_name);
}

module_init(kretprobe_init)
module_exit(kretprobe_exit)
MODULE_LICENSE("GPL");
```

The highlighted `maxactive` variable is the number of reserved storage for return addresses in the `kretprobe` probe, and by default, it is the number of CPUs (or twice the number of CPUs in preemptive systems with a maximum of 10). If `maxactive` is too low, some probes will be missed.

The complete examples, including Yocto recipes, can be found in the source that accompanies the book.

See also

▸ The kprobes documentation on the Linux kernel at `https://git.kernel.org/cgit/linux/kernel/git/torvalds/linux.git/tree/Documentation/kprobes.txt`

Using dynamic kernel events

Although dynamic tracing is a very useful feature, custom kernel modules is not a user-friendly interface. Fortunately, the Linux kernel has been extended with the support of `kprobe` events, which allow us to set `kprobes` probes using a `debugfs` interface.

Getting ready

To make use of this feature, we need to configure our kernel with the `CONFIG_KPROBE_EVENT` configuration variable.

How to do it...

The `debugfs` interface adds probes via the `/sys/kernel/debug/tracing/kprobe_events` file. For example, to add a `kprobe` called `example_probe` to the `do_sys_open` function, you can execute the following command:

```
# echo 'p:example_probe do_sys_open dfd=%r0 filename=%r1 flags=%r2
  mode=%r3' > /sys/kernel/debug/tracing/kprobe_events
```

The probe will print the function's argument list, according to the function's declaration arguments as seen in the funcion's definition below:

```
long do_sys_open(int dfd, const char __user *filename, int flags,
  umode_t mode);
```

You can then manage kprobes through the sysfs as follows:

▸ To see all the registered probes:

```
# cat /sys/kernel/debug/tracing/kprobe_events
p:kprobes/example_probe do_sys_open dfd=%r0 filename=%r1
    flags=%r2 mode=%r3
```

▸ To print the probe format:

```
# cat
    /sys/kernel/debug/tracing/events/kprobes/example_probe/format
name: example_probe
ID: 1235
format:
        field:unsigned short common_type;          offset:0;
    size:2; signed:0;
        field:unsigned char common_flags;          offset:2;
    size:1; signed:0;
        field:unsigned char common_preempt_count;
    offset:3;          size:1; signed:0;
        field:int common_pid;    offset:4;          size:4;
    signed:1;
        field:unsigned long __probe_ip; offset:8;
    size:4; signed:0;
        field:u32 dfd;  offset:12;        size:4; signed:0;
        field:u32 filename;        offset:16;        size:4;
    signed:0;
        field:u32 flags;            offset:20;        size:4;
    signed:0;
        field:u32 mode; offset:24;        size:4; signed:0;
print fmt: "(%lx) dfd=%lx filename=%lx flags=%lx mode=%lx",
    REC->__probe_ip, REC->dfd, REC->filename, REC->flags, REC-
    >mode
```

▸ To enable the probe use the following command:

```
# echo 1 >
    /sys/kernel/debug/tracing/events/kprobes/example_probe/enable
```

▸ To see the probe output on either the trace or trace_pipe files:

```
# cat /sys/kernel/debug/tracing/trace
# tracer: nop
#
```

```
# entries-in-buffer/entries-written: 59/59    #P:4
#
#                                   _------=> irqs-off
#                                  / _-----=> need-resched
#                                 | / _----=> hardirq/softirq
#                                 || / _--=> preempt-depth
#                                 ||| /      delay
#            TASK-PID    CPU#    ||||    TIMESTAMP  FUNCTION
#              | |         |     ||||        |         |
         sh-737    [000] d...  1610.378856: example_probe:
  (do_sys_open+0x0/0x184) dfd=ffffff9c filename=f88488
  flags=20241 mode=16
         sh-737    [000] d...  1660.888921: example_probe:
  (do_sys_open+0x0/0x184) dfd=ffffff9c filename=f88a88
  flags=20241 mode=16
```

▸ To clear the probe (after disabling it):

```
# echo '-:example_probe' >>
  /sys/kernel/debug/tracing/kprobe_events
```

▸ To clear all probes:

```
# echo > /sys/kernel/debug/tracing/kprobe_events
```

▸ To check the number of hit and missed events:

```
# cat /sys/kernel/debug/tracing/kprobe_profile
example_probe                              78                    0
```

With the format being as follows:

```
<event name> <hits> <miss-hits>
```

How it works...

To set a probe we use the following syntax:

```
<type>:<event name> <symbol> <fetch arguments>
```

Let's explain each of the mentioned parameters:

- ▸ `type`: This is either `p` for `kprobe` or `r` for a return probe.
- ▸ `event name`: This is optional and has the format `<group/event>`. If the group name is omitted, it defaults to `kprobes`, and if the event name is omitted, it is autogenerated based on the symbol. When an event name is given, it adds a directory under `/sys/kernel/debug/tracing/events/kprobes/` with the following content:
  - ❏ `id`: This is the ID of the probe event
  - ❏ `filter`: This specifies user filtering rules
  - ❏ `format`: This is the format of the probe event
  - ❏ `enabled`: This is used to enable or disable the probe event
- ▸ `symbol`: This is either the symbol name plus an optional offset or the memory address where the probe is to be inserted.
- ▸ `fetch arguments`: These are optional and represent the information to extract with a maximum of 128 arguments. They have the following format:

  `<name>=<offset>(<argument>):<type>`

  Lets explain each of the mentioned parameters:
  - ❏ `name`: This sets the argument name
  - ❏ `offset`: This adds an offset to the address argument
  - ❏ `argument`: This can be of the following format:

  `%<register>`: This fetches the specified register. For ARM these are:

  > `r0 to r10`
  >
  > `fp`
  >
  > `ip`
  >
  > `sp`
  >
  > `lr`
  >
  > `pc`
  >
  > `cpsr`
  >
  > `ORIG_r0`

  `@<address>`: This fetches the memory at the specified kernel address

  `@<symbol><offset>`: This fetches the memory at the specified symbol and optional offset

  `$stack`: This fetches the stack address

`$stack<N>`: This fetches the *n*th entry of the stack

And for return probes we have:

`$retval`: This fetches the return value

❑ `type`: This one sets the argument type used by `kprobe` to access the memory from the following options:

u8,u16,u32,u64, for unsigned types

s8,s16,s32,s64, for signed types

string, for null terminated strings

bitfield, with the following format:

`b<bit-width>@<bit-offset>/<container-size>`

There's more...

Current versions of the Linux kernel (from v3.14 onwards) also have support for user space probe events (uprobes), with a similar interface to the one for the `kprobes` events.

Exploring Yocto's tracing and profiling tools

Tracing and profiling tools are used to increase the performance, efficiency, and quality of both, applications and systems. User space tracing and profiling tools make use of performance counters and static and dynamic tracing functionality that the Linux kernel offers, as we have seen in the previous recipes.

Getting ready

Tracing enables us to log an application's activity so that its behavior can be analyzed, optimized, and corrected.

Yocto offers several tracing tools including:

- ▶ **trace-cmd**: This is a command line interface to the `ftrace` kernel subsystem, and **kernelshark**, a graphical interface to trace-cmd.
- ▶ **perf**: This is a tool that originated in the Linux kernel as a command line interface to its performance counter events subsystem. It has since then expanded and added several other tracing mechanisms.

> ▸ **blktrace**: This is a tool that provides information about the block layer input/output.

> ▸ **Linux Trace Toolkit Next Generation** (**LTTng**): This is a tool that allows for correlated tracing of the Linux kernel, applications, and libraries. Yocto also includes **babeltrace**, a tool to translate the traces into human readable logs.

> ▸ **SystemTap**: This is a tool to dynamically instrument the Linux kernel.

Profiling refers to a group of techniques used to measure an application's consumed resources and the time taken to execute an application. The data is then used to improve the application's performance and optimize it. Some of the aforementioned tools such as perf and SystemTap have evolved to become powerful tracing and profiling tools.

Apart from the enlisted tracing tools, which can also be used for profiling, Yocto offers several other profiling tools:

> ▸ **OProfile**: This is a statistical profiler for Linux that profiles all running code with low overhead.

> ▸ **Powertop**: This is a tool used to analyze the system's power consumption and power management.

> ▸ **Latencytop**: This is a tool used to analyze system latencies.

> ▸ **Sysprof**: This tool is included for Intel architectures on X11 graphical images. It does not work on ARM architectures.

How to do it...

These tools can be added to your target image either individually or with the `tools-profile` feature. To use the tools, we also need to include debug information in our applications. To this extent we should use the `-dbg` version of the packages, or better, configure Yocto so that debug information is generated with the `dbg-pkgs` image feature. To add both features to your images, add the following to your project's `conf/local.conf` file:

```
EXTRA_IMAGE_FEATURES = "tools-profile dbg-pkgs"
```

The `-sdk` version of target images already adds these features.

There's more...

Apart from these tools, Yocto also offers the standard monitoring tools available on a Linux system. Some examples are:

> ▸ **htop**: This tool is available in the `meta-oe` layer and provides process monitoring.

> ▸ **iotop**: This tool is also included in the `meta-oe` layer and provides block device I/O statistics by process.

- ▶ **procps**: This one is available in Poky and includes the following tools:
    - ❑ **ps**: This tool is used to list and provide process statuses.
    - ❑ **vmstat**: This is used for virtual memory statistics.
    - ❑ **uptime**: This is useful for load averages monitoring.
    - ❑ **free**: This is used for memory usage monitoring. Remember to take kernel caches into account.
    - ❑ **slabtop**: This one provides memory usage statistics for the kernel slab allocator.

- ▶ **sysstat**: This is available in Poky and contains, among others, the following tools:
    - ❑ **pidstat**: This is another option for process statistics.
    - ❑ **iostat**: This one provides block I/O statistics.
    - ❑ **mpstat**: This tool provides multi-processor statistics.

And Yocto also offers the following network tools:

- ▶ **tcpdump**: This networking tool is included in the `meta-networking` layer in `meta-openembedded`. It captures and analyzes network traffic.

- ▶ **netstat**: This is part of the `net-tools` package in Poky. It provides network protocol statistics.

- ▶ **ss**: This tool is included in the `iproute2` package in Poky. It provides sockets statistics.

Tracing and profiling with perf

The perf Linux tool can instrument the Linux kernel with both hardware and software performance counter events as well as static and dynamic kernel trace points. For this, it uses the kernel functionality we have seen in previous recipes, providing a common interface to all of them.

This tool can be used to debug, troubleshoot, optimize, and measure applications, workloads, or the full system, which covers the processor, kernel, and applications. Perf is probably the most complete of the tracing and profiling tools available for a Linux system.

Getting ready

The perf source is part of the Linux kernel. To include perf in your system, add the following to your `conf/local.conf` file:

```
IMAGE_INSTALL_append = " perf"
```

Perf is also part of the `tools-profile` image feature, so you can also add it with the following:

```
EXTRA_IMAGE_FEATURES += "tools-profile"
```

Perf is also included in the `-sdk` images.

To take the maximum advantage of this tool, we need to have symbols both in user space applications and libraries, as well as the Linux kernel. For this, we need to avoid stripping binaries by adding the following to the `conf/local.conf` configuration file:

```
INHIBIT_PACKAGE_STRIP = "1"
```

Also, adding the debug information of the applications by adding the following is recommended:

```
EXTRA_IMAGE_FEATURES += "dbg-pkgs"
```

By default, the debug information is placed in a `.debug` directory in the same location as the binary it corresponds to. But perf needs a central location to look for all debug information. So, to configure our debug information with a structure that perf understands, we also need the following in our `conf/local.conf` configuration file:

```
PACKAGE_DEBUG_SPLIT_STYLE = 'debug-file-directory'
```

Finally, configure the Linux kernel with the `CONFIG_DEBUG_INFO` configuration variable to include debug information, `CONFIG_KALLSYMS` to add debug symbols into the kernel, and `CONFIG_FRAME_POINTER` to be able to see complete stack traces.

> As we saw in the *Using the kernel's performance counters* recipe, we will also need to pass `maxcpus=1` (or `maxcpus=0` to disable SMP) to the Linux kernel in order to use the i.MX6 PMU, due to the sharing of the PMU interrupt between all cores. Also, in order to use the PMU on i.MX6 processors, the SoC needs to receive at least 4 JTAG clock cycles after power on reset. This is documented in the errata number *ERR006259*.

At the time of writing, the `meta-fsl-arm` layer for Yocto 1.7 disables some of perf features. To be able to follow the upcoming examples, remove the following line from the `meta-fsl-arm` layer's `/opt/yocto/fsl-community-bsp/sources/meta-fsl-arm/conf/machine/include/imx-base.inc` file:

```
-PERF_FEATURES_ENABLE = ""
```

Newer Yocto releases will include this by default.

How to do it...

Perf can be used to provide a default set of event statistics for a particular workload with:

```
# perf stat <command>
```

For example, a single ping will provide the following output:

```
# perf stat ping -c 1 192.168.1.1
PING 192.168.1.1 (192.168.1.1): 56 data bytes
64 bytes from 192.168.1.1: seq=0 ttl=64 time=6.489 ms

--- 192.168.1.1 ping statistics ---
1 packets transmitted, 1 packets received, 0% packet loss
round-trip min/avg/max = 6.489/6.489/6.489 ms


 Performance counter stats for 'ping -c 1 192.168.1.1':

          8.984333 task-clock                #    0.360 CPUs utilized
                15 context-switches          #    0.002 M/sec
                 0 cpu-migrations            #    0.000 K/sec
               140 page-faults               #    0.016 M/sec
           3433188 cycles                    #    0.382 GHz
            123948 stalled-cycles-frontend   #    3.61% frontend
cycles idle
            418329 stalled-cycles-backend    #   12.18% backend
cycles idle
            234497 instructions              #    0.07   insns per
cycle
                                             #    1.78   stalled
cycles per insn
             22649 branches                  #    2.521 M/sec
              8123 branch-misses             #   35.86% of all
branches

       0.024962333 seconds time elapsed
```

If we are only interested in a particular set of events, we can specify the events we want to output information from using the -e option.

We can also sample data and store it so that it can be later analyzed:

```
# perf record <command>
```

Better still, we can add stack backtraces with the `-g` option:

```
# perf record -g -- ping -c 1 192.168.1.1
```

The result will be stored on a `perf.data` file which we would then analyze with:

```
# perf report
```

Its output can be seen in the following screenshot:

```
Samples: 22  of event 'cycles', Event count (approx.): 2307629
+   20.76%  ping  [kernel.kallsyms]   [k] queue_work_on
+   18.23%  ping  [kernel.kallsyms]   [k] do_page_fault
+   10.02%  ping  [kernel.kallsyms]   [k] __percpu_counter_add
+    9.80%  ping  [kernel.kallsyms]   [k] handle_mm_fault
+    8.26%  ping  ld-2.19.so          [.] __udivsi3
+    7.59%  ping  [kernel.kallsyms]   [k] filemap_fault
+    6.82%  ping  [kernel.kallsyms]   [k] __memzero
+    5.95%  ping  ld-2.19.so          [.] open_verify
+    4.96%  ping  [kernel.kallsyms]   [k] __sync_icache_dcache
+    3.84%  ping  ld-2.19.so          [.] _dl_start
+    2.58%  ping  [kernel.kallsyms]   [k] padzero
+    1.02%  ping  [kernel.kallsyms]   [k] do_brk
+    0.15%  ping  [kernel.kallsyms]   [k] mprotect_fixup
+    0.03%  ping  [kernel.kallsyms]   [k] perf_event_comm
```

The functions order may be customized with the `--sort` option.

We can see how perf has resolved both user space and kernel symbols. Perf will read kernel symbols from the Linux kernel ELF file under `/boot`. If it is stored in a non-standard location, we can optionally pass its location with a `-k` option. If it does not find it, it will fall back to using `/proc/kallsyms`, where the Linux kernel exports the kernel symbols to user space when built with the `CONFIG_KALLSYMS` configuration variable.

> If a perf report is not showing kernel symbols, it may be because the ELF file does not match the running kernel. You can try to rename it and see if using `/proc/kallsyms` works.
>
> Also, to obtain complete backtraces, applications need to be compiled with debug optimization by using the `DEBUG_BUILD` configuration variable, as we saw earlier in this chapter.

By default, Perf uses a **newt** interface (TUI) that needs the `expand` utility, part of coreutils. If coreutils is not included in your root filesystem, you can ask for a text-only output with:

```
# perf report -stdio
```

After executing the preceding command we get the following output:

```
# ========
# captured on: Fri Mar  6 21:34:41 2015
# hostname : ccimx6sbc
# os release : 3.10.54-dey+g8f13306f52e0
# perf version : 3.10.54
# arch : armv7l
# nrcpus online : 4
# nrcpus avail : 1
# cpudesc : (null)
# total memory : 0 kB
# cmdline :
# event : name = cycles, type = 0, config = 0x0, config1 = 0x0, config2 = 0x0, excl_usr = 0, excl_kern = 0, excl_host = 0, excl_guest = 1, precise_ip = 0
# pmu mappings: not available
# ========
#
# Samples: 22  of event 'cycles'
# Event count (approx.): 2307629
#
# Overhead  Command     Shared Object              Symbol
# ........  ........    ..................         ........................
#
  [31m 20.76%[m[m    ping  [kernel.kallsyms]  [k] queue_work_on
            |
            --- queue_work_on
                tty_flip_buffer_push
                pty_write
                do_output_char
                process_output
                n_tty_write
                tty_write
                vfs_write
                SyS_write
                ret_fast_syscall
                __GI___libc_write
               |
               |[31m--50.86%--[m[m[m0x676e6970
               |[31m--49.14%--[m[m[...]
  [31m 18.23%[m[m    ping  [kernel.kallsyms]  [k] do_page_fault
            |
            --- do_page_fault
                do_DataAbort
                __dabt_usr
               |
               |[31m--51.41%--[m[m strcmp
               |
               |[31m--48.59%--[m[m _dl_addr
```

We can see all the functions called with the following columns:

- ▸ **Overhead**: This represents the percentage of the sampling data corresponding to that function.
- ▸ **Command**: This refers to the name of the command passed to the perf record.
- ▸ **Shared Object**: This represents the ELF image name (`kernel.kallsyms` will appear for the kernel).
- ▸ **Privilege Level**: It has the following modes:
  - ❑ for user mode
  - ❑ `k` for kernel mode
  - ❑ `g` for virtualized guest kernel
  - ❑ `u` for virtualized host user space
  - ❑ `H` for hypervisor
- ▸ **Symbol**: This is the resolved symbol name.

In the TUI interface, we can press enter on a function name to access a sub-menu, which will give us the following output:

```
Annotate strcmp
Zoom into ping(1020) thread
Zoom into libc-2.19.so DSO
Browse map details
Run scripts for samples of thread [ping]
Run scripts for samples of symbol [do_page_fault]
Run scripts for all samples
Switch to another data file in PWD
Exit
```

From this we can, for example, annotate the code as shown in the following screenshot:

```
do_page_fault
                  Disassembly of section .text:

                  80018be4 <do_page_fault>:
                  mov    ip,
                  push   {r4, r5, r6, r7, r8, r9, sl, fp, ip, lr, pc}
                  sub    fp, ip, #4
                  sub    sp, sp, #116    ; 0x74
                  mov    r3,
                  bic    r5, r3, #8128   ; 0x1fc0
                  bic    r3, r5, #63     ; 0x3f
                  mov    r6,
                  mov    r4,
                  ldr    r2, [r2, #64]   ; 0x40
                  ands   r1, r1, #2048   ; 0x800
                  ldr    r9, [r3, #12]
                  str    r1, [fp, #-128] ; 0x80
                  mov    r8,
                  moveq  r3, #40 ; 0x28
                  movne  r3, #41 ; 0x29
                  tst    r2, #128        ; 0x80
                  str    r3, [fp, #-124] ; 0x7c
                  ldr    r7, [r9, #196]  ; 0xc4
                  bne    80018c38 <do_page_fault+0x54>
                  cpsie  i
      50.00       bic    r3, r5, #63     ; 0x3f
                  ldr    r3, [r3, #4]
                  bics   r1, r3, #1073741824     ; 0x40000000
                  bne    80018d4c <do_page_fault+0x168>
```

If using text mode, we can also get annotated output with:

```
# perf annotate -d <command>
```

Perf can also do system-wide profiling instead of focusing on a specific workload. For example, to monitor the system for five seconds, we would execute the following command:

```
# perf stat -a sleep 5
Performance counter stats for 'sleep 5':
```

```
      5006.660002 task-clock              #    1.000 CPUs
utilized[100.00%]
              324 context-switches        #    0.065 K/sec
[100.00%]
                0 cpu-migrations          #    0.000 K/sec
[100.00%]
              126 page-faults             #    0.025 K/sec
         12200175 cycles                  #    0.002 GHz [100.00%]
          2844703 stalled-cycles-frontend #   23.32% frontend
cycles idle    [100.00%]
          9152564 stalled-cycles-backend  #   75.02% backend
cycles idle    [100.00%]
          4645466 instructions            #    0.38  insns per
cycle
                                          #    1.97  stalled
cycles per insn [100.00%]
           479051 branches                #    0.096 M/sec
[100.00%]
           222903 branch-misses           #   46.53% of all
branches


      5.006115001 seconds time elapsed
```

Or to sample the system for five seconds, we will execute the following command:

```
# perf record -a -g -- sleep 5
```

When using system-wide measurements the command is just used as measurement duration. For this, the `sleep` command will not consume extra cycles.

How it works...

The perf tool provides statistics for both user and kernel events occurring in the system. It can instrument in two modes:

- **Event counting** (`perf stat`): This counts events in kernel context and prints statistics at the end. It has the least overhead.
- **Event sampling** (`perf record`): This writes the gathered data to a file at a given sampling period. The data can then be read as profiling (`perf report`) or trace data (`perf script`). Gathering data to a file can be resource intensive and the file can quickly grow in size.

By default, perf counts events for all the threads in the given command, including child processes, until the command finishes or is interrupted.

A generic way to run perf is as follows:

```
perf stat|record [-e <comma separated event list> --filter '<expr>']
  [-o <filename>] [--] <command> [<arguments>]
```

Let's explain the preceding code in detail:

 ▸ e: This specifies an event list to use instead of the default set of events. An event filter can also be specified, with its syntax explained in the Linux kernel source documentation at `Documentation/trace/events.txt`.

 ▸ o: This specifies the output file name, by default `perf.data`.

 ▸ --: This is used as a separator when the command needs arguments.

It can also start or sample a running process by passing the `-p <pid>` option.

We can obtain a list of all available events by executing the following command:

```
# perf list
```

Or on a specific subsystem with the following command:

```
# perf list '<subsystem>:*'
```

You can also access raw PMU events directly by using the `r<event>` event, for example, to read the data cache misses on an ARM core:

```
# perf stat -e r3 sleep 5
```

Unless specified, the perf record will sample hardware events at an average rate of 1000 Hz, but the rate can be modified with the `-F <freq>` argument. Tracepoints will be counted on each occurrence.

Reading tracing data

Perf records samples and stores tracing data in a file. The raw timestamped trace data can be seen with:

```
# perf script
```

After executing the command we get the following output:

```
# ========
# captured on: Fri Mar  6 21:44:19 2015
# hostname : ccimx6sbc
# os release : 3.10.54-dey+g8f13306f52e0
# perf version : 3.10.54
# arch : armv7l
# nrcpus online : 4
# nrcpus avail : 1
# cpudesc : (null)
# total memory : 0 kB
# cmdline :
# event : name = cycles, type = 0, config = 0x0, config1 = 0x0, config2 = 0x0, excl_usr = 0, excl_kern = 0, excl_host = 0, excl_guest = 1, precise_ip = 0
# pmu mappings: not available
# ========
#
perf  1045 [000]   620.536754: cycles:
            8066c690 smp_call_function_single ([kernel.kallsyms])
            80083ca0 cpu_function_call ([kernel.kallsyms])
            80083eb8 perf_event_enable ([kernel.kallsyms])
            80084260 perf_event_for_each_child ([kernel.kallsyms])
            80086104 perf_ioctl ([kernel.kallsyms])
            800d9ac4 do_vfs_ioctl ([kernel.kallsyms])
            800d9cdc sys_ioctl ([kernel.kallsyms])
            8000e480 ret_fast_syscall ([kernel.kallsyms])
            769bc8cc __GI___ioctl (/lib/libc-2.19.so)
            7eafcadc [unknown] ([unknown])

perf  1045 [000]   620.536770: cycles:
            8066c690 smp_call_function_single ([kernel.kallsyms])
            80083ca0 cpu_function_call ([kernel.kallsyms])
            80083eb8 perf_event_enable ([kernel.kallsyms])
            80084260 perf_event_for_each_child ([kernel.kallsyms])
            80086104 perf_ioctl ([kernel.kallsyms])
            800d9ac4 do_vfs_ioctl ([kernel.kallsyms])
            800d9cdc sys_ioctl ([kernel.kallsyms])
            8000e480 ret_fast_syscall ([kernel.kallsyms])
            769bc8cc __GI___ioctl (/lib/libc-2.19.so)
            7eafcadc [unknown] ([unknown])
```

As we have seen, we can use a perf report to look at the sampled data formatted for profiling analysis, but we can also generate python scripts that we can then modify to change the way the data is presented, by running the following line of code:

 # perf script -g python

This will generate a `perf-script.py` script that looks as follows:

```
import os
import sys

sys.path.append(os.environ['PERF_EXEC_PATH'] + \
        '/scripts/python/Perf-Trace-Util/lib/Perf/Trace')

from perf_trace_context import *
from Core import *

def trace_begin():
        print "in trace_begin"

def trace_end():
        print "in trace_end"

def trace_unhandled(event_name, context, event_fields_dict):
                print ' '.join(['%s=%s'%(k,str(v))for k,v in sorted(event_fields_dict.items())])

def print_header(event_name, cpu, secs, nsecs, pid, comm):
        print "%-20s %5u %05u.%09u %8u %-20s " % \
        (event_name, cpu, secs, nsecs, pid, comm),
```

To run the script, use the following command:

```
# perf script -s perf-script.py
```

You need to install the `perf-python` package in our target image. You can add this to your image with:

```
    IMAGE_INSTALL_append = " perf-python"
```

Now you will get a similar output as with the `perf` script earlier. But now you can modify the print statements in the python code to post process the sampled data to your specific needs.

There's more...

Perf can use dynamic events to extend the event list to any location where `kprobe` can be placed. For this, configure the kernel for `kprobe` and `uprobe` support (if available), as seen in the *Using dynamic kernel events* recipe earlier.

To add a probe point in a specific function execute the following command:

```
# perf probe --add "tcp_sendmsg"
Added new event:
  probe:tcp_sendmsg    (on tcp_sendmsg)
```

You can now use it in all perf tools, such as profiling the download of a file:

```
# perf record -e probe:tcp_sendmsg -a -g -- wget
  http://downloads.yoctoproject.org/releases/yocto/yocto-
  1.7.1/RELEASENOTES
Connecting to downloads.yoctoproject.org (198.145.29.10:80)
RELEASENOTES          100% |**********************************************
*************************************| 11924    0:00:00 ETA
[ perf record: Woken up 1 times to write data ]
[ perf record: Captured and wrote 0.025 MB perf.data (~1074 samples)
  ]
```

And you can view the profiling data executing the following command:

```
# perf report
```

And then you get the following output:

```
Samples: 14  of event 'probe:tcp_sendmsg', Event count (approx.): 14
-  92.86%  dropbear  [kernel.kallsyms]  [k] tcp_sendmsg
       tcp_sendmsg
       sock_aio_write
       do_sync_readv_writev
       do_readv_writev
       vfs_writev
       SyS_writev
       ret_fast_syscall
       __libc_writev
       0
    7.14%     wget  [kernel.kallsyms]   [k] tcp_sendmsg
       tcp_sendmsg
       sock_aio_write
       do_sync_write
       vfs_write
       SyS_write
       ret_fast_syscall
       __GI___libc_write
```

> You may need to configure DNS servers in your target for the `wget` command as seen in the preceding code to work. To use Google's public DNS servers, you can add the following to your `/etc/resolv.conf` file:
>
> `nameserver 8.8.8.8`
>
> `nameserver 8.8.4.4`

You can then delete the probe with:

```
# perf probe --del tcp_sendmsg
```

/sys/kernel/debug//tracing/uprobe_events file does not exist - please rebuild kernel with CONFIG_UPROBE_EVENT.

Removed event: probe:tcp_sendmsg

Profile charts

System behavior can be visualized using a perf timechart. To gather data, run:

```
# perf timechart record -- <command> <arguments>
```

And to turn it into an `svg` file use the following command:

```
# perf timechart
```

Using perf as strace substitute

Perf can be used as an alternative to strace but with much less overhead with the following syntax:

```
# perf trace record <command>
```

However, the Yocto recipe for perf does not currently build this support. We can see the missing library in the compilation log:

```
Makefile:681: No libaudit.h found, disables 'trace' tool, please
    install audit-libs-devel or libaudit-dev
```

See also

▸ A list of the available ARM i.MX6 PMU events at `http://infocenter.arm.com/help/index.jsp?topic=/com.arm.doc.ddi0388f/BEHGGDJC.html`

▸ An extended tutorial in the use of perf at `https://perf.wiki.kernel.org/index.php/Tutorial`

▸ Some advanced examples at Brendan Gregg's perf site `http://www.brendangregg.com/perf.html`

Using SystemTap

SystemTap is a GPLv2 licensed system wide tool that allows you to gather tracing and profiling data from a running Linux system. The user writes a `systemtap` script, which is then compiled into a Linux kernel module linked against the same kernel source it is going to run under.

The script sets events and handlers, which are called by the kernel module on the specified events triggering. For this, it uses the `kprobes` and `uprobes` (if available) interfaces in the kernel, as we saw in the *Using dynamic kernel events* recipe before.

Getting ready

To use SystemTap, we need to add it to our target image either by adding it specifically, as in:

```
IMAGE_INSTALL_append = " systemtap"
```

We can also add it by using the `tools-profile` image feature, or an `-sdk` image.

We will also need an SSH server running on the target. This is already available on the -sdk image; otherwise we can add one to our image with the following:

```
EXTRA_IMAGE_FEATURES += "ssh-server-openssh"
```

We will also need to compile the kernel with the CONFIG_DEBUG_INFO configuration variable to include debug information, as well as performance events counters and kprobes as explained in previous recipes.

How to do it...

To use systemtap on a Yocto system, we need to run the crosstap utility in the host, passing it the systemtap script to run. For example, to run the sys_open.stp sample script, we can run the following code:

```
probe begin
{
        print("Monitoring starts\n")
        printf("%6s %6s %16s\n", "UID", "PID", "NAME");
}

probe kernel.function("sys_open")
{
        printf("%6d %6d %16s\n", uid(), pid(), execname());
}

probe timer.s(60)
{
        print("Monitoring ends\n")
        exit()
}
```

We would run the following commands:

```
$ source setup-environment wandboard-quad
$ crosstap root@<target_ip> sys_open.stp
```

Yocto does not support running scripts on the target, as that would require building modules on the target, and that is untested.

How it works...

SystemTap scripts are written with its own C/awk like language. They enable us to trace events by instrumenting the kernel code at different locations, such as:

- Beginning and end of SystemTap sessions
- Entry, return, or specific offset of kernel and user space functions
- Timer events
- Performance hardware counter events

They also enable us to extract data, such as:

- Thread, process, or user ID
- Current CPU
- Process name
- Time
- Local variables
- Kernel and user space backtraces

Additionally, SystemTap also offers the ability to analyze the gathered data, and for different probes to work together. SystemTap includes a wide selection of example scripts and a framework for creating script libraries that can be shared. These tapsets are installed by default and can be extended by the user's own scripts. When a symbol is not defined in a script, SystemTap will search the tapset library for it.

See also

- The tapset reference at `https://sourceware.org/systemtap/tapsets/`
- All examples included in the source at `https://sourceware.org/systemtap/examples/`
- A reference to the systemtap scripting language at `https://sourceware.org/systemtap/langref/`

Using OProfile

OProfile is a statistical profiler released under the GNU GPL license. The version included in the Yocto 1.7 release is a system-wide profiler, which uses the legacy profiling mode with a kernel module to sample hardware performance counters data and a user space daemon to write them to a file. More recent Yocto releases use newer versions that use the performance events subsystem, which we introduced in the *Using the kernel's performance counters* recipe, so they are able to profile processes and workloads as well.

The version included in Yocto 1.7 consists of a kernel module, a user space daemon to collect sample data, and several profiling tools to analyze captured data.

This recipe will focus on the OProfile version included in the 1.7 Yocto release.

Getting ready

To include OProfile in your system, add the following to your `conf/local.conf` file:

```
IMAGE_INSTALL_append += " oprofile"
```

OProfile is also part of the `tools-profile` image feature, so you can also add it with:

```
EXTRA_IMAGE_FEATURES += "tools-profile"
```

OProfile is also included in the `-sdk` images.

OProfile does not need debugging symbols in applications unless annotated results are needed. For callgraph analysis, the binaries must have stack frames information so they should be build with debug optimization by setting the `DEBUG_BUILD` variable in the `conf/local.conf` file:

```
DEBUG_BUILD = "1"
```

To build the kernel driver, configure the Linux kernel with profiling support, `CONFIG_PROFILING`, and the `CONFIG_OPROFILE` configuration variable to build the OProfile module.

OProfile uses the hardware counters support in the SoC, but it can also work on a timer-based mode. To work with the timer-based model, you need to pass the `oprofile.timer=1` kernel argument to the Linux kernel, or load the OProfile module with:

```
# modprobe oprofile timer=1
```

> Because OProfile relies on the i.MX6 performance counters, we still need to boot with `maxcpus=1` for it to work. This restricts the profiling in i.MX6 SoCs to one core.

How to do it...

To profile a single ping, start a profiling session as follows:

```
# opcontrol --start --vmlinux=/boot/vmlinux --callgraph 5
Using 2.6+ OProfile kernel interface.
Reading module info.
Using log file /var/lib/oprofile/samples/oprofiled.log
Daemon started.
Profiler running.
```

Then run the workload to profile, for example, a single ping:

```
# ping -c 1 192.168.1.1
PING 192.168.1.1 (192.168.1.1): 56 data bytes
64 bytes from 192.168.1.1: seq=0 ttl=64 time=5.421 ms

--- 192.168.1.1 ping statistics ---
1 packets transmitted, 1 packets received, 0% packet loss
round-trip min/avg/max = 5.421/5.421/5.421 ms
```

And stop collecting data with:

```
 # opcontrol --stop
```

> We will get a parsing error if the kernel image name contains special characters. To avoid it, we can use a symbolic link as follows:
>
> ```
> # ln -s /boot/vmlinux-3.10.17-1.0.2-
>   wandboard+gbe8d6872b5eb /boot/vmlinux
> ```
>
> Also, if you see the following error:
>
> ```
> Count 100000 for event CPU_CYCLES is below the minimum
> 1500000
> ```
>
> You will need to change the reset count of the `CPU_CYCLES` event to that minimum, with:
>
> ```
> # opcontrol --setup --event=CPU_CYCLES:1500000
> ```

You can then view the collected data with:

```
# opreport -f
Using /var/lib/oprofile/samples/ for samples directory.
CPU: ARM Cortex-A9, speed 996000 MHz (estimated)
Counted CPU_CYCLES events (CPU cycle) with a unit mask of 0x00 (No
  unit mask) count 1500000
CPU_CYCLES:150...|
  samples|      %|
------------------
     401 83.0228 /boot/vmlinux-3.10.17-1.0.2-wandboard+gbe8d6872b5eb
      31  6.4182 /bin/bash
      28  5.7971 /lib/libc-2.20.so
      18  3.7267 /lib/ld-2.20.so
       3  0.6211 /usr/bin/oprofiled
       1  0.2070 /usr/bin/ophelp
       1  0.2070 /usr/sbin/sshd
```

And an excerpt for output with callgraph and symbols is as follows:

```
# opreport -cl
Using /var/lib/oprofile/samples/ for samples directory.
warning: [heap] (tgid:790 range:0x3db000-0x4bc000) could not be
  found.
warning: [stack] (tgid:785 range:0x7ee11000-0x7ee32000) could not be
  found.
CPU: ARM Cortex-A9, speed 996000 MHz (estimated)
Counted CPU_CYCLES events (CPU cycle) with a unit mask of 0x00 (No
  unit mask) count 1500000
samples  %         app name                 symbol name
-----------------------------------------------------------------------
------
   102     48.8038  vmlinux-3.10.17-1.0.2-wandboard+gbe8d6872b5eb
   __do_softirq
   107     51.1962  vmlinux-3.10.17-1.0.2-wandboard+gbe8d6872b5eb
   do_softirq
102     21.1180  vmlinux-3.10.17-1.0.2-wandboard+gbe8d6872b5eb
   __do_softirq
   102     47.4419  vmlinux-3.10.17-1.0.2-wandboard+gbe8d6872b5eb
   __do_softirq
```

```
102       47.4419   vmlinux-3.10.17-1.0.2-wandboard+gbe8d6872b5eb
 __do_softirq [self]
7          3.2558   vmlinux-3.10.17-1.0.2-wandboard+gbe8d6872b5eb
net_rx_action
4          1.8605   vmlinux-3.10.17-1.0.2-wandboard+gbe8d6872b5eb
run_timer_softirq
-----------------------------------------------------------------
----------
31         6.4182   bash                      /bin/bash
```

How it works...

The OProfile daemon records data continuously, accumulating data from multiple runs. Use the `--start` and `--stop` options to start and stop accumulating new data. If you want to start collecting data from scratch, use the `--reset` option first.

Before running a profiling session, you need to configure the OProfile daemon to run with or without kernel profiling. Specifying the kernel profiling option is the only compulsory configuration variable.

In order to configure the OProfile daemon, stop it first (if running) with the `--shutdown` option. The `--stop` option will only stop data collection, but will not kill the daemon.

To configure OProfile without kernel profiling you execute the following command:

```
opcontrol --no-vmlinux <options>
```

And to configure the kernel profiling, we can run the following command:

```
opcontrol --vmlinux=/boot/path/to/vmlinux <options>
```

Both of these will configure the daemon and load the OProfile kernel module, if needed. Some common options are:

- `--separate=<type>`: This controls how the profiled data is separated into different files, with type being:
  - **none**: This does not separate profiles.
  - **library**: This separates shared libraries profiles per application. The sample file name will include the name of library and the executable.
  - **kernel**: This adds kernel profiling.
  - **thread**: This adds per thread profiles.
  - **cpu**: This adds per CPU profiles.
  - **all**: This does all of the above.

▶ `--callgrah=<depth>`: This logs called and calling functions as well as the time spent in functions.

Once the daemon is configured, you can start a profiling session.

To check the current configuration, you execute:

```
# opcontrol --status
Daemon not running
Session-dir: /var/lib/oprofile
Separate options: library kernel
vmlinux file: /boot/vmlinux
Image filter: none
Call-graph depth: 5
```

The sampled data is stored in the `/var/lib/oprofile/samples/` directory.

We can then analyze the collected data with:

```
opreport <options>
```

Some useful options include:

▶ `-c`: This shows callgraph information, if available.

▶ `-g`: This shows the source file and line number for each symbol.

▶ `-f`: This shows full object paths.

▶ `-o`: This provides the output to the specified file instead of `stdout`.

OProfile mounts a pseudo filesystem in `/dev/oprofile` which is used to report and receive configuration from user space. It also contains a character device node used to pass sampled data from the kernel module to the user space daemon.

There's more...

Yocto includes a graphical user interface for OProfile that can be run in the host. However, it is not part of Poky and needs to be downloaded and installed separately.

Refer to the `oprofileui` repository at `https://git.yoctoproject.org/cgit/cgit.cgi/oprofileui/` for a README with instructions, or to the *Yocto Project's Profiling and Tracing Manual* at http://www.yoctoproject.org/docs/1.7.1/profile-manual/profile-manual.html.

See also

▸ The project's home page for more information about OProfile at `http://oprofile.sourceforge.net/news/`

Using LTTng

LTTng is a set of dual licensed GPLv2 and LGPL tracing and profiling tools for both applications and kernel. It produces binary trace files in the production optimized **Compact Trace Format** (**CTF**), which can then be analyzed by tools, such as **babeltrace**.

Getting ready

To include the different LTTng tools in your system, add the following to your `conf/local.conf` file:

```
IMAGE_INSTALL_append = " lttng-tools lttng-modules lttng-ust"
```

They are also part of the `tools-profile` image feature, so you can also add them with:

```
EXTRA_IMAGE_FEATURES += "tools-profile"
```

These are also included in the `-sdk` images.

> At the time of writing, Yocto 1.7 excludes `lttng-modules` from the `tools-profile` feature and `sdk` images for ARM; so they have to be added manually.

The LTTng command-line tool is the main user interface to LTTng. It can be used to trace both the Linux kernel—using the kernel tracing interfaces we have seen in previous recipes—as well as instrumented user space applications.

How to do it...

A kernel profiling session workflow is as follows:

1. Create a profiling session with:

   ```
   # lttng create test-session
   Session test-session created.
   Traces will be written in /home/root/lttng-traces/test-session-20150117-174945
   ```

2. Enable the events you want to trace with:

```
# lttng enable-event --kernel sched_switch,sched_process_fork
Warning: No tracing group detected
Kernel event sched_switch created in channel channel0
Kernel event sched_process_fork created in channel channel0
```

You can get a list of the available kernel events with:

```
# lttng list --kernel
```

This corresponds to the static tracepoint events available in the Linux kernel.

3. Now, you are ready to start sampling profiling data:

```
# lttng start
Tracing started for session test-session
```

4. Run the workload you want to profile:

```
# ping -c 1 192.168.1.1
```

5. When the command finishes or is interrupted, stop the gathering of profiling data:

```
# lttng stop
Waiting for data availability.
Tracing stopped for session test-session
```

6. Finally, destroy the profiling session using the following command. Note that this keeps the tracing data and only destroys the session.

```
# lttng destroy
Session test-session destroyed
```

7. To view the profiling data so that it is readable by humans, start babeltrace with:

```
# babeltrace /home/root/lttng-traces/test-session-20150117-
  174945
```

The profiling data can also be copied to the host to be analyzed.

User space applications and libraries need to be instrumented so that they can be profiled. This is done by linking them with the liblttng-ust library.

Applications can then make use of the `tracef` function call, which has the same format as `printf()`, to output traces. For example, to instrument the example `helloworld.c` application we saw in previous chapters, modify the source in `meta-custom/recipes-example/helloworld/helloworld-1.0/helloworld.c` as follows:

```
#include <stdio.h>
#include <lttng/tracef.h>

main(void)
{
    printf("Hello World");
    tracef("I said: %s", "Hello World");
}
```

Modify its Yocto recipe in `meta-custom/recipes-example/helloworld/helloworld_1.0.bb` as follows:

```
DESCRIPTION = "Simple helloworld application"
SECTION = "examples"
LICENSE = "MIT"
LIC_FILES_CHKSUM =
    "file://${COMMON_LICENSE_DIR}/MIT;md5=0835ade698e0bcf8506ecda2f7b4
    f302"


SRC_URI = "file://helloworld.c"
DEPENDS = "lttng-ust"


S = "${WORKDIR}"

do_compile() {
            ${CC} helloworld.c -llttng-ust -o helloworld
}

do_install() {
            install -d ${D}${bindir}
            install -m 0755 helloworld ${D}${bindir}
}
```

Then build the package, copy it to the target, and start a profiling session as follows:

1. Create a profiling session by executing the following command:

   ```
   # lttng create test-user-session
   Session test-user-session created.
   Traces will be written in /home/root/lttng-traces/test-user-
      session-20150117-185731
   ```

2. Enable the events you want to profile—in this case, all the user space events:

   ```
   # lttng enable-event -u -a
   Warning: No tracing group detected
   All UST events are enabled in channel channel0
   ```

3. Start to gather profiling data:

   ```
   # lttng start
   Tracing started for session test-user-session
   ```

4. Run the workload—in this case, the instrumented hello world example program:

   ```
   # helloworld
   Hello World
   ```

5. Once it finishes, stop gathering data:

   ```
   # lttng stop
   Waiting for data availability.
   Tracing stopped for session test-user-session
   ```

6. Without destroying the session, you can start `babeltrace` executing:

   ```
   # lttng view
   [18:58:22.625557512] (+0.001278334) wandboard-quad
      lttng_ust_tracef:event: { cpu_id = 0 }, { _msg_length = 19,
      msg = "I said: Hello World" }
   ```

7. Finally, you can destroy the profiling session:

   ```
   # lttng destroy test-user-session
   Session test-user-session destroyed
   ```

How it works...

Kernel tracing is done using the tracing functionalities available in the Linux kernel, as we have seen in previous recipes. For the following examples to work, the Linux kernel must be configured appropriately as seen in the corresponding recipes earlier.

LTTng provides a common user interface to control some of the kernel tracing features we saw previously, such as the following:

> **Static tracepoint events**:
>
> You can enable specific static tracepoint events with:
>
> ```
> # lttng enable-event <comma separated event list> -k
> ```
>
> You can enable all tracepoints with:
>
> ```
> # lttng enable-event -a -k --tracepoint
> ```
>
> You can also enable all syscalls with:
>
> ```
> # lttng enable-event -a -k --syscall
> ```
>
> You can enable all tracepoints and syscalls with:
>
> ```
> # lttng enable-event -a -k
> ```
>
> **Dynamic tracepoint events**:
>
> You can also add dynamic tracepoints with:
>
> ```
> # lttng enable-event <probe_name> -k --probe <symbol>+<offset>
> ```
> You can also add them with:
>
> ```
> # lttng enable-event <probe_name> -k --probe <address>
> ```
>
> **Function tracing**:
>
> You can also use the function tracing kernel functionality with:
>
> ```
> # lttng enable-event <probe_name> -k --function <symbol>
> ```
>
> **Performance counter events**:
>
> And the hardware performance counters, for example for the CPU cycles, with the following command:
>
> ```
> # lttng add-context -t perf:cpu:cpu-cycles -k
> ```
>
> Use the `add-context --help` option to list further context options and perf counters.

Extending application profiling

Further applications tracing flexibility can be achieved with the `tracepoint()` call by writing a template file (`.tp`), and using the `lttng-gen-tp` script along with the source file. This generates an object file that can then be linked to your application.

At the time of writing, Yocto has no standard way to cross-instrument user space applications, but it can be done natively using an `-sdk` image, or adding the following image features to the `conf/local.conf` file:

```
EXTRA_IMAGE_FEATURES += "tools-sdk dev-pkgs"
```

For example, define a tracepoint `hw.tp` file as follows:

```
TRACEPOINT_EVENT(
    hello_world_trace_provider,
    hw_tracepoint,
    TP_ARGS(
        int, my_integer_arg,
        char*, my_string_arg
    ),
    TP_FIELDS(
        ctf_string(my_string_field, my_string_arg)
        ctf_integer(int, my_integer_field, my_integer_arg)
    )
)
```

Pass this through the `lttng-gen-tp` tool to obtain `hw.c`, `hw.h`, and `hw.o` files:

 # lttng-gen-tp hw.tp

> Note that the `lttng-gen-tp` tool is not installed with the `lttng-ust` package, but with the `lttng-ust-bin` package. This has to be added to be the target image, for example, by adding the following in your `conf/local.conf` file:
>
> **IMAGE_INSTALL_append = " lttng-ust-bin"**

You can now add the `hw.h` header file to your helloworld application that is in the `helloworld.c` file and use the `tracepoint()` call as follows:

```
#include <stdio.h>
#include "hw.h"

main(void)
{
    printf("Hello World");
```

```
        tracepoint(hello_world_trace_provider,  hw_tracepoint, 1, "I
    said: Hello World");
}
```

Now link your application with the native `gcc` as follows:

```
# gcc -o hw helloworld.c hw.o -llttng-ust -ldl
```

> Note that in order to use `gcc` on the target, we need to build one of the `-sdk` images, or add some extra features to our image, such as:
>
> **EXTRA_IMAGE_FEATURES = "tools-sdk dev-pkgs"**

To profile your application, do the following:

1. Create a profiling session:

    ```
    # lttng create test-session
    Spawning a session daemon
    Warning: No tracing group detected
    Session test-session created.
    Traces will be written in /home/root/lttng-traces/test-
        session-20150117-195930
    ```

2. Enable the specific event you want to profile:

    ```
    # lttng enable-event --userspace
        hello_world_trace_provider:hw_tracepoint
    Warning: No tracing group detected
    UST event hello_world_trace_provider:hw_tracepoint created in
        channel channel0
    ```

3. Start gathering profiling data:

    ```
    # lttng start
    Tracing started for session test-session
    ```

4. Run the workload to profile—in this case the helloworld application:

    ```
    #./hw
    Hello World
    ```

5. Stop gathering data:

    ```
    # lttng stop
    ```

6. Now start `babeltrace` with:

    ```
    # lttng view
    ```

    ```
    [20:00:43.537630037] (+?.?????????) wandboard-quad
      hello_world_trace_provider:hw_tracepoint: { cpu_id = 0 }, {
      my_string_field = "I said: Hello World", my_integer_field =
      1 }
    ```

7. Finally, destroy the profiling session:

    ```
    # lttng destroy test-session
    ```

There's more...

You can also use the Trace Compass application or Eclipse plugin to analyze the traces in the host by visiting `http://projects.eclipse.org/projects/tools.tracecompass/downloads`. A stable release was not yet available at the time of writing.

See also

*   Details on using LTTng at `http://lttng.org/docs/`
*   Details about the instrumenting of C applications at `http://lttng.org/docs/#doc-c-application`
*   A `tracepoint()` example in the `lttng-ust` source at `http://git.lttng.org/?p=lttng-ust.git;a=tree;f=tests/hello;h=4ae310caf62a8321a253fa84a04982edab52829c;hb=HEAD`

Using blktrace

There are a few tools available to perform block devices I/O monitoring and profiling.

Starting with `iotop` which we mentioned in the *Exploring Yocto's tracing and profiling tools* recipe, which gives a general idea of the throughput on a system and a particular process. Or `iostat`, which provides many more statistics regarding CPU usage and device utilization, but does not provide per process details. And finally `blktrace` that is a GPLv2 licensed tool which monitors specific block devices I/O at a low level, and can also compute **I/O operations per second (IOPS)**.

This recipe will explain how to use `blktrace` to trace block devices and `blkparse`, to convert the traces into human readable format.

Getting ready

To use `blktrace` and `blkparse`, you can add them to the target image by adding it specifically, as in:

```
IMAGE_INSTALL_append = " blktrace"
```

Alternately, you can also use the `tools-profile` image feature, or an `-sdk` image.

You will also need to configure the Linux kernel with `CONFIG_FTRACE` and `CONFIG_BLK_DEV_IO_TRACE` to be able to trace block I/O actions.

When profiling a block device, it is important to minimize the effect of the tracing on the results; for example, not storing the tracing data on the block device being profiled.

There are several ways to achieve this:

- ▸ Running the trace from a different block device.
- ▸ Running the trace from a RAM-based `tmpfs` device (such as `/var/volatile`). Running from a memory-based device will limit the amount of tracing data that can be stored though.
- ▸ Running the trace from a network-mounted filesystem.
- ▸ Running the trace over the network.

Also, the filesystem being used in the block device to profile is an important factor, as filesystem features such as journalism will distort the I/O statistics. Flash filesystems, even if they are presented to user space as block devices, cannot be profiled with `blktrace`.

How to do it...

Let's imagine you want to profile the I/O for the microSD card device on the Wandboard. By booting the system from the network, as seen in the *Configuring network booting for a development setup* recipe from *Chapter 1, The Build System*, you can avoid unnecessary access to the device by the system.

For this example, we will mount as an ext2 partition to avoid journalism, but other tweaks may be needed for effective profiling of a specific workload:

```
# mount -t ext2 /dev/mmcblk0p2 /mnt
EXT2-fs (mmcblk0p2): warning: mounting ext3 filesystem as ext2
EXT2-fs (mmcblk0p2): warning: mounting unchecked fs, running e2fsck
  is recommended
```

The workflow to profile a specific workload is as follows:

1. Start `blktrace` to gather tracing data on the `/dev/mmcblk0` device with:

   ```
   # blktrace /dev/mmcblk0
   ```

2. Start the workload to profile, for example, the creation of a 10 KB file. Open an SSH connection to the target and execute:

   ```
   # dd if=/dev/urandom of=/mnt/home/root/random-10k-file bs=1k
     count=10 conv=fsync

   10+0 records in

   10+0 records out

   10240 bytes (10 kB) copied, 0.00585167 s, 1.7 MB/s
   ```

3. Stop the profiling on the console with *Ctrl + C*. This will create a file in the same directory called `mmcblk0.blktrace.0`. You will see the following output:

   ```
   ^C=== mmcblk0 ===
     CPU  0:                   30 events,        2 KiB data
     Total:                   30 events (dropped 0),        2
     KiB data
   ```

Some useful options for `blktrace` are:

▶ -w: This is used to run only for the specified number of seconds

▶ -a: This adds a mask to the current file, where the masks can be:

   ❑ `barrier`: This refers to the barrier attribute

   ❑ `complete`: This refers to an operation completed by the driver

   ❑ `fs`: These are the FS requests

   ❑ `issue`: This option refers to operations issued to the driver

   ❑ `pc`: This refers to packet command events

   ❑ `queue`: This option represents queue operations

   ❑ `read`: This refers to read traces

   ❑ `requeue`: This is used for requeue operations

   ❑ `sync`: This represents synchronous attributes

   ❑ `write`: This refers to write traces

How it works...

Once you have gathered the tracing data, you can process it with `blkparse` as follows:

 # blkparse mmcblk0

This provides an `stdout` output for all the gathered data, and a final summary, as follows:

```
Input file mmcblk0.blktrace.0 added
179,0    0         1    0.000000000   521  A   W 1138688 + 8 <-
    (179,2) 1114112
179,0    0         2    0.000003666   521  Q   W 1138688 + 8
    [kworker/u8:0]
179,0    0         3    0.000025333   521  G   W 1138688 + 8
    [kworker/u8:0]
179,0    0         4    0.000031000   521  P   N [kworker/u8:0]
179,0    0         5    0.000044666   521  I   W 1138688 + 8
    [kworker/u8:0]
179,0    0         0    0.000056666     0  m   N cfq519A
    insert_request
179,0    0         0    0.000063000     0  m   N cfq519A
    add_to_rr
179,0    0         6    0.000081000   521  U   N [kworker/u8:0] 1
179,0    0         0    0.000121000     0  m   N cfq workload
    slice:6
179,0    0         0    0.000132666     0  m   N cfq519A
    set_active wl_class:0 wl_type:0
179,0    0         0    0.000141333     0  m   N cfq519A   Not
    idling. st->count:1
179,0    0         0    0.000150000     0  m   N cfq519A   fifo=
    (null)
179,0    0         0    0.000156000     0  m   N cfq519A
    dispatch_insert
179,0    0         0    0.000167666     0  m   N cfq519A
    dispatched a request
179,0    0         0    0.000175000     0  m   N cfq519A   activate
    rq, drv=1
179,0    0         7    0.000181333    83  D   W 1138688 + 8
    [mmcqd/2]
179,0    0         8    0.735417000    83  C   W 1138688 + 8 [0]
179,0    0         0    0.739904333     0  m   N cfq519A   complete
    rqnoidle 0
179,0    0         0    0.739910000     0  m   N cfq519A
    set_slice=4
179,0    0         0    0.739912000     0  m   N cfq schedule
    dispatch
CPU0 (mmcblk0):
```

```
Reads Queued:          0,        0KiB  Writes Queued:1,4KiB
Read Dispatches:       0,        0KiB  Write Dispatches:1,4KiB
Reads Requeued:        0               Writes Requeued:0
Reads Completed:       0,        0KiB  Writes Completed:1,4KiB
Read Merges:           0,        0KiB  Write Merges:0,0KiB
Read depth:            0               Write depth:1
IO unplugs:            1               Timer unplugs:0


Throughput (R/W): 0KiB/s / 5KiB/s
Events (mmcblk0): 20 entries
Skips: 0 forward (0 -   0.0%)
```

The output format from `blkparse` is:

```
179,0    0        7       0.000181333    83   D   W 1138688 + 8
   [mmcqd/2]
```

This corresponds to:

```
<mayor,minor> <cpu> <seq_nr> <timestamp> <pid> <actions> <rwbs>
   <start block> + <nr of blocks> <command>
```

The columns correspond to:

▸ A: I/O remapped to a different device

▸ B: I/O bounced

▸ C: I/O completed

▸ D: I/O issued to driver

▸ F: I/O front merged with request on queue

▸ G: Get request

▸ I: I/O inserted into request queue

▸ M: I/O back merged with request on queue

▸ P: Plug request

▸ Q: I/O handled by request queue code

▸ S: Sleep request

▸ T: Unplug due to timeout

▸ U: Unplug request

▸ X: Split

The RWBS field corresponds to:

- ▶ R: Read
- ▶ W: Write
- ▶ B: Barrier
- ▶ S: Synchronous

Another way of tracing non-disruptively is using live monitoring, that is, piping the output of `blktrace` to `blkparse` directly without writing anything to disk, as follows:

```
# blktrace /dev/mmcblk0 -o - | blkparse -i -
```

This can also be done in just one line:

```
# btrace /dev/mmcblk0
```

There's more...

The `blktrace` command can also send the tracing data over the network so that it is stored on a different device.

For this, start `blktrace` on the target system as follows:

```
# blktrace -l /dev/mmcblk0
```

And on another device, run another instance as follows:

```
$ blktrace -d /dev/mmcblk0 -h <target_ip>
```

Back to the target, you can now execute the specific workload you want to trace:

```
# dd if=/dev/urandom of=/mnt/home/root/random-10k-file bs=1k count=10
  conv=fsync
10+0 records in
10+0 records out
10240 bytes (10 kB) copied, 0.00585167 s, 1.7 MB/s
```

Once it finishes, interrupt the remote `blktrace` with *Ctrl + C*. A summary will be printed at both the target and the host.

You can now run `blkparse` to process the gathered data.

Index

O

[PACKT] open source
PUBLISHING · community experience distilled

Thank you for buying
Embedded Linux Projects Using Yocto Project Cookbook

About Packt Publishing

Packt, pronounced 'packed', published its first book, *Mastering phpMyAdmin for Effective MySQL Management*, in April 2004, and subsequently continued to specialize in publishing highly focused books on specific technologies and solutions.

Our books and publications share the experiences of your fellow IT professionals in adapting and customizing today's systems, applications, and frameworks. Our solution-based books give you the knowledge and power to customize the software and technologies you're using to get the job done. Packt books are more specific and less general than the IT books you have seen in the past. Our unique business model allows us to bring you more focused information, giving you more of what you need to know, and less of what you don't.

Packt is a modern yet unique publishing company that focuses on producing quality, cutting-edge books for communities of developers, administrators, and newbies alike. For more information, please visit our website at www.packtpub.com.

About Packt Open Source

In 2010, Packt launched two new brands, Packt Open Source and Packt Enterprise, in order to continue its focus on specialization. This book is part of the Packt open source brand, home to books published on software built around open source licenses, and offering information to anybody from advanced developers to budding web designers. The Open Source brand also runs Packt's open source Royalty Scheme, by which Packt gives a royalty to each open source project about whose software a book is sold.

Writing for Packt

We welcome all inquiries from people who are interested in authoring. Book proposals should be sent to author@packtpub.com. If your book idea is still at an early stage and you would like to discuss it first before writing a formal book proposal, then please contact us; one of our commissioning editors will get in touch with you.

We're not just looking for published authors; if you have strong technical skills but no writing experience, our experienced editors can help you develop a writing career, or simply get some additional reward for your expertise.

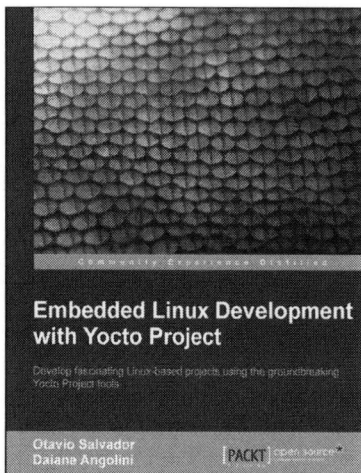

Embedded Linux Development with Yocto Project

ISBN: 978-1-78328-233-3   Paperback: 142 pages

Develop fascinating Linux-based projects using the groundbreaking Yocto Project tools

1. Optimize Yocto Project's capabilities to develop captivating embedded Linux projects.

2. Facilitates efficient system development by helping you avoid known pitfalls.

3. Demonstrates concepts in a practical and easy-to-understand way.

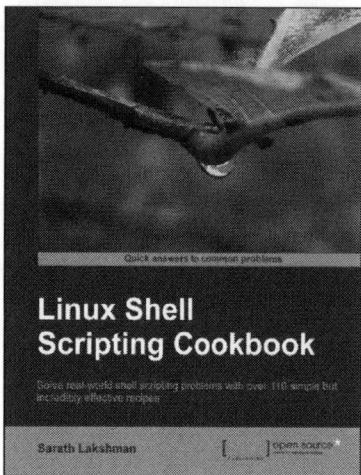

Linux Shell Scripting Cookbook

ISBN: 978-1-84951-376-0   Paperback: 360 pages

Solve real-world shell scripting problems with over 110 simple but incredibly effective recipes

1. Master the art of crafting one-liner command sequence to perform tasks such as text processing, digging data from files, and lot more.

2. Practical problem solving techniques adherent to the latest Linux platform.

3. Packed with easy-to-follow examples to exercise all the features of the Linux shell scripting language.

Please check **www.PacktPub.com** for information on our titles

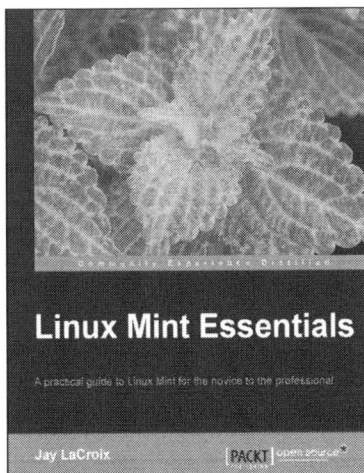

Linux Mint Essentials

ISBN: 978-1-78216-815-7   Paperback: 324 pages

A practical guide to Linux Mint for the novice to the professional

1. Learn to use Linux Mint like a pro, starting with the installation and going all the way through maintaining your system.

2. Covers everything you need to know in order to be productive, including browsing the Internet, creating documents, and installing software.

3. Hands-on activities reinforce your knowledge.

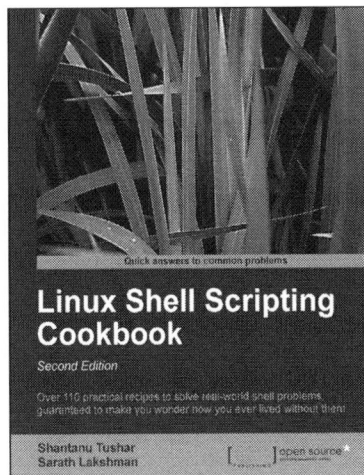

Linux Shell Scripting Cookbook

Second Edition

ISBN: 978-1-78216-274-2   Paperback: 384 pages

Over 110 practical recipes to solve real-world shell problems, guaranteed to make you wonder how you ever lived without them

1. Master the art of crafting one-liner command sequence to perform text processing, digging data from files, backups to sysadmin tools, and a lot more.

2. And if powerful text processing isn't enough, see how to make your scripts interact with the web-services like Twitter, Gmail.

3. Explores the possibilities with the shell in a simple and elegant way - you will see how to effectively solve problems in your day to day life.

Please check **www.PacktPub.com** for information on our titles

Printed in Great Britain
by Amazon

Embedded Linux Projects Using Yocto Project Cookbook

The embedded Linux world is standardizing around Yocto Project as the best integration framework to create reliable embedded Linux products. Yocto Project effectively shortens the time it takes to develop and maintain an embedded Linux product, and it increases its reliability and robustness by using proven and tested components.

This book begins with the installation of a professional embedded Yocto setup, then advises you on best practices, and finally explains how to quickly get hands on with the Freescale ARM ecosystem and community layer, using the affordable and open source Wandboard embedded board.

What this book will do for you...

- Optimize your Yocto setup to speed up development and debug build issues

- Introduce development workflows for the U-Boot and the Linux kernel, including debugging and optimization methodologies

- Customize your root filesystem with both already supported and new Yocto packages

- Understand the open source licensing requirements and how to comply with them when cohabiting with proprietary programs

- Bring professional embedded Yocto products to market in a timely manner

- Optimize your production systems by reducing the size of both the Linux kernel and root filesystems

Inside the Cookbook...

- A straightforward and easy-to-follow format

- A selection of the most important tasks and problems

- Carefully organized instructions for solving the problem efficiently

- Clear explanations of what you did

- Apply the solution to other situations

$ 49.99 US
£ 32.99 UK

ISBN 978-1-78439-518-6

9 781784 395186

54999

Prices do not include
local sales tax or VAT
where applicable

[PACKT] open source*
PUBLISHING   community experience distilled

Visit **www.PacktPub.com** for books, eBooks,
code, downloads, and PacktLib.